The Impact of CASE Technology on Software Processes

SERIES ON SOFTWARE ENGINEERING AND KNOWLEDGE ENGINEERING

Series Editor-in-Chief
S K CHANG (*University of Pittsburgh, USA*)

Vol. 1 Knowledge-Based Software Development for Real-Time Distributed Systems
Jeffrey J-P Tsai and Thomas J Weigert (Univ. Illinois)

Vol. 2 Advances in Software Engineering and Knowledge Engineering
edited by Vincenzo Ambriola (Univ. Pisa) *and Genoveffa Tortora* (Univ. Salerno)

Vol. 3 The Impact of CASE Technology on Software Processes
edited by Daniel E Cooke (Univ. Texas)

Forthcoming title:

Acquisition of Software Engineering Knowledge
edited by Robert G. Reynolds (Wayne State Univ.)

Series on Software Engineering and Knowledge Engineering

Vol. 3

The Impact of CASE Technology on Software Processes

Series Editor

S K Chang

Editor

Daniel E Cooke
University of Texas, USA

World Scientific
Singapore • New Jersey • London • Hong Kong

Published by

World Scientific Publishing Co. Pte. Ltd.

P O Box 128, Farrer Road, Singapore 9128

USA office: Suite 1B, 1060 Main Street, River Edge, NJ 07661

UK office: 73 Lynton Mead, Totteridge, London N20 8DH

THE IMPACT OF CASE TECHNOLOGY ON SOFTWARE PROCESSES

ISBN 981-02-1027-2

Printed in Singapore by Utopia Press.

CONTENTS

AN INTRODUCTION TO THE ISSUES OF COMPUTER AIDED SOFTWARE ENGINEERING

DANIEL E. COOKE

Computer Science Department, University of Texas El Paso, El Paso, Texas 79968-0518, USA

ABSTRACT

The intent of this introduction is to provide a backdrop for the papers which follow. As such, several reservations and concerns about the field of Computer Aided Software Engineering (i.e., CASE) in general are raised. The concerns and worries certainly do not apply to all CASE tools and, indeed, are not based upon the efforts of the other authors who present papers here. Simply put, we would be remiss if we did not include in this volume some basis for critical evaluation of CASE tools and CASE Research.

1. Introduction

Much has happened in the area of Computer Aided Software Engineering (CASE) in the past several years. Research efforts abound and new products are continually appearing. Claims of productivity improvement have ranged from 30 to 300 per cent. Unfortunately, there is little in the way of empirical studies to support or refute such claims. The best studies available concerning productivity (and/or quality) improvement rely upon the perceptions of managers [7]. The field needs studies which compare traditional software development with software development using CASE. One such study, by Granger, compared a control group which developed software in a traditional setting and a treatment group which developed software using a CASE tool [5]. This study showed improvement in both productivity and quality in the treatment group (where quality was measured in terms of how well the product met the original specification). The software system produced in the Granger study was approximately 2000 lines of Pascal code.

Studies of the effect of CASE on larger scale projects are needed. Also needed are studies to determine the impact of CASE on software maintenance. Suppose a CASE tool improves the quality and productivity for the software development phases, but tends to make maintenance activities more complex and costly. Since maintenance activities account for more than half of the total software cost [6], the CASE tool might actually reduce productivity, when one considers productivity over the entirety of the software life cycle.

A CASE tool falls into one of two major classes. The most common tools are those which provide automation to support current software process models (SPM's). Current models include the waterfall, the spiral, etc. The second class of tools are those which extend problem solving abstractions beyond the current procedural programming languages (i.e., beyond languages like Pascal, Ada, C, etc.). These tools are likely to form the basis of new software process models.

The classes of tools introduced here are different from the traditional upper, middle, and lower CASE tools discussed elsewhere. Upper CASE tools typically focus on computer aided planning, middle CASE on analysis and design activities, and lower CASE tools support software development [4]. The two classes of tools introduced here correspond better to Balzer's two levels of effort in Software Process Model automation.

In Balzer's first level are tools to assist in software development in the near term. This level contains all tools which automate activities within the current problem solving environment. In the second level, tools to affect the long term exist, namely tools which advance the current problem solving environment [1].

An underlying assumption is that a given software process model is based primarily on the last language used for problem specification prior to turning the solution over to the computer. For the most part, software engineering was born and has matured around a single class of very precise specification languages, the procedural programming languages. There are two observations which follow from this view of software specification:

(1) A true next generation language will very likely result in a new software process model; and
(2) In specifying software, the software engineer is actually specifying a specification.

The goal of this introduction is to provide a backdrop for understanding current research in CASE, CASE technology transfer issues, and the papers which are collected in this volume.

2. CASE Research Efforts

2.1. *Introduction*

In general, CASE tools are developed for the purpose of automating the software process. This section discusses the problems and promise of both informal and formal approaches to the development of CASE tools.

2.2. *Informal efforts toward CASE*

The empirical development of any CASE tool reflects the tendency of software developers to identify features which are common to all the software products they have developed within some well-defined problem domain. Unfortunately, an understanding of past successes in software development does not assure an understanding of the process of software development — it only assures that if future problems are more or less like past problems, they can probably be solved. In the empirical approach there is uncertainty about future success. A related problem in the empirical development of tools occurs when a tool fails to solve some new problem. In the empirical approach there is a strong tendency to add features to the tool which will help it solve the new problem. There exists the danger that such tools will grow until they reach a size where they are no longer useable or manageable. Furthermore, as features are added to a tool, one typically finds that several abstraction levels result, leading to an incoherence in the tools.

In order to understand the problem of incoherence consider the following analogous example. Suppose, in Pascal, there existed features which permitted the programmer to *dip* into the assembler language level abstraction. If this were possible, it would become necessary for the programmer to understand the problem solution at the procedural programming language level as well as the assembler level. Consider the resulting increase in software maintenance complexity. In order to successfully alter a program, the maintainer might need to understand the interaction between the machine code generated by the Pascal compiler and the assembler code he/she had embedded in the software.

Many empirically developed tools also support the features needed to maintain multiple, simultaneous views of a specification. The uncertainty as to whether views are consistent may lead to major drawbacks to tool use. The concern here, is that an understanding of the relationships among the multiple views of an object software product is not always achieved in the development of all CASE products. In other words, if there is not a precise understanding of the interactions among the views of the object being specified, then how is it possible to truly understand that object? This approach to the development of tools is reminiscent of the *ad hoc* production of "Artificial Intelligence" tools witnessed in the 1980s. Such techniques may result in damage to the area of CASE in general, as these techniques damaged AI more recently.

On the other hand, the empirical approaches to software automation may result in a greater understanding of the problems that can be solved in certain domains and, consequently, lead to excellent development tools. Moreover, if it is eventually possible to generalize problem solving techniques which are common to all domains, then much will be gained from the informal approaches.

2.3. *Formal approaches to software automation*

There are, however, problems with many formal approaches to software development tools. It is not enough to show a set of significant problems that can be solved by some novel approach to software development. For example, if a specification language is to be used as the basis for transformation to a program, several properties of the language and the transformation should be proven. The language, in order to be considered formal, needs a precise, formal semantic. The formal semantic will eliminate concern over the potential for ambiguity in interpreting the meaning of a statement given in the language. If possible, the fact that the language can solve any Turing computable problem should be proven as well as the general correctness of the program transformation technique. Finally, it is important to be able to reason about the specified programs [3].

However, it may be expecting too much of a semantic to provide for both a truth-preserving transformation to programs *and* an ability to reason about intended programs. It may be better to develop separate languages and/or semantics. One finds a true difficulty, for example, in developing a transformation from a logical expression to a unit of programming code. This difficulty is due, in part, to the fact that first order predicate calculus is used to state universal truths, while the truth of a logical expression in a program is ascertained with respect to an existing state of the program's execution.

3. Technology Transfer Issues

3.1. *Introduction*

A complete understanding of the benefits of Computer Aided Software

Engineering (CASE) technology has not yet been reached. This single fact may tend to impede the spread of CASE tools in the workplace and actually increase the potential for CASE tools to evolve into shelfware. The lack of reliable knowledge concerning the potential of CASE may indeed increase the tendency of software developers to keep "the devil they know". Therefore, one might argue that the discussions concerning CASE technology transfer are premature. Nonetheless, ignoring the issues of technology transfer may cause tool developers to lose sight of the forest for the trees. In other words, the process of developing CASE tools should not ignore the potential impact of the tool on a target software development organization. In this section the issues of CASE technology transfer are explored.

3.2. *What is technology transfer?*

Technology transfer is a measured and disciplined approach to matching new tools and techniques to organizations which are best prepared to embrace the new methods and tools. In order for one to truly understand the transfer of some technology, it is necessary to:

(1) Understand the benefits of the tool;
(2) Understand the costs involved in using the tool; and
(3) Determine when one can conclude that the technology has indeed been transferred.

If technology transfer is unsuccessful, CASE could suffer a premature death in the software engineering profession. This death would not necessarily be due to the merit (or lack thereof) of CASE, but possibly due to an unmeasured and disorganized approach to technology transfer. In the face of increasing software costs, it is inappropriate to gamble with a technology which could reduce the costs associated with software development [2]. CASE technology transfer is a very delicate endeavor due to the issues which surround the technology.

3.3. *What are the benefits versus the cost of using CASE?*

One of the current problems with CASE is that no underlying theory exists upon which theoretical investigation may be based. Therefore, it is not possible to provide formal guarantees concerning the benefits offered by current CASE technology. This is an especially critical shortcoming of those tools which assist in software production through code generation. For critical software systems it is desirable for the CASE tools to possess certain properties which will guarantee the correctness of the software the tools produce. The lack of a theory in program generation suggests that we cannot yet realize the true impact of code generators. If the potential for pitfalls of CASE products cannot be predicted, technology transfer falls more into the realm of guesswork. In other words, the goal of technology transfer is to match the "best" product with an organization which can "best" utilize it. If the potential for success of a product is to some extent unknown, then technology transfer cannot proceed effectively.

If CASE technology is to be transferred effectively, its benefit to a given organization must be well known. There may be times when the benefit of the technology does not justify the effort of transfer. Current estimations concerning the impact of CASE tools on productivity and quality enhancement focus largely on systems analysis and are often based on the perceptions of software managers [7]. Although the referenced study is an excellent one, the authors admit that, "The intuitive claims about improved productivity made by CASE vendors have been supported by this research, while the amount of productivity improvement was not investigated" [7]. In other words, the amount of actual improvement in productivity and quality remains unmeasured.

The fact that most of the effort in understanding the effect of CASE technology has focused strictly on software production supports the notion that the organizational impact of CASE remains largely unknown. What is the effect of CASE on maintenance and the software development life cycle in general? What learning curves are involved in the technology transition period? In the absence of answers to these questions, it is impossible to ascertain when an organization is prepared for the new CASE technology and what the organization can expect during the transition period.

To further aggravate CASE technology transfer, the industry is young enough to have not yet experienced the natural industry "shakeouts" which invoke the principle of "survival of the fittest". Inferior products cannot typically compete with good ones. A recent survey found sixty vendors offering CASE products [2]. There is little doubt that there were more than sixty vendors marketing CASE tools at the time the survey was conducted. Furthermore, it is indeed true that new vendors have introduced CASE products since the survey.

3.4. *What are the costs involved in using the tool?*

There can be many costs involved in using CASE tools. For example, the learning curves involved in using CASE tools should be considered before using the tool in a software development project. Some tools are so large that no single person is likely to be an expert with the entire tool. CASE tool specialists may be needed in order to complete a project. This may present the problem where one specialist may not understand how his/her actions may affect the work of other specialists.

One may also find that a CASE tool provides a benefit in one area and presents major costs in another. For example, a CASE tool might help the engineer a great deal with developing code, but the tool may impede the ability to maintain the code.

Other costs which may result from the use of CASE tools include the loss efficiency in the code generated by a tool; job dissatisfaction on the part of the software engineer; etc.

3.5. *How does one know when the CASE technology has been transferred?*

If it is true that technology transfer has not taken place until the organization embracing the technology has adapted itself to best utilize the technology, one may conclude that it took fifteen to twenty years to transfer the procedural programming languages into most software development organizations. In other words, the whole field of software engineering was originally established in order to discover the techniques and methods an organization should follow in order to best utilize third generation languages in solving problems. Until structured programming/design techniques, programmer organizations, etc. were promoted by software engineering, the software development community had not adapted itself to best utilize these languages.

Given the historical perspective, it seems clear that there exist levels of effectiveness of technology transfer. Completeness of transfer might be gauged with respect to some level of sophistication in using the technology. For example, the most primitive level of transfer might require the organization to completely abandon the old tools and begin using the new tools. Subsequent levels of sophistication in tool use might then be based upon measures of how the organization evolves and adapts itself to use the tool more effectively.

4. The Papers Contained in this Book

In this section the intent is to direct the reader's attention to significant aspects of the respective papers. These papers contain other ideas and results of significance. For these related results the authors speak for themselves.

Certainly, an objective is to gather a sense of what the impact of CASE should be. In other words, there is a danger that CASE researchers may work on tools for the sake of the tools and ignore the desired impact on software development processes. This concern is related to Raymond Yeh's comment that "a new wave of tools for software evolution focus not only on the [software] product, but on the process [of developing software] itself."

The remainder of this book is divided into the following parts:

1. The Impact of CASE in General
2. CASE Tools and CASE Tool Integration
3. Management Benefits of CASE
4. Software Process Modeling
5. Educating Software Engineers for CASE

4.1. *The impact of CASE in general*

Dr Raymond Yeh's paper discusses the symbiotic relationship between a software development environment and the tools used for software development. Implicit is the idea that tools affect the environment as much as the environment affects the tools. Dr. Yeh is careful to respect the interaction between tools and their environments, but does offer more universal features a software process model should provide. These features are largely based upon the conflicting needs of any software development environment. One should expect a CASE tool to provide these universal features but leave itself configurable to differing environments. Dr. Yeh underscores the importance of the validation of software specifications through rapid prototyping and points the way towards an appropriate next goal: Specification To Executable Program.

Drs. Gail Corbitt, Ronald Norman, and Mark Butler assess the organizational impact of CASE based on a theory of social change. According to the theory, change involves at least three phases. In each phase, people undergoing the change exhibit identifiable behaviors. Using force field analysis, Dr. Corbitt and colleagues demonstrate that the theory of social change can be used to explain the behavior of an organization adopting CASE technology. Thus, a well-known theory may be used to predict the impact of CASE on software development processes.

4.2. *CASE tools and CASE tool integration*

Much of the success of a software project depends upon the validation of software specifications. Software engineers write and verify programs based on specifications with an implicit belief that the specifications are valid. Unfortunately, the belief is not necessarily a well-founded belief. Therefore, software process models of the future must focus much more on the validation of software specifications. Research in rapid prototyping has contributed a great deal to our knowledge concerning the validation of software specifications. Dr. Luqi's paper focuses on rapid prototyping and the importance of validation. Through Dr. Luqi's expertise and an example rapid prototyping language, the reader learns the desirable features of a rapid prototyping language. These desirable features provide substantive clues as to the nature of software validation. From Dr. Luqi one learns the role of rapid prototyping in CASE and the nature of software validation in the software process model.

W. D. Hurley discusses the integration of the separate processes followed in user interface design and software development. The major notion here, is that the form of a system is its user interface and the content of a system is its actual functionality. Currently, the processes involved in user interface design often stand apart from the processes followed in developing software. Hurley suggests the use of CASE tools to explore the possibility of developing a unified methodology which intertwines the user interface design and software development activities. A tool and method is needed to ensure that user interface developers and software developers produce mutually consistent results.

Documentation of software is a major concern in any software project. Jason Wang and Peter Ng present results concerning the design and prototype of an intelligent document processing system called TEXPROS. Using TEXPROS, the authors claim that much of the activity of change control and configuration management can be automated. Consequently, the benefits of automating documentation may accrue over the entire life of a software product.

S. Chen, W. T. Tsai, and X. Chen introduce an implemented system which provides an object-oriented environment to assist in the maintenance of Assembly Programs. This system supports version control, ripple effect analysis, and program documentation. SAMEA is an integrated environment for software maintenance at the assembly program level. Many of the techniques developed for SAMEA apply, as well, to the maintenance of software developed in higher level languages.

Drs. Papazoglou, Marinos, and Bourbakis focus on the stratum of programming involving the integration of CASE tools. They suggest the use of an

Object Management System (OMS) for the purpose of organizing the integration of CASE tools which may operate on different platforms and according to different methodologies. This paper introduces the primitive operations which an OMS should offer. From these primitives the reader learns how to organize and approach the problems inherent in the integration of CASE tools. Furthermore, one recognizes the significance of having a person in the software development organization who is capable of forming the toolset (or workbench) which is best suited for a given software project and for which integration issues are resolvable.

4.3. *Management benefits of CASE*

Mr. Greg Boone's paper provides a more general notion of the organizational impact of CASE. He discusses what the experience has been and what it could be. He advocates the position that software engineering should take on more of an engineering orientation. Therefore, he focuses on the appropriate mindset of an organization adopting CASE technology. This paper provides an excellent view of the appropriate cultural and social aspects of CASE adoption as well as an engineering approach to managing change in an organization.

Mr. Boone also introduces the notion of stratification of programming effort. On one level there exist programmers who develop and integrate general purpose tools for problem solving. On another level are those programmers who make use of these tools to solve problems within their respective domains of expertise.

John Baker's paper discusses the CASE environment in terms of its potential benefit for management activity (i.e., many of his figures are projected and not yet substantiated). However, Baker does present management techniques which should become more effective when used in a CASE environment. In particular, Baker claims that the impact of CASE should lead to more effective management by exception and participatory management.

4.4. *Software process modeling*

Robert Lai introduces a formalism, developed by the Software Product Consortium, to help describe and analyze arbitrary software models. The formalism, PASTA, is designed to help software engineers study the impact of process models and consequently build better ones.

A similar result is presented by Wolfgang Deiters, Volker Gruhn, and Herbert Weber. An implemented system called, MELMAC, is discussed with a focus on how FUNSOFT, a software process modeling language, can be used for modeling, analyzing, and enacting a software process model. In particular, Deiters *et. al.* focus on support for software process model evolution.

4.5. *Educating software engineers for CASE*

Joseph Urban and Patrick Bobbie discuss the impact of education on CASE. In order to realize the complete benefit of CASE, CASE must ultimately impact undergraduate education. The impact of CASE technology cannot be known until the technology is effectively transferred. In order to transfer CASE technology it is necessary to begin educating future software engineers concerning CASE. Therefore, CASE must eventually impact the education of undergraduate software engineers in order for the full impact of CASE to be understood.

5. Acknowledgments

Research sponsored by the Air Force Office of Scientific Research (AFSC), under contract F49620-89-C-0074 and F49620-93-1-0152. The United States Government is authorized to reproduce and distribute reprints for governmental purposes notwithstanding any copyright notation hereon. I also acknowledge the help of countless reviewers. I am greatly indebted to S. K. Chang, W. C. McCoy, and my former student, John F. Kennedy.

Papers by Yeh, Corbitt *et. al.*, Luqi, Hurley, Wang *et. al.*, Chen *et. al.*, Papazoglou *et. al.*, Boone, Baker, and Urban *et. al.* originally appeared in special issues of the *International Journal of Software Engineering and Knowledge Engineering*.

References

1. R. Balzer, T. E. Cheetham, and C. Green, "Software technology in the 1990s: using a new paradigm", *Computer* (November, 1983) 39–45.
2. D. E. Cooke, "A plan for a national center of excellence for Computer Aided Software Engineering", NSWC #N60921-89-C-A182, 1990. Private communication.
3. D. E. Cooke, "An issue of the next generation of problem solving environments", *J. Syst. Integration*, **1**, 2 (1992) 39–52.
4. M. L. Gibson, "The CASE Philosophy", *BYTE* (April, 1989) 209–218.
5. M. Granger and R. Pick, "Computer-Aided Software Engineering impact on the software development process: An Experiment", *Proc. Twenty-Fourth Annual Hawaii Int. Conf. System Sciences*, Vol. III, ed., Jay F. Nunamaker, Jr. (IEEE

Computer Society Press, 1991) pp. 28–35.
6. Luqi and D. Cooke, "The management of uncertainty in software development", *Proc. Sixteenth Annual Int. Computer Software and Applications Conf.* (IEEE Computer Society Press, 1992), pp. 381–386.
7. R. J. Norman and J. E. Nunamaker, Jr., "CASE productivity preceptions of software engineering professionals", *CACM* **32**, 9 (1989) 1102–1108.

The Impact of CASE in General

SYSTEM DEVELOPMENT AS A WICKED PROBLEM

RAYMOND T. YEH

International Software Systems, Inc., 9430 Research Boulevard, Echelon IV, Suite 250, Austin, Texas 78759–6543, USA

ABSTRACT

Many problems in the software industry today result from our ignorance that system development belongs to a class of problems that are "wicked" in nature. This paper discusses key attributes of wicked problems and suggests a basic set of principles based on experiences from good practices in the field to deal with the attributes of wicked problems. As a result of these principles, new process paradigms are needed. Automation of the alternative process and further research on downsizing mainframe applications to distributed applications are also discussed here.

1. Introduction

Major corporations around the world are facing a real dilemma in software development. MIS departments are already overburdened maintaining the inventory of existing Cobol programs. Maintenance consumes about 80% of the software budget, and the ever increasing demand for applications strains the dwindling resource for new development. User groups have been taking the software development task into their own hands using PCs and 4GLs, but they have not used a disciplined approach. As a consequence, they are making the same mistakes as their own mainframe Cobol developers made some 20 years ago, and are creating their own maintenance mess.

Complicating the existing MIS predicaments is the fact that business structures have been changing during the 1980s and change is expected to accelerate in the 1990s. The result will be the transformation of the traditional functional hierarchical organization primarily supported by white collar workers, into Network-oriented organizations primarily supported by knowledge workers. This puts new demands on the MIS department which must support this organizational transformation. Clearly, the availability of powerful computers-on-a chip, inexpensive memory, and matured networking capability offers tremendous potential for cooperative processing to support such organizational changes. This potential, however, is limited by software.

Since it is impossible to train enough new personnel to meet the demand for cooperative applications, the challenges we face today is how to transform (not rewrite) a high percentage of existing code into distributed code, and how to do system development better, faster, and cheaper in order to support organizational changes. This paper addresses these challenges by examining the fundamental issues of software evolution and by pointing out some possible new paths to solutions.

2. Evolution of software development models

In order to manage the increasing breadth and complexity of software systems, several development models have been used during the past 35 years. The "code and fix" model used in the 1950s and early 1960s provided too much flexibility. The resulting systems were difficult to test and maintain. The Waterfall Model [1] provided more structure. This model stressed extensive documentation and testing, frequent customer involvement, and "building systems twice" because requirements and design are too difficult to get right the first time. Unfortunately, this model was adopted in practice with more rigidity and structure than suggested, and "building it twice" turned into once, then fix it." As such, waterfall development as practiced now has a single version product focus.

The Evolutionary model [2] provided a multiple-version product focus by suggesting expanding operational product growth incrementally as a means of expanding the products as requirements evolve. This model explicitly acknowledged the fact that it is not generally possible to completely define the requirements of complex systems up front. The importance of a process focus in software development is clearly explained by Humphrey's maturity level study [3]. The spiral model [4] was the first to explicitly introduce multiple cycles of planning, prototyping, etc., for risk management and dynamic process organization.

It seems that these previously mentioned process models and practices are all aimed to achieve efficiency by wrestling with three fundamental points of conflicting needs:

- stability vs flexibility

- modularity vs essential interconnectivity
- broad, long-term scope vs narrow, immediate focus

These are indeed difficult balancing acts. Therefore, despite the evolution of models, many experts, e.g., Parnas, Brooks, etc., [5, 6] suggest that dramatically new processes and methods are needed to tackle the software problem. Indeed, several new paradigms that place heavy emphasis on prototyping and reuse as a means of minimizing risks and achieving higher productivity, have been proposed by Campbell, Faulk and Weiss, Royce, and Yeh [7–9]. We believe that a way to find alternative solutions is to first understand the fundamental nature of the software problem, and then to synthesize a set of basic principles, based on past practical experience, so that we can properly deal with the class of problems to which software belongs.

3. The Nature of the Software Problem

The breadth and complexity of the software problem, in our opinion, are typical of a class of problems known as "wicked" problems [10] or "ill structured" problems [11]. Wicked problems have several diverse elements; they are difficult to define until they are nearly solved. The Waterfall model is an example of the classical systems approach to problem solving. The classical systems approach involves first understanding the problem, then gathering information and analyzing it, and finally generating solutions, testing them, and modifying them. However, it is generally inadequate for dealing with "wicked" problems. In the following paragraphs we shall briefly discuss some of the relevant characteristics of wicked problems and examine the basic principles of dealing with them.

Five major characteristics of wicked problems are relevant to software development.

1. *The problem formulation and its solution cannot be separated.*
   In typical, large software systems, requirements cannot be completely defined until the bulk of the system is built and used. But, the system cannot be built without specifying what is to be built. Thus, the activities of requirements, design, build, evaluate, and use need to occur in a more ongoing, intertwined, and mutually supporting way, rather than proceeding along the lines of *a priori* definitions as is usually the case today.

2. *There are no rules to determine when a solution is complete.*
   A wicked problem, in a sense, is never completely solved. Improvements

can always be made and judgement is subjective rather than mathematical. Experience has shown that software systems can always be improved. To deal with this, it is necessary to focus on building a base to support improvement rather than to focus on single delivery.

3. *Symptoms and causes cannot be distinguished.*
   It is common in software systems that problems may be due to a mixture of coding error, incomplete design, or poor requirement expression. These may in turn be due to faulty engineering, ineffective communications, or poor management. Corrective actions based on simplistic diagnoses that fail to analyze the broad, complex nature of the problem usually only temporarily mask the problems and create deeper problems. To deal with this kind of issue, risk and responsibility must be distributed and shared so as to encourage problem identification and willingness to take action.
4. *Wicked problems are substantially unique.*
   Since software systems will continue to grow along with human intellect, it will not be possible to assign bounds to the problem set. There will always be problems which are unprecedented. However, a wicked problem may be tamed over time or be presented in a tame fashion. To deal with this attribute, we need to understand a specific application domain for reusing the knowledge.
5. *Exhaustive and definite problem formulation are not generally possible.*
   To deal with this problem, we need to recognize the fact that expertise is usually distributed and that different stakeholders, from project leader to customers, of the targeted system must be involved in the development process, especially in the requirements definition phase. Furthermore, prototyping is a good way to obtain early feedback and encourage consensus building.

These five characteristics lead to a set of nasty attributes which are common among large software systems. Such systems are:

- Hard to define
- Hard to plan
- Hard to manage
- Hard to schedule
- Hard to test

4. Basic Principles

While problems of software engineering have often been brought to the forefront of discussion, many large, complex systems have been successfully built. Good managers, supplement standard processes with their own "bag-of-tricks" to tackle wickedness and deliver quality software. These practices and lessons, learned from modern manufacturing processes, have provided a rich environment from which a number of guiding principles can be synthesized for tackling wicked problems. We introduce six such principles here: Separation of concerns (or modularity); Co-evolution; Iterations; Continual improvement; Objectifications; and Inclusion.

1. *Separation of Concerns*
   This principle focuses on using subdivision and decomposition to deal with complexity. This "divide and conquer" principle needs no further elaboration.
2. *Co-evolution*
   This principle emphasizes the fact that many activities in the engineering process are closely related. Co-evolution implies that a good engineering process should allow overlapping phases and that activities within different phases can proceed in parallel. This principle specifically addresses the wicked problem attribute that problem formulation and solution cannot always be separated.
3. *Proto-Iteration*
   Iteration means converging upon a desired result through a series of steps. It applies when a single cycle of operations is unlikely to produce the overall desired result. It also applies when end goals are fuzzy and repeated efforts to attain interim results help to define the desired results. Proto stands for prototyping. So, proto-iteration is the principle of cautiously exploring the unknown with repeated small prototypes to minimize risks.
4. *Continual Improvement*
   This principle is a philosophy of seeking success by not counting on getting something right the first time, but rather by making continual improvement an internalized habit. For example, Humphrey [2] suggested that the highest software maturity level is the one that is not only repeatable, defined, and managed, but is optimized by collecting and using feedback to improve the process itself.

5. *Objectification*
   This principle requires making the basis of judgement explicit and communicating it to others. It implies the successful exchange of information as well as the underlying reasons and rationale. For complex product development involving teams of people, applying this principle is critical to the success of the project.
6. *Inclusion*
   "Inclusion" refers to the practice of employing more widespread, ongoing participation of diverse, needed, and affected people in the development process. Sharing risks and responsibility encourages commitment, risk-taking, and focusing on problem solving rather than finger pointing. Diversity of participation also helps to identify problems that may be obvious to one group, but subtle to others. For example, inclusion means users should be closely involved in an ongoing requirements process.

It should be clear that these principles do combine to deal with the wicked problem attributes described in the previous section. The following table provides a clear picture.

Table 1. Basic principles to tackle wicked problems.

Wicked Problem Attributes	Basic Priciples to Deal With This Attribute
1. Problem formulation and solution cannot be separated	Co-evolution; separation of concerns; iteration
2. There are no stopping rules to determine that a solution is complete	Continual improvement; separation of concerns
3. Symptoms and causes cannot be distinguished	Separation of concerns, inclusion; objectification
4. Uniqueness	Separation of concerns; objectification; iteration
5. Exhautive and definite formulation are not possible and no finite set of operations	Inclusion; separation of concerns

5. Taming The Beast

The two fundamental software challenges discussed in Sec. 1 are:

- How to develop software faster, better, and cheaper?
- How to transform existing huge applications that reside on mainframes to cooperative applications residing on workstations connected by networks?

Does our understanding of the nature of the software problem help us meet these two challenges?

5.1. *A framework for an alternative process model*

The six principles for tackling wicked problems suggested in the previous section can be used to evaluate any new process or process models. We shall describe here a framework for such models.

Most models are concerned primarily with the activity structure. An activity designates important activities and related artifacts over time. It generally contains definitions of tasks, work products, and plans and schedules for relating tasks and coordinating events. We believe that there are at least three concerns in any process model, namely: the Engineering process; Project management; and Process management.

An engineering process is comprised of several activities or subprocesses, and the organization of these activities. These activities are related and sometimes must co-evolve together. For example, the activity of defining requirements must co-evolve with that of defining the architecture. If these activities are not synchronized, requirements become uncertain and development objectives become risky. Activities may overlap in time and may proceed in parallel based on the co-evolution and separation-of-concerns principle. Finally, as a result of the objectification and inclusion principles, prototyping should be part of the process.

Based on the objectification and inclusion principles, project management must be concerned not only with the activity structure, but with the "communication structure." A communication structure designates important information exchanges over time among systems, projects, technical models, or roles. It identifies the major concerns and roles, along with their responsibilities, dependencies, and interconnecting communication channels. Figure 1 depicts the important role of planning for communication which is ignored by traditional models [13].

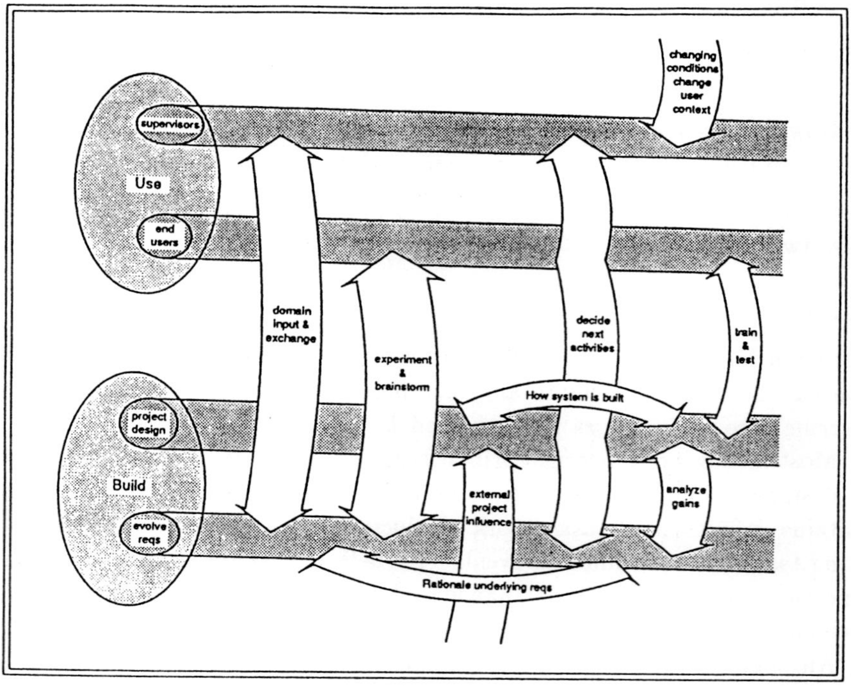

Fig. 1. An example of planning for communication.

Although many alternative processes have been recently proposed, one that closely follows the guideline of a good model described above, is the Rapid Iterative Production Prototyping (RIPP) model practiced by DuPont's IEA [14] during the past several years. RIPP uses prototyping as a key mechanism to explore the wickedness of a problem and to provide "time boxes" for delivering systems incrementally, as illustrated in Fig. 2. The prototypes become production subsystems if user/customer consensus is obtained. They are called production prototypes only to acknowledge the fact that business rules and hence system requirements will continue to change, and hence, subject the underlying systems to constant change. In the RIPP process, communication channels among stakeholders are clearly established through review boards. A key advantage of a process model, such as RIPP, which satisfies the general guidelines mentioned in this section is the rapid convergence of the expectation gap, as illustrated in Fig. 3.

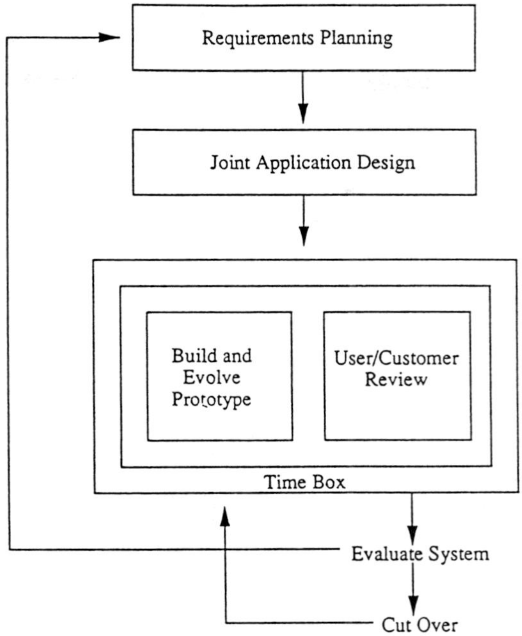

Fig. 2. View of the RIPP model.

We have used RIPP as an example of a wave of new models for software evolution that focus not only on the product, but on the process itself, and that use prototyping as a key method for interacting with users and managing risks.

It should be noted that rapid iteration via prototypes is possible only through automation. In the next section, we shall describe some key components of the software engineering environment needed to support development processes like RIPP.

5.2. *Process automation*

Major improvements in software productivity derived primarily from the introduction of new language systems as we moved from machine language to assembly language to 3GLs. In our opinion, the key concept needed to support a prototyping-driven process, such as RIPP, is the Specification To Executable Program or STEP technology.

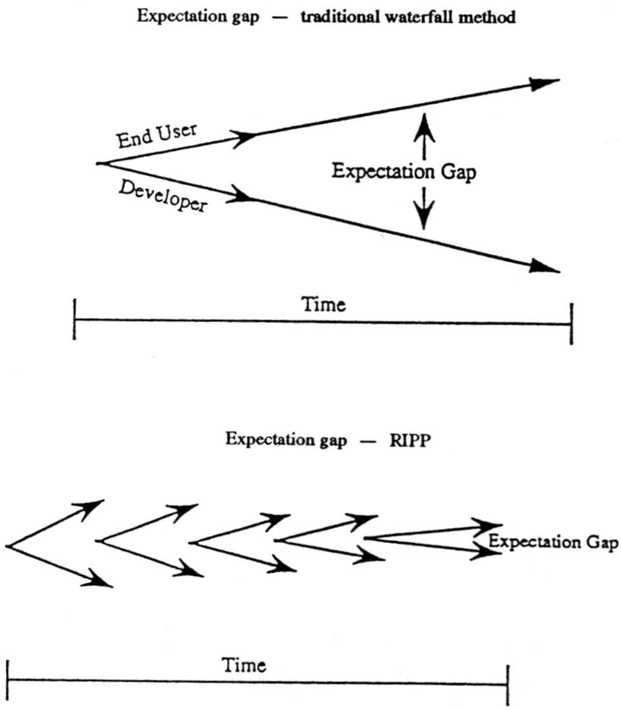

Fig. 3. Expectation of two process models.

We believe that software specification technology has reached a level of maturity capable of leading us to the next natural evolution in language systems. A STEP subsystem in a software engineering environment should consist of the following components, as depicted in Fig. 4.

a. An easily customizable end-user interface builder;
b. An executable, graphical specification language system that includes:
   1. A specification compiler
   2. Various prototyping facilities
c. Support for reuse
d. Support for design validation
e. Built in domain specific knowledge bases

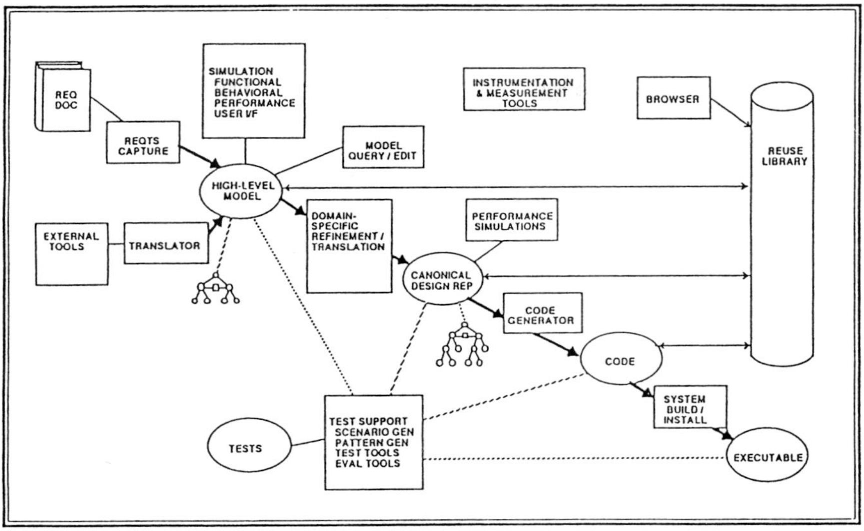

Fig. 4. Key components of a STEP subsystem.

A specification language is the centerpiece of a STEP subsystem. It will have two levels: a presentation level that supports different application domains, and a canonical representation level that provides code generation capability. Note that a presentation level that is customized to each application domain is needed in order to allow users to concentrate on problem logic rather than on idiosyncrasies of language or environment.

Based on the principle of separation-of-concerns, we envision that prototypes are quickly built to assess different aspects of the system: end-user interface, behavior, functionality, and performance before the automatic code generation phase. This executable specification and the ability to reuse specifications combine into a powerful capability that has the following benefits:

a. Rapid convergence of end-user expectation and system behavior.
b. Dramatic reduction of maintenance costs through 100% code generation.
c. Rapid response to requirements changes.
d. Significant improvement in productivity and quality due to paradigm shift as depicted in Fig. 5.

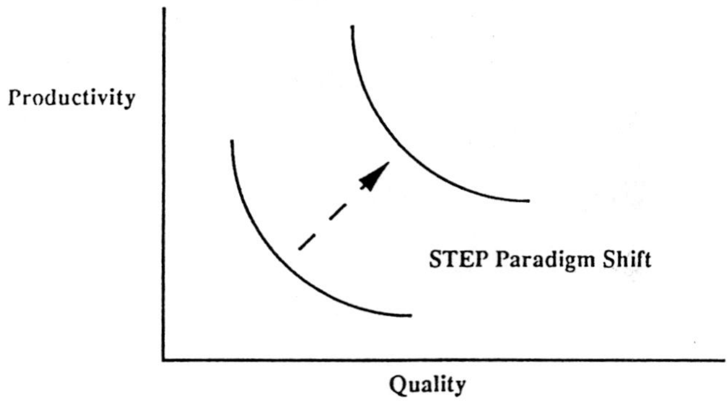

Fig. 5.

It is the inevitable emergence of modern methodology such as RIPP and STEP technology, in our opinion, that will enable software application development to be better, faster and cheaper, as suggested by Meadows [15].

5.3. *Downsizing mainframe applications to cooperative applications on connected workstations*

This is a formidable challenge that is facing corporate MIS directors now and will for years to come. We certainly cannot afford the time and human resources needed to rewrite all the mainframe code. We also cannot find a sufficient number of good programmers to be trained on how to write distributed, parallel programs. We believe a fundamental approach to meeting these challenges lies in "component engineering," which consists of three basic elements.

1. *Program Understanding and Component Identification*
   Given the premise that we will not even attempt to rewrite all the mainframe code, we must first try to understand that we have to identify key components, and perhaps try to restructure it for distributed environments. There are many approaches to understanding a piece of software using complexity measures or visualization attempts. We contend that the fundamental question in programming is how program blocks are put together. If we consider the fact that programming language constructs are essentially composition operators that "glue" these blocks together, then identification

of the "essential" blocks of an application will represent a key discovery. Because then it is possible to "reglue" these blocks into different structures. This leads to our next issue.

2. *Component Composition*
   In sequential programming, we use several basic composition operators, such as sequential composition, choice composition, and various loop structures. The challenge in distributed programming is to identify a small number of key composition operators that can systematically develop large programs by putting smaller program blocks together. With such operators, it is then possible to systematically reglue programming blocks of a large sequential program. The work done by Chandy [16] shows great potential. Such program composition and reuse are closely related, this leads to our next issue.
3. *Component Creation and Reuse*
   Experience has shown that successful software reuse needs to be domain specific. Clearly, reuse of designs or specifications can help to alleviate some of the programming personnel shortage for cooperative applications. We believe that a higher level of reuse lies in the techniques area. The rule of thumb is that in each application domain, a small number of problem solving techniques may be heavily used to solve a major portion of the problems in the domain. Thus, application design templates based on these problem solving techniques would be of great value in improving the productivity of developing cooperative applications.

We are of the opinion that solutions to component engineering, coupled with new processes and STEP technology introduced in the previous subsection, will lead to major breakthroughs for software development in the 1990s.

6. Concluding Remarks

This position paper is written with the intention of exposing the wicked nature of software development, and pointing to some potentially large pay-off solutions in the near future. As such, we did not choose to elaborate on the technical feasibility of the solution suggested. We would like to state here that the technology suggested are already in development. In fact, some commercial products are already in existence and more technologically advanced products are certain to appear in the near future.

Acknowledgments

The author is indebted to many colleagues who have helped in the formulation of the concepts discussed in this paper. They are Mani Chandy, Chenho Kung, Bill Gilmore, Roland Mittermeir, Dave Naumann, Tom Meadows, Win Royce, and George Sumrall.

References

1. W. W. Royce, "Managing the development of large software systems: concepts and techniques," *Proc. WESCON* (August 1970).
2. D. D. McCraken and M. A. Jackson, "Life cycle concept considered harmful," *Softw. Eng. Notes*, ACM (1982).
3. W. S. Humphrey, *Managing the Software Process* (Addison-Wesley, 1989).
4. B. Boehm, "A spiral model of software development and enhancement," *Comput.* **215** (1988).
5. D. Parnas, "Software aspects of strategic defense systems", *Commentaries of the ACM* **28**, 12 (1985).
6. F. P. Brooks, "No silver bullet: essence and accidents of software engineering," *Information Processing '86*, ed. H. J. Kegler (Elsevier, 1986).
7. G. H. Campbell, Jr., S. R. Faulk and D. M. Weiss, "Introduction to synthesis," *Software Productivity Consortium* (June, 1990).
8. W. W. Royce, "The requirements development process — present and future," *Requirements Engineering and Rapid Prototyping Workshop*, TTCP XTP-2, Eatontown, NJ. Hosted by U.S. Army CECOM CSE, Ft. Monmouth, NJ (1989).
9. R. T. Yeh, "Specification compilers, a step towards next generation CASE systems," *System Builder* (April/May 1990).
10. H. Rittel, "On the planning crisis: systems analysis of the first and second generations'," *Bedriftsøkonomen*, NR. 8, Norway (1972).
11. H. A. Simon, "The structure of ill structured problems," *Artif. Intell.* (1973) 181–201.
12. W. S. Humphrey, *Managing the Software Process* (Addison-Wesley, 1989).
13. W. Gilmore and D. Naumann, Draft report on recommended CECOM software development process model (International Software Systems, Inc., December 1990).
14. S. Schultz, *Personal Communications on RIPP Methodology* (1990); *Rapid Iterative Production Prototyping Guide* (Dupont Information Engineering Associates, 1989).
15. T. Meadows, *A Development Revolution — The Inevitable Emergence of RAD and STEP Technologies* (SYSCORP International, Inc., 1990).
16. K. M. Chandy and S. Taylor, "A primer for program composition notation," California Institute of Technology (June 1990).

Further Reading

R. Fink, "Using joint application design (JAD) techniques to accelerate the requirements definition process, *Requirements Engineering and Rapid Prototyping Workshop*, TTCP XTP-2, Eatontown, NJ. Hosted by U.S. Army CECOM CSE, Ft. Monmouth, NJ (1989).

C. Floyd, "Outline of a paradigm change in software engineering," *ACM SIGSOFT Soft. Eng. Notes* **13**, 2 (1987).

Luqi, V. Berzins and R. T. Yeh, "A prototyping language for real-time software," *IEEE Trans. Softw. Eng.* **14**, 10 (1988) 1409–1423.

J. S. Morrison, "A wicked problem — software testing in large scale systems," *American Programmer Magazine* (1991).

P. A. Ng and R. T. Yeh, *Modern Software Engineering, Foundations and Current Perspectives* (Van Nostrand Reinhold, 1990).

D. Parnas and P. Clements, "A rational design process: how and why to fake it," *Trans. Softw. Eng.* **12**, 2.

C. Tully (ed.), 1988, "Representing and enacting the software process," *Proc. 4th Int. Software Process Workshop*, Moretonhampstead, Devon, UK, ACM Press: *ACMSIG Softw. Eng. Notes* **14**, 4(1989).

About the Author

Raymond T. Yeh taught at Penn State, University of Texas at Austin, and University of Maryland. He is founder of two companies. His current interest is in building customizable software environments.

ASSESSING PROXIMITY TO FRUITION: A CASE STUDY OF THE PHASES IN CASE TECHNOLOGY TRANSFER

GAIL F. CORBITT
Accounting and Management Science Department, California State University, Chico, CA 95929-0011, USA

RONALD J. NORMAN
Information and Decision Systems Department, San Diego State University, San Diego, CA 92182-0127, USA

and

MARK C. BUTLER
Management Department, San Diego State University, San Diego, CA 92182, USA

ABSTRACT

Using the Lewin theory of planned change as a theoretical model, this study tests three hypotheses related to the three phase approach to change. An Action Research Model is used to gather data from 75 participants in CASE technology transfer in the Information Systems Department of a large insurance company. Five groups of people representing management and various levels of CASE usage participate in the study. In addition to group discussion, standardized questionnaires and individual Force Field Analyses are used to collect the data.

In general the null hypotheses are rejected. The results appear to support at least three stages of change during CASE technology transfer. The groups differed with respect to content and magnitude of problems in the environment. In addition, during the moving phase it appears users may actually be more disillusioned with the change than non-users, however, the nature of the forces is more personal and indicates that they are personally involved with the move. While these people may be more negative than non-users, they are also moving closer to full implementation than those who have not started the moving process.

There have been a number of implementation theories in Information Systems (I.S.) and Management Science (M.S.) that suggest that the implementation process is a phased process [1, 11, 12]. In addition, I.S. professionals have recognized that a planned change approach to system implementation may be of some benefit [3, 15, 16]. Rather than evaluate the various models and identify common threads, the purpose of the current study is to take one of these theories and test its value within the context of system implementation, specifically in CASE (Computer-Aided Software Engineering) implementation.

In an overview of popular planned change models in the field of management, the one theory that appeared to be the best at explaining reality is that of Kurt Lewin [4]. While there are models with more than three phases such as that proposed by the Boston Consulting Group and Rogers [8], research tends to support a minimum of three phases; unfreezing, moving and refreezing [15].

The question remaining is whether or not Lewin's theory is supported by data in actual system implementations. In other words, are there at least three phases that an organization goes through when implementing CASE, and if so, is there a way to determine where the organization (as well as individuals within the organization) is with respect to the end result, which is successful use of the system (in this study, the CASE tool in question)?

This question is important from two perspectives; that of the practitioner and that of the research community. The practitioner is of course concerned with results, how close is the organization to realizing the benefits of CASE and, how much longer will implementation take? The research community also can realize benefits from a test of a prominent theory. As a behavioral science I.S. research needs to develop theory, test theory and create models that not only describe reality but can eventually predict outcomes. Just as with the field of medicine, it is not enough to state what the theories are or to cite anecdotal evidence to support what is in retrospect "common sense." Rather the researcher needs to take well founded theories and test these theories in empirical settings. Unfortunately, the "lab" for I.S. research is an ever changing environment and the best we can expect is to observe the environment at fixed points in time and study it. There are several approaches to the study to I.S. research, but the most useful to both practitioner and researcher is an Action Research Model [9, 13]. This is the approach used to gather the data in the current study.

1. Rationale: A Review of Relevant Literature

Based on actual social change situations studied in the 1940s, Kurt Lewin and associates developed what has become the foundation of a theory of social change [4]. This theory has been used widely in the field of organizational development and organizational behavior [7]. In comparison to management, however, the application of the Lewin theory to system implementation (including M.S. modeling) has been a relatively recent phenomenon. Schultz and Slevin mention the use of Lewin's theory only as a foundation of work done by Sorenson and Zand [11, 12].

While there are many interesting aspects to the overall theory of change proposed by Lewin, the key elements are that:

1. change involves at least three identifiable phases, unfreezing, moving and refreezing, and
2. the forces associated with each phase are different.

During the unfreezing phase, for example, the negative forces generally outweigh the positive. In this phase, in order to prepare the environment for change, the users of the system need to psychologically get ready for change. There is some discomfort with the threat to the status quo and in general an atmosphere of support for the change is developed that may even include some guilt anxiety if a person does not change [10].

As the positive forces begin to outweigh the negative, the user becomes more ready to move to the new system. This is the second or moving phase of the change. During this phase the user alters behavior, seeks and finds solutions to problems, and incorporates the needed adjustments in work or lifestyle in order to facilitate the change. The theory states that the favoring forces continue to grow until a new level of acceptance is achieved.

At the third level, refreezing occurs when the new behavior becomes the new status quo. The users confirm and support the change openly and look for evidence that the change is effective. In other words, the new behavior or system is more comfortable and affirming than the original behavior or system.

Within the context of CASE implementation, the needs assessment and feasibility phases of the Systems Development Life Cycle correspond to the unfreezing phases. Once the system development tools are chosen the moving phase begins where the analyst/designer learns the tools, adjusts the current methodology so that the tools can be used more efficiently and develops end-user systems using the new tools. As usage begins, the moving phase is hopefully advanced enough so that the benefits of the new system outweigh the resistance and natural inertia [3] that occur with any system implementation. Refreezing occurs when the new system is fixed in the environment, i.e., reversion to the old system is not possible, and when the analysts/designers prefer the new over the old.

A key component of this theory is that the constellation of forces, both positive and negative, associated with each phase of the change can be identified and measured. Thus, a tool, referred to as Force Field Analysis, is used to identify the constellation of forces. According to the theory, as the users move through the phases the positive forces outweigh the negative in increasing magnitude. It is this measurability of forces that appeals to the researcher. If indeed the forces can be identified, can be measured and support the general theory then this largely descriptive tool can be used to test and develop a more prescriptive model. The beginning stages of testing are to see if the theory can be supported with data.

The most cited study that actually did gather data to test the Lewin theory is that of Zand and Sorenson [15], also reported as Sorenson and Zand [12]. These researchers applied the Lewin theory to the field of M.S. and Operations Research modeling, where they conclude that the Lewin change framework "may be used to understand and improve the ongoing change efforts of management scientists as well as those of managers and staff specialists in an organization" [15, p. 543].

While the Zand and Sorenson data found support for the three stage model of change proposed by Lewin, the data were largely post-hoc in nature where management scientists were asked to recall projects and then associate forces that favored or hindered their success. In short, even though the data collection after the fact may be more subjective than data gathered while the implementation is occurring, there was support for the Lewin theory of change within a systems context.

The question remaining is whether or not the theory is applicable across system settings. Applying the theory to CASE implementation, the following hypotheses are considered:

- HT1 Within the implementation of a CASE tool there are at least three identifiable phases of adoption.
- HT2 The forces characterizing each phase are different both in content and in magnitude.
- HT3 There are more positive forces associated with each successive phase, i.e., Refreezing is the most positive, Unfreezing is the least positive, and Moving is in between these two extremes.

2. Methodology

Using an Action Research Model to gather data, an information system's development (ISD) department within a large insurance company was contacted. The ISD department had been trying to implement a CASE tool and methodology for two years with "limited success." Management was considering a new tool that could be used with the existing CASE tools and, before purchasing the new tool, wanted to know if the existing organization could handle yet another change. The task of the researchers is to assess the current environment in order to determine the organization's capacity to accommodate another change.

As part of the assessment the researchers see this application as a way to determine where the organization is with respect to the current changes. In other words, applying the Lewin model to this environment, where is this ISD department with respect to the CASE tool and methodology already in place? The environment lends itself to this application for several reasons:

1. The organization has 75 people in its ISD department so that data can be gathered from several individuals, making observed comparisons meaningful;
2. There are users as well as non-users of the tools within the same department, increasing the likelihood that different phases can be observed at the same point in time, and
3. Management is receptive to the idea of research, and welcomes with openness our desire to probe the environment in detail.

Management's support of the research project indicates an open trusting environment which is a prerequisite for change [2, 14, 15]. Thus an unhealthy environment is not the focus of the study so the change itself can be the focus of study. If the Lewin theory holds, one expects there to be a difference between users and non-users with respect to their receptivity to the current change as well as to the pending change, i.e., the introduction of the new IPSE (Integrated Project Support Environment) product.

Translating the three theoretical hypotheses into working null hypotheses in this environment produces the following:

HN(1): All people in the ISD department are the same with respect to the change, i.e., view the change as being in a similar place (phase) with respect to time and value to the organization.

HN(2): The forces associated with the current change are the same for users and non-users both in magnitude and content.

HN(3): If people are in different places with respect to adopting the change (i.e., NH(1) is rejected) there is no difference in the magnitude of positive forces between groups in each identifiable phase.

While t-tests for differences between groups can be used to test HN(2) and HN(3), the test for phase (HN1) is more subjective. A standardized instrument is used to assess each person's overall view of how the organization reacts to change in general across the following dimensions: time frame, organizational focus, planning, change mode, management, structure, perspective, motivation, development, communication, and leadership. This instrument is based on the work of Nelson and Burns [6]. In addition, all participants are asked to identify the major problems facing the organization as they continue to adopt the CASE tools. If there is no difference, similar problems should surface with each group of people interviewed. In other words, if everyone is in the same place with respect to the change, there is no difference in how the change is viewed and the problems associated with the change are similar across all levels within the ISD department.

Another way to assess the presence of phases is to see if the characteristics of the groups match those described by Lewin and Schein [10]. These are outlined above and can be used as a point of reference. For example, one expects people in the unfreezing stage to question the need for change and in general question the psychological support within the organization for the change proposed [15].

In order to facilitate complete participation by all individuals in the organization, management agreed to release the employees for half day sessions to meet behind closed doors with the research team. Five groups are formed and consist of the following:

1. Management,
2. Support services,
3. More experienced users,
4. Less experienced users, and
5. Non-users.

The support group consists of system development support in the form of training, database administration, quality assurance, etc. The users outnumbered the non-users two to one so the users are assigned by management to one of the user group sessions based on experience with the tools. The agenda for each group meeting is the same. After brief introductions and guarantees of anonymity, the standardized instrument is handed out, scored and collected for further analysis. An open discussion is then conducted where each group generates the significant problems associated with moving the organization to the new CASE tool environment. The problems are recorded and voted on by group participants.

The top problem is then analyzed using Force Field Analysis wherein positive and negative forces are identified by the group as a whole and then the entire list of forces, both positive and negative, are individually assigned weights. In other words for each item on the list each person draws a line indicating the strength that the force has for them personally. The longer the line the stronger the force. These individual rankings are then gathered along with the list of problems and the voting results. Data are compiled by group and then analyzed and compared. Individuals within each group are kept anonymous and group means are reported and used for feedback to management.

Table 1. Profile of each group with respect to general mode for change.

	CHANGE MODE		
Group	N	Mean	Standard Deviation
Management	11	1.82	.386
Support	21	1.81	.499
Users(1)	14	1.79	.773
Users(2)	15	1.73	.442
Non-users	14	2.21	.674
TOTAL	75	1.87	.572

t-test results: $p < .05$ no difference between groups.

3. Results

The profile of each group can be identified as Table 1. For purposes of testing the hypotheses in the remaining sections of this paper, the users are combined into one group when comparisons are made. (The data in Table 1 support the notion that the groups of users were not significantly different from each other). Table 1 reports the results of the score (using a four point scale) on the change mode dimension of the standardized instrument. The participants rated the organization using a four point scale that describes the organization as reactive (1), responsive (2), proactive (3), or developing (4).

During the administration of the study the planned agenda was followed except in the management group. This group did complete the standardized instrument, but time was spent on topics that detracted from the research. This group shared their visions of what the environment would be with the changes fully implemented and as a result, did not generate problems. They did complete a Force Field Analysis associated with the forces surrounding the achievement of their own vision. This, however, makes comparison with the other groups more difficult, especially as hypotheses are tested. Consequently, management is excluded in the presentation of results.

The first hypothesis predicts no difference in time or place with respect to the change. Looking at the top three problems generated by each group, Table 2, it is clear that the groups are in different places with the change. The Support group, for example, sees the major problems as further implementation of the tools. They see many benefits to the new methodology and understand that development needs to be done differently using the new tools. They see role definition and priorities for accomplishing the change as major problems.

Table 2. Top three problems by group.

	Support Group
1.	How to incorporate new tools into the environment in order to achieve goals
2.	Definition of roles of all participants so that all groups can know role and support each other.
3.	How to prioritize the changes and consolidate support
	Users
1.	How to incorporate tools into existing concepts and expertise currently available
2.	How to achieve expected levels of output and productivity
3.	How to handle the magnitude of the change — multiple tools and multiple learning curves
	Non-users
1.	Need to address growing resentment and dissatisfaction with the user community as their needs are not met by new systems
2.	Quality of decision that selected tools — "are these the right tools for us?"
3.	Identify goals and needs of new tools

The User groups are consistent in their view of the problems, centering around how to do their work using the tools. Few people see benefits from the new tools, or even how all the pieces of development (generated by parts of the tools) fit together. The number one problem for these people is how to produce work using the tools when the learning curve is taking so long. This is similar to the support group, but at a higher level of detail. None of the participants in the User groups sees the "big picture." They see the change as inevitable but for the most part are struggling with how to get there in the least amount of time. A particularly appropriate analogy summarizes the major problems this group faces as this: "we have been given a room full of parts and materials and are being asked to build an airplane wing. None of us has seen an airplane wing and we have no blueprints."

In contrast the Non-user group sees the major problems as those associated with the end-user, the users of the systems being developed. For the most part this group questions the need for change and yet sees that many of the existing systems need revamping. It is interesting to note that this is the only group that raised the issue of whether or not the tools chosen were the right ones.

With respect to hypothesis 1, based on the characteristics of the people in the groups along with the content analysis of problems generated by each group, the researchers concluded that there were three distinctly different groups within the organization and that they were in different places with respect to the change. Not only were the problems generated different in content, but the discussion surfaced a fair amount of conflict between the three groups. Non-users questioned their place in the organization given that everyone else had been trained on the new methodology/tools and yet they "were the ones keeping the lights on and doing all the work." The Users saw the Support group as "prima donnas" waiting for the Users to produce something so the Support people would have something to do. The Support people have difficulty understanding why implementation is taking so long and have little empathy for the learning curve with which the users struggle.

The first null hypothesis is therefore rejected. It is the conclusion of the researchers that the Non-users have characteristics associated with the unfreezing stage (are not yet moving or ready to move), the Users are in various stages of moving, and the Support group have refrozen, even though they have not fully experienced the move. Management appears to be more in line with the Support group, although the problem analysis cannot be used to confirm this.

Table 3 is used to evaluate the second null hypothesis: that the forces between groups are the same. Given that there is a statistical difference among groups, the second null hypothesis is also rejected in favor of the theoretical hypothesis. The unfreezing group has a net negative force of −24.5 per person, compared to a positive 5.4 per person in the support group who appears to have refrozen. The highest negative value of −62.1 per user belongs to the group believed to be moving. While the theory predicts a positive net force among movers these data suggest that moving may go through its own stages of disillusionment with the positive coupled with overwhelming negatives while the move is taking place. In fact, the experienced users had a significantly higher net negative than did the less experienced users. (More is said about this in the conclusions and implications section.)

Table 3. Force field analysis results by group.

	POSITIVE		NEGATIVE		NET	
	Total	Average	Total	Average	Total	Average
Support	739	73.9	683	68.5	56	+5.4
Users	811	28.0	2613	90.1	−1802	−62.1
Non-Users	156	11.1	499	35.6	− 343	−24.5

(all numbers are stated in centimeters)
Statistical difference observed between each pair of groups at $p < .01$.

In order to look at the content portion of the second hypothesis, Tables 4 and 5 list the top five positive and negative forces respectively identified by each group. (If there are fewer than five forces listed in the Table it means the list is exhaustive.) It is difficult to draw conclusions from the data as presented, so a panel of five experts were asked to categorize each of the forces by its source or the nature of its content. When this was done, consensus was reached and beside each item on the lists in Tables 4 and 5, the category of the item is listed. While it is difficult to draw concrete conclusions, one observation is that the User group is the only group with forces that are viewed as individual or internal to the person. In other words, the Users are concerned with the personal frustration experienced in using the tools, the high learning curve and the fact that no known positive benefits have been experienced from the system. On the positive side, they see that learning the tools provides them with personal growth and job enrichment and, in general, is supportive of them and their fellow workers.

The other two groups have forces that are largely external to the individual. Those in the unfreezing stage question the value of the new tools in light of the existing system and see others (Management and Support in particular) as being the source for potential negatives. The refrozen group also has an external focus with technical aspects of the system as positive and management as the primary source for negative forces. Thus, while the conclusions are tenuous, the forces do appear to vary in content from at least the User group versus those who are not moving (the Non-users) or those who have already moved (Support).

Table 4. Content of positive forces by group.

CATEGORY		
		Support Group
V/T	1.	Good documentation
I	2.	Gives gains in productivity
T	3.	Uses leading edge technology
T	4.	Develops "big picture" view of system
P/M	5.	Provides for consistency and standards across projects
		Users
P/T	1.	Provides for a common data repository
I	2.	Provides for personal growth and job enlargement
I	3.	Supports good people doing good work
O	4.	Supports strategic goals of the organization
I	5.	Produces higher expectations of people (staff and end users)
		Non-users
T/P	1.	Outputs from new tools look good
O	2.	Likelihood that people can use tools to meet needs if tied to evaluation
P	3.	Increased system flexibility and capability

Legend

V = Vendor	I = Individual
T = Technical	E = End-user related
S = Support of system	M = Management
P = Project related	O = Organizational

Table 5. Content of negative forces by group.

CATEGORY		
		Support Group
O	1.	Magnitude of change — too much forces us to do too much as so we cannot be specialists
P/M	2.	Goals of the new CASE environment/system are unknown or unclear
M	3.	Management lacks understanding of whole change taking place
M	4.	Different interpretations of tools allows staff to deviate from standards
M	5.	Lack of unified direction at mid-management level
		Users
P	1.	Increases project development time — too much emphasis on target dates
S	2.	Lack of internal available support
I	3.	High frustration level when using the tools
I	4.	Long learning curves (management does not understand this)
I	5.	Positives are still unknown—have not been experienced yet
		Non-users
E	1.	End-users needs are not being met by existing personnel
S	2.	Lack of support to existing systems
T	3.	Too much emphasis on tools
M	4.	Lack of management support to get job done
T	5.	New systems cannot do what old systems do

Legend

V = Vendor	I = Individual
T = Technical	E = End-user related
S = Support of system	M = Management
P = Project related	O = Organizational

The final hypothesis is that related to the direction of the magnitude of forces and again the data in Table 3 are used to test the null hypothesis which predicts no difference in direction. The theory predicts that the unfrozen group has more negative than positive, the refrozen group more positive than negative with the movers in between. In fact, the Lewin model alludes to a curvilinear function similar to that in Fig. 1, with a more or less steady increase in the positive forces as the negative or restraining forces are sought out and addressed.

While the null hypothesis is rejected, the forces do differ in magnitude, the Users have a lower net negative value than that for Non-users. Apparently the movement of forces may be more similar to the pattern presented in Fig. 2. In fact, the data in this study seem to indicate that during the disillusionment phase of moving the negative may reach a point lower than that experienced during unfreezing.

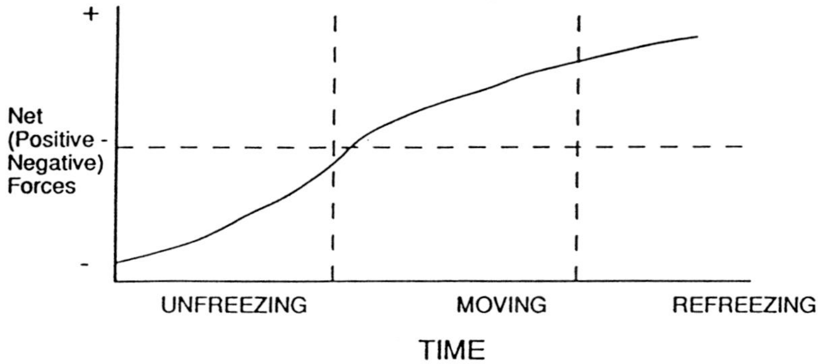

Fig. 1. Theoretical movement of constellation of forces as change progresses.

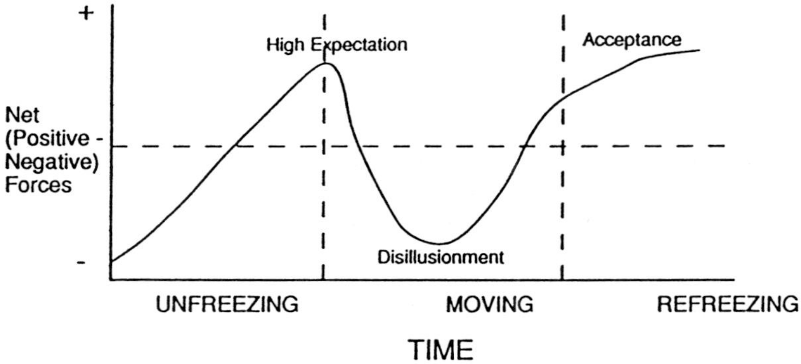

Fig. 2. Patterns of change for two years internalization process (adopted from Morrison 1989).

4. Conclusions and Implications

In a study of social change, the quantifiable data must be looked at in tandem with qualifiable results. This study has used Force Field Analysis as a tool to test the appropriateness of the Lewin model for change to that of CASE implementation. In general the Lewin theory is supported by the data in this study. There were at least three identifiable groups within the ISD department and they were in different places with respect to the change taking place. Both the quantifiable and qualifying data support this finding.

The interesting side notes about the data are that the magnitude of the forces (i.e., more positive than negative) may not be as indicative of where individuals are with respect to the change as much as the nature of the forces themselves. For example, during the unfreezing stage a person is likely to question the decision about the system of choice: "Why is this tool used?", "Did management make a mistake?", and the like. Similarly, the unfrozen potential user looks externally for problems: management isn't supportive, the end-users may not accept this, etc.

By the time the person enters the moving phase, he/she may actually be more disillusioned than those who are still questioning the decision. At the same time, the problems and forces surrounding the move are largely internal: how does this affect me and my job? What can I do to cut the learning curve and be more productive? As a side note, during the solution phase of this project, the users offered as a solution to work half days on Saturdays at no extra pay to help learn the tools faster, if management would get them some locally available expertise to help with the learning curve. In short, they developed personal commitment to the change.

Less is actually known about the refrozen group. The data seem to indicate that they have gone through the moving phase, but since the Support staff do not work with all the tools, they only had to learn a portion of what the project development people (Users and Non-users) master. It is somewhat like the person who needs to lose five pounds, buys a diet book and follows the program for two weeks and loses the five pounds. This person cannot understand why their colleague who has to lose 50 pounds cannot achieve the same success, after all it is all in the book. The magnitude of the change for the Users of the tools and for the Support staff which is highly specialized is not comparable. Yet this group is ready to move on to something new and put considerable pressure on those still in the throws of moving to "come on board." The lack of empathy for the Users among the Support team was evident in this study and creates some difficult problems for management. In particular, strategies are needed that bring all groups closer in line with the change process so that they can begin to feel like part of a team. The Support people need to get more involved in the moving phase and the Non-users need to begin to move so that the organization can move forward with the change instead of two extremes (unfrozen and refrozen) groups pulling at the middle group.

From a research perspective, the supporting data for the Lewin model, modified by the Morrison diagram (Fig. 2) give new insight into the nature of the change process during CASE technology transfer. It may be possible, with further study, to develop a predictive tool so that assessment of where each person or groups of persons are with respect to a particular change can be validated. This gives better understanding to the change process as it applies to systems. What is needed now is verification of the data in this study across other system environments in general. With respect to CASE implementation, a replication of the data across different CASE tools is needed as well as a broader base of data, i.e., more people, more sites and possibly longitudinal data looking at the changes that take place in forces (both in magnitude and content) from the beginning of the process to the end.

Thus, the answer to the question: "How much longer will it be until we are fully implemented on CASE?" may depend largely on the nature of the negative forces in the environment. The good news is that internal forces, those things personal to the person making the change, even though they may be negative, may mean that the person is moving towards fruition.

References

1. A. Bean, R. Neal, M. Radnor and D. Tanser, "Structural and behavioral correlates of implementation in U.S. business organizations," *Implementation Operations Research/Management* (Elseiver, 1975) pp. 77–132.
2. R. W. Boss, "Trust and managerial problem solving revisted," *Group and Organizational Studies* **3**, 3 (1978) 331–342.
3. P. Keen, "Information systems and organizational change," *Commun. ACM* **24**, 1 (1981) 24–33.
4. K. Lewin, "Group decision and social change", *Readings in Social Psychology* (Henry Holt and Co., 1952) pp. 459–473.
5. D. E. Morrison, "Making change user-friendly: managing the impact on technology on people," *Inf. Executive* (Spring 1989).
6. L. Nelson and F. L. Burns, "High performance programming: a framework for transforming organizations" *Transforming Work*, ed. J. D. Adams (1984) pp. 225–242.
7. S. P. Robbins, *Organizational Behavior*, 5th ed. (Prentice-Hall, 1991).
8. E. Rogers, *Diffusion of Innovations* (The Free Press, 1972).

9. A. Sandberg, "Socio-technical design, trade union strategies and action research," *Research Methods in Information Systems*, eds. E. Mumford *et. al.* (Elsevier, 1985) pp. 79–99.
10. E. H. Schein, "The mechanism of change" *Interpersonal Dynamics*, eds. W. Bennis, E. Schein, F. Steele and D. Berlew (Dorsey, 1964) pp. 362–378.
11. R. Schultz, M. Ginzberg and H. Lucas, "A structural model of implementation," *Implementing Operations Research/Management Science*, eds. R. Schultz and D. Slevin (Elsevier, 1984) pp. 55–88.
12. R. E. Sorenson and D. E. Zand, "Improving implementation of OR/MS models by applying in the Lewin–Schein theory of change," *Implementing Operations Research/Management Science*, eds. R. Schultz and D. Slevin (Elsevier, 1984) pp. 217–236.
13. T. Wood-Harper, "Research methods in information systems: using action research," *Research Methods in Information Systems*, eds. E. Mumford *et. al.* (Elsevier, 1985) pp. 169–191.
14. D. E. Zand, "Trust and managerial effectiveness," *Admin. Sci. Quart.* **17**, 2 (1972) 229–239.
15. D. E. Zand and R. E. Sorenson, "Theory of change and the effective use of management science," *Admin. Sci. Quart.* **20**, 4 (1975) 532–545.
16. R. W. Zmud and J. F. Cox, "The implementation process: a change approach," *MIS Quart.* **3**, 2 (1979) 35–43.

CASE Tools and CASE Tool Integration

THE ROLE OF PROTOTYPING LANGUAGES IN CASE*

LUQI

Computer Science Department, Naval Postgraduate School, Monterey, CA 93943, USA

ABSTRACT

Prototyping languages form a new category in the computer language family. They are different from the commonly familiar computer languages because they are used to support a higher level of automation at early phases of software development as well as throughout the entire process. They are used to create mechanically processable and executable descriptions or models of proposed software systems. Prototyping languages are also used to firm up requirements via frequent modifications and demonstrations of the models in an iterative process of prototype evolution. The benefits of a prototyping language are fully realized when it is used with its computer-aided prototyping system (CAPS). In this paper, we describe the background, requirements, characteristics, computational features, and general principles for the design of prototyping languages. An example of a prototyping language design is used to illustrate these concepts.

1. Introduction

Computer Aided Prototyping Systems (CAPS) should be used to prototype large, parallel, distributed, real-time, and knowledge-based systems because the requirements for design of such software systems are difficult to assess, leading to demand for prototyping support in these areas [17, 29]. The formal prototyping languages needed to build CAPS form a special category in the computer language family.

Rapid prototyping languages are used to create software prototypes, which are mechanically processable and executable descriptions or simplified models of proposed software systems. They are also used to modify the models frequently in an iterative prototype evolution process for the purpose of firming up the requirements. Figure 1 illustrates the prototyping process, which consists

*This research was supported by the National Science Foundation under grant number CCR-9058453.

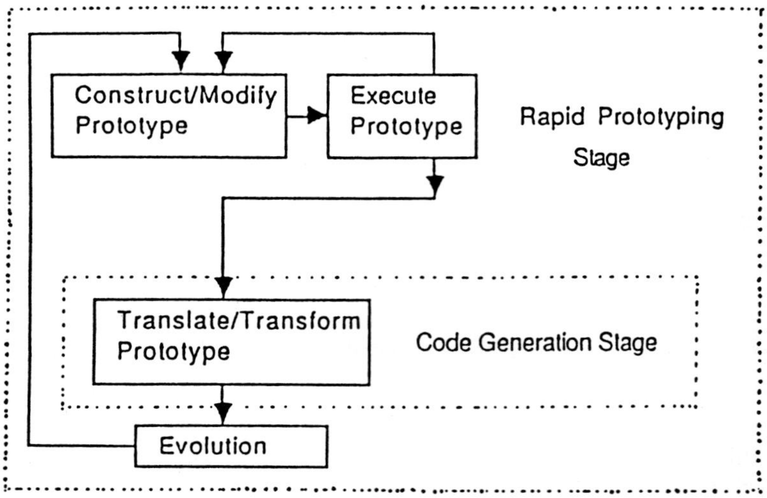

Fig. 1. Rapid prototyping process.

of two stages: prototype construction and code generation. The prototyping stage firms up software requirements through iterative negotiations between customers and designers via examination of executable prototypes. The designer adjusts the requirements and modifies the prototype accordingly based on feedback from the customer until the customer agrees on the requirements. The code generation stage focuses on augmenting the prototype to generate the production code. Prototypes are built to gain information to guide analysis and design, and support automatic generation of the production code.

A rapid prototyping language intended to apply to a variety of software systems is an ambitious goal that raises many interesting research problems [8]. Goals for such a language have to include the modeling of those systems, providing a fundamental mechanism for the integration of the tools in its CAPS, and computer-aided transformations of prototypes into implementations of the production version of the software. Solutions to these problems are essential for achieving significant improvements in the quality and productivity of the software development process [31].

It is useful to briefly examine the history of computer languages. The terminology for describing languages has been changing dramatically with implementation technology. Originally any compiled programming language was a very high level language. As systems became more complex, the meaning of the term shifted towards design languages which can describe system structure without introducing low level implementation details and can define generalized components that can be adapted to many different situations. Technologies improved to the point where programming languages could support abstraction and generalization, e.g., Ada and Smalltalk. Systems became even larger, and the meaning of the term shifted again, towards languages describing what a system is supposed to do, without specifying how the system is to accomplish its goals. As technology advances, some of these specification languages are becoming executable. The term "very high level language" is not precisely defined, since the concept of a very high level language is a moving target that depends on the current state of compiler technology and the speed, memory capacity, and cost of available hardware. Currently it refers to languages with abstractions and powerful mathematical constructs used in the early stages of the traditional software life cycle, such as domain modeling languages, specification languages, design languages, and prototyping languages.

As compiler and hardware technology improves, the gaps among these high level computer language categories are getting smaller and may eventually disappear. Programming languages are getting more expressive and more flexible, and are supporting more abstract descriptions of the processes to be carried out, while specification and design languages are incorporating larger executable subsets [5, 32]. In the near future these types of languages will remain distinct to more effectively support different classes of tools. Programming languages will support optimizing compilers whose main objective is to produce efficient implementations. Specification and design languages will support tools for requirements analysis and proving the correctness of designs and implementations. Protyping languages will support tools for prototype construction, demonstration and production code generation.

The theory and technology of computer languages has become sufficient to support exploratory development of a general purpose rapid prototyping language. In 1985, a special purpose rapid prototyping language PSDL (Prototype System Description Language) and its CAPS were published in [34] for rapid prototyping in the development of large and real-time systems [17]. In the past years, the feasibility study for the tools in the CAPS has shown great promise [1]. The design and implementation of a rapid prototyping language can benefit from past work on specification, design, and programming languages. Many such languages previously designed for programming, design or specification were used or intended to be used for prototyping purposes in different degrees. In the 1970's, the SETL programming language was designed based on set theory and already had the primitive concepts for integrating high level mathematics with an execution capability [28]. Other languages that have been used for prototyping at the programming level include APL, SNOBOL, LISP, and PROLOG. The Gypsy language from UT Austin provides a simple basis for representing, executing, and proving correctness of communicating processes [9]. Research on real-time modeling and scheduling provides fundamental support for the design of hard real-time systems [22]. Work on attribute grammars paved the road to automated approaches for prototyping special purpose languages [10, 27]. The GIST system at ISI has explored computer-aided requirements modeling with the aid of symbolic evaluation and English paraphrasing [7, 30]. The OBSERV system has used abstract ports coupled with graphical interconnection-facilities to support rapid prototyping and exploratory design [35]. The Argus project at MIT has explored implementation of atomic transactions in distributed systems [15]. The wide spectrum language Refine from Reasoning systems [26], the DRACO system from UC Irvine [24], and the CIP project from Munich [2] have explored the feasibility of using transformations to realize specifications.

The strength of a specification language is its simplicity, abstraction, clarity of expression, and means for rigorous logical reasoning [3]. The strengths of a design language are its expressiveness and support for recording goals and justifications. A common weakness of specification and design languages is lack of efficient facilities for execution or lack of any effective means for execution. The strength of most programming languages is supporting efficient execution, while common weaknesses are the need for specifying many details and lack of facilities for recording goals and justifications in a formal way. A prototyping language should integrate the strengths and functions of specification and design languages with the capability for execution. Because of the wide range of goals for prototyping languages, design decisions for those languages are difficult to make. It is helpful to examine the functions of a prototyping language in the rapid prototyping process before further discussion of language principles.

2. CAPS and Prototyping Languages

In the rapid prototyping process, software prototypes must be constructed quickly and at low to be practical. The prototyping language and its CAPS are used for:

- Rapidly building and modifying prototypes,
- Simplifying the design of complex systems,
- Demonstrating prototype systems to users,
- Evaluating and checking proposed design, and
- Efficiently and reliably transforming prototypes into production code.

A prototyping language has no obligation to give detailed algorithms for all components of the system as long as it is descriptive and executable. Its CAPS should automatically supply algorithmic details needed for execution, help the designer manipulate, analyze, demonstrate, and explain the prototype, and help the development team transform the prototype into a production version of the system. The design of the prototyping language is subject to the need of supporting the software tools in a CAPS system.

2.1. *Tools in a computer aided prototyping system (CAPS)*

Prototyping with computer-aided tools makes a rapid process possible. A CAPS designed for supporting a special prototyping language should make it easy to specify, construct, demonstrate, understand, explain, and modify a software prototype. The language provides the basic communication and representation medium for all the tools in a CAPS system. In the CAPS proposed in [17], guidelines for decomposing software modules, reusable components, a prototyping interface, a design database, and a software base management system with inference capabilities make the process possible.

The tool set should provide facilities for analyzing the consistency of a prototype design. Some of the properties that should be checked include:

- Type consistency,
- Feasibility of timing constraints,
- Consistency between the levels of a hierarchical description,
- Preconditions on input parameters and generic parameters,
- Constraints on relative rates of producer and consumer processes,
- Absence of deadlocks in distributed and parallel systems,
- Absence of unhandled exceptions.

In addition to providing facilities for constructing and checking the internal consistency of a prototype, the tool set should provide facilities for generating input data, debugging, displaying output, and evaluating the results of prototype execution in terms of the same semantic model used for the design of the prototype.

To support user validation and system evolution, a prototyping language should interface to a facility for maintaining the correspondence between requirements and design decisions. Tools are needed for determining which parts of a prototype are affected by a requirements change, and which requirements are affected by a proposed change to the behavior of a prototype.

The tool set should also provide a design database for maintaining the design history, to capture dependencies between different versions of the system and to record alternative designs that were considered [6, 11, 19, 25]. This database should be capable of recording and maintaining constraints between the components of a prototype. An issue in the design of such a database is the relation between the prototyping language used for representing the design objects in the database, and representations for the attributes, relationships, and constraints used by the CAPS tools. The information in the designer's view of the language is a subset of the information in the tool views, since tools often add additional attributes to the entities defined by the language for recording the results of analysis and synthesis procedures. Since the tool set is likely to grow, the representation of design objects should be extendible without affecting the interfaces to existing tools.

2.2. *The purpose of a prototyping language*

A prototyping language is used by both people and software tools. To support the human users, a prototyping language should be easy to write, understand, and modify. To support the tools, the language should be easy to analyze and transform mechanically. The requirements for prototyping language follow.

A prototyping language should be clear and simple. This implies uniform structure, a small number of orthogonal constructs, and general interpretations without special cases or restrictions. To support automated tools, the language should have a simple syntax and a precisely defined meaning. The underlying model should have a mathematical basis to support execution, rigorous reasoning, and transformations. The model should also support tools for communication with untrained people. Such tools should provide graphical summary views, English paraphrasing, and explanation facilities.

A prototyping language should be powerful and concise. It should enable brief prototype definitions for a wide variety of software systems, including the tools in the CAPS. The language and the tools should support abstractions, incomplete descriptions, and automated design completion. The language should support abstractions for concurrency, synchronization, and timing constraints in addition to traditional functional, data, and control abstractions. The constructs of the language should match decisions made by the designer more closely than the operations performed by the processor, to make prototype descriptions easy to understand and change. The designer should be able to specify only the essential attributes of a proposed system, and the tools should supply default values for all attributes needed for execution of a software prototype. To avoid complicating the language, high level abstractions should be expressed as standard pre-defined components in a knowledge base whenever it is possible to do so without extending the language.

A prototyping language should localize design decisions and interactions between system components or pieces of knowledge in the knowledge base. These features allow independently designed subsystems of complex systems to cooperate without unexpected interference, simplify concurrency issues, and aid in scheduling.

A prototyping language should be able to represent black-box specifications. Specifications are needed for documenting prototypes, retrieving reusable software components, and verifying implementations via automated testing and proofs. Such descriptions also form the basis for automated synthesis capabilities, inheritance of common properties and constraints, and consistency checking. This part of the language may contain non-computable constructs such as unbounded logical quantifiers to gain expressive power.

The language should be able to represent clear-box design information. This information includes interconnections of subcomponents, dependencies between components, design goals such as invariant constraints, and criteria for choosing between alternative designs. The language should have facilities for adapting components to new uses and making small perturbations on their behavior without examining the details of the internal implementation of the components, to make it easier to reuse components.

The language should have an expressive executable subset. This subset should be easily recognizable both by people and automated tools. It should be possible to transform or augment expressions of the language outside the executable subset to make them recognizably executable.

The language should support the construction of efficient implementations by augmenting the prototype description with annotations. These annotations should describe additional constraints or lower level design decisions. This enables developers to treat optimization as a refinement step where additional information is added to the original descriptions, rather than a complete redefinition of the system. This avoids repeated description of the same information in different ways, and reduces opportunities for making errors.

It must be possible to run test cases and gather data in a practical amount of time. Efficiency does not have the highest priority in a prototyping language, but it cannot be ignored completely. Thus execution mechanisms based on exhaustive enumeration are insufficient for a prototyping language, although they may be supplied as a default to enable execution of small test cases even in the absence of information about more efficient execution strategies. The language should therefore support relatively efficient execution mechanisms, tools for locating performance bottlenecks, and incremental optimizations transformations to improve prototypes that are impractically slow.

Real-time constraints require execution times to be predictable, although not necessarily very fast. Prototypes of real-time systems may operate in simulated time or linearly scaled real time, but the actual execution times for the production version must be predictable within accurate bounds.

3. Examples of a Prototyping Language

The rapid prototyping language PSDL [17, 18, 34] and its CAPS were designed to support prototyping of large, parallel, and real-time systems. The CAPS provides a designer interface for constructing, analyzing, and modifying a prototype, along with execution facilities which realize timing constraints with respect to either actual or linearly scaled real-time.

PSDL encourages localized descriptions and software structures, to aid the designer in constructing and modifying understandable models of complex systems. The language has a simple and expressive computational model based on modified dataflow augmented with non-procedural constraints. The elements of the model are operators and data streams. Every operator is a state machine and some operators are functions, i.e., machines with an empty set of state variables and a single internal state. Every data stream carries values of an abstract type, and some streams carry exception values.

The computational model was developed based on two main concerns: ease of use by human designers, and ease of processing by the tools in the CAPS. Data flow diagrams have been widely used in requirements analysis, partially because they are easy to understand both by developers and by customers. This motivated us to adopt a graphical notation in PSDL, based on operators and data flows. However, the data flow diagrams commonly used in informal, manual approaches to requirements analysis are not sufficiently precise to support execution and analysis of real-time behavior of a proposed system. The behavior of a classical data flow diagram is not completely determined because the diagram shows only the data that can flow through the system, and does not specify the cause and effect relationships and the timing properties that determine the details of system behavior. We added annotations to the graphics to express this information, and found that this was sufficient to enable automatic execution and real-time scheduling by the CAPS tools.

A PSDL prototype consists of a hierarchically structured set of definitions for operators and types. Each definition has a *specification part* for black-box descriptions and *implementation part* for clear-box descriptions. The specifications are used both for documentation of the prototype and for retrieval of reusable software components. A specification is executable without further information from the designer if the CAPS can automatically retrieve, adapt, and combine the reusable software components in its software base to match the specification. In cases where this is not possible, the designer must develop an implementation part decomposing the specified system into more primitive subsystems and provide black-box specifications for each of the subsystems. The decomposition is done in terms of the PSDL computational model, using augmented data flow diagrams.

An augmented data flow diagram is a directed graph, annotated with control constraints and timing constraints. The nodes in an augmented data flow diagram represent operators, the edges represent data streams, and the numbers associated with the nodes represent maximum execution times. The diagram has a graphical representation and the constraints have a text representation, as illustrated in Fig. 2. The example shows a simple control system illustrating some typical features of embedded software. The filter performs a smoothing operation to reduce the noise in the sensor data, and the controller uses the filtered sensor data to determine how to respond to commands from a human operator, which are transmitted to the embedded system via a switch on the operator's control panel. A simple smoothing filter might take the form

$$\text{new state\_variable} = \text{w}^*\text{old state\_variable} + (1.0\text{-w})^* \text{ sensor\_data}$$

where the weight w is a real number between 0 and 1 that must be chosen to provide the best trade-off between response time and sensitivity to noise. The example has a minimal specification part with an informal description.

```
OPERATOR control_system
SPECIFICATION
  INPUT operator_switch: boolean, sensor_data: real
  OUTPUT control_signal: real
  STATES state_variable: real INITIALLY 0.0
  DESCRIPTION { top level of a simple embedded system }
END

IMPLEMENTATION
  GRAPH
```

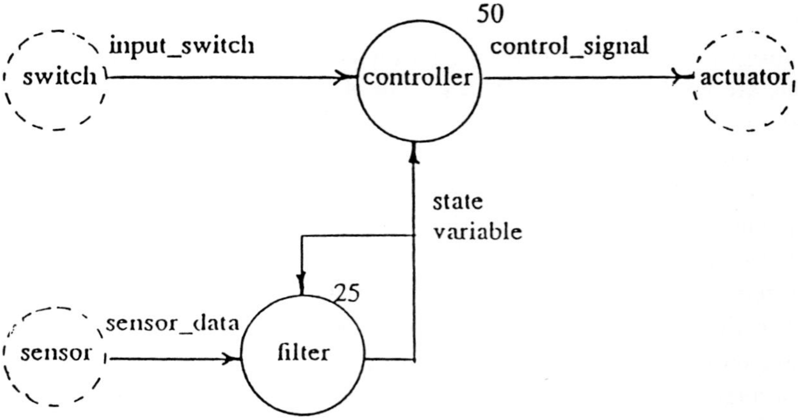


```
  CONTROL CONSTRAINTS
    OPERATOR filter PERIOD 100 ms
    OPERATOR controller TRIGGERED BY ALL input_switch
      MAXIMUM RESPONSE TIME 200 ms
      MINIMUM CALLING PERIOD 200 ms
END
```

Fig. 2. Example of an augmented data flow diagram in PSDL.

The implementation part contains a graph showing the decomposition of the system into two subsystems, and the control constraints give control and timing information. The control constraints and the timing constraints determine both the conditions under which the operators are triggered and the buffering disciplines for the data streams. In general, control constrains can express conditional execution or output, and can control exceptions and timers. PSDL timers are used to control durations of states, and can be thought of as software stopwatches.

Timing constraints can be added to operators to define hard real-time deadlines for time-critical operators. Timing constraints can express sporadic data-driven execution as well as periodic execution. In Fig. 2 both operators are time-critical. The *filter* operator must be fired periodically, every 100 milliseconds. The *controller* operator is fired sporadically, whenever a new value for the *input-switch* arrives, and must complete execution within 200 milliseconds of the arrival of the new value.

There are two possible buffering disciplines for a data stream; *dataflow* and *sampled.* Dataflow streams act as first-in-first-out buffers, and are used for synchronizing data-driven computations. Sampled streams act as continuously available sources of data which can be read or updated on demand, and are used for connecting unsynchronized operators which can fire at different or unpredictable rates. Data streams have dataflow buffers if and only if they appear in a TRIGGERED BY ALL control constraint. In Fig. 2, the streams *input_switch* and *control_signal* are dataflow streams, while *sensor_data* and *state_variable* are sampled streams. The triggering conditions express requirements for the *controller* and the *actuator* to respond exactly once to every new value in the streams *input_switch* and *control_signal.* The other streams must be sampled because the filter operator must operate at fixed times and values may be written into the *sensor_data* stream or read from the *state_variable* stream at unpredictable times.

The PSDL translator [1] generates Ada code for interconnecting operators appearing in an augmented dataflow diagram. Figure 3 shows a simplified version of the Ada code that would be generated for the example in Fig. 2 if the operator *filter* and *controller* are realized by reusable components from the above software base. In the example we assume these components are Ada procedures with the same names as the corresponding PSDL operators. There are two different kinds of code generated: buffer declarations and driver code. Buffers are instances of pre-defined generic packages corresponding to the two buffering disciplines for PSDL data streams, with variants for declaring the initial values of streams that represent state variables for state machines. The driver procedures *controller_driver* and *filter_driver* realize the control constraints and perform the data stream operations. These procedures are called from the static schedule tasks at times determined by a pre-computed static schedule.

(a) generated buffer declarations and initialization

```
input_switch_buffer is new fifo_buffer(boolean);
sensor_data_buffer is new sampled_buffer(real);
state_variable_buffer is new state_variable(real, 0.0);
```

(b) generated driver code

```
procedure controller_driver is
   input_switch: boolean;
   state_variable, control_signal: real;
begin
   if input_switch_buffer.new_data then
      input_switch_buffer.read(input_switch);
      state_variable_buffer.read(state_variable);
      controller(input_switch, state_variable, control_signal);
      control_signal_buffer.write(control_signal);
   end if;
end controller_driver;

procedure filter_driver is
   sensor_data, state_variable: real;
begin
   if true then
      sensor_data_buffer.read(sensor_data);
      state_variable_buffer.read(state_variable);
      filter (sensor_data, state_variable)
      state_variable_buffer, write (state_variable)
   end if;
end filter_driver;
```

Fig. 3. General Ada code for the control_system.

The timing constraints associated with time-critical operators are realized by the static scheduler in CAPS. A static schedule for the operators in Fig. 2 is shown in Fig. 4. This schedule repeats every 400 milliseconds. Since there is no explicit deadline given for the *filter* operator, the deadline defaults to the maximum execution time, and the operator is scheduled at intervals exactly 100 milliseconds apart. The initial firing of the *filter* is scheduled before the initial firing of the *controller* because of the precedence relation created by the data stream *state_variable*. The *controller* is scheduled so that a response to any request can be completed within 200 milliseconds of the request, regardless of when the request occurs. Each instance of the *controller* in the schedule is responsible for handling only those requests that arrive after the previous instance of the *controller* has started execution. The instance of the *controller* that starts at time 275 is interleaved with an execution of the *filter*. This is permissible because operators do not interact except via data streams. These interruptions are realized in Ada by making the calls to *filter_driver* and *controller_driver* from two tasks with different priorities. There are short periods of time at the beginning and at the end of each execution of an operator when such interruptions cannot be scheduled, because of atomic read and write operations on the data streams.

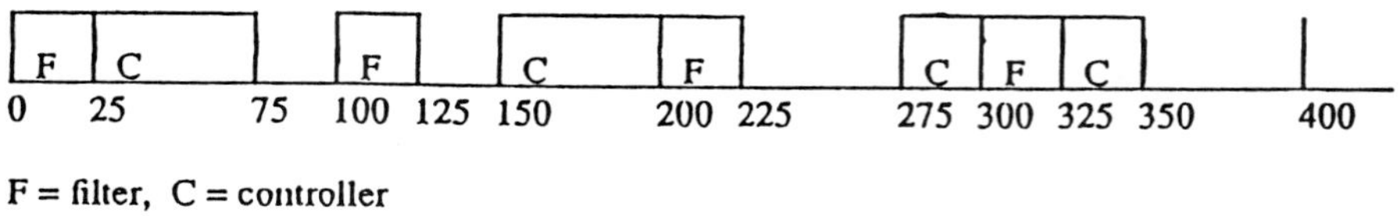

Fig. 4. Static schedule for the control_system.

PSDL was designed so that operators can interact only via data streams. This locality property simplifies the design and modification of prototypes by ensuring that operators can be executed in parallel without interference and can interact only via the documented interfaces, and also makes it easier to construct schedules. The locality property is realized by the absence of a mechanism for transmitting objects with internal states along data streams and scoping rules that do not allow direct nonlocal data references.

4. Designing a Prototyping Language

A prototyping language should simplify the designer's view of the system and support automated means for bridging the gap between this simplified view and the detailed algorithmic descriptions currently needed for efficient execution. The CAPS system should provide mechanisms for execution, static analysis, preparation of test cases, display and analysis of results, and debugging to allow the prototype designers to work entirely within the simplified view.

4.1. *Static and dynamic properties*

Static properties of a computer language must be fixed before a system is executed, while dynamic properties can be changed as the system runs. Prototyping languages should support dynamic treatment of objects such as data types, operators, and timing constraints to support flexible demonstrations and prototyping of adaptive systems. For example, programs that can manipulate data types, programs, and schedules at run-time can adapt to unanticipated circumstances more readily than those that cannot.

This goal is hard to meet, because static declarations allow tools to provide more information about a proposed system and enable more efficient execution techniques. A prototyping language with many dynamic features requires type checking, interpreter calls or compilation, loading, linking, and scheduling to be done as the system runs. These facilities are difficult to implement efficiently, and are not supported by the class of languages usually used for production versions. Uniform guarantees of type correctness, clean termination, or meeting hard real-time constraints may not be possible without static restrictions on these properties. Thus a prototyping language should be able to represent optional static restrictions, and CAPS should support transformations adding explicit static restrictions to improve efficiency or predictability.

4.2. *Computational model*

The models underlying a prototyping language provide the common ground for the associated set of tools. The semantic model for the language provides the basis for automated analysis, while the computational model provides the basis for execution. One of the main challenges in developing a prototyping language is finding models that can coherently span the range of applications required.

There is no common model of expert systems available for rapid prototyping. First order logic is one of the most familiar models for reasoning, but it has been criticized for its weaknesses, such as difficulties in handling uncertain information, representing heuristic methods for speeding up conclusions, and performing nonmonotonic reasoning. Many other kinds of logic have been proposed, but there has been no consensus on whether there is a single logic suitable for constructing all types of expert systems, or which variety of logic is the most promising. Some approaches to expert systems use models other than logic, such as semantic networks, Bayesian statistics, and production systems. It is not clear which approach will yield the best results in the long run.

There is also no commonly accepted model for representing real-time constraints. Some approaches that have been explored include temporal logic, state machines, mode charts, augmented data flow diagrams, Petri nets, and

I/O automata. The model for a prototyping language should be chosen to enhance the application of recent results in logic, graph theory, and combinatorics to provide an effective execution mechanism. Other unexplored areas include effective models for real-time databases and real-time communications networks. Since different models appear to be best for different purposes, practical prototyping languages should seek a unified way to support multiple models. This requires careful attention to the interactions between the language and the set of pre-defined components that can be supplied by the CAPS.

4.3. *Execution support*

A knowledge-based approach is needed to provide adequate execution support for a prototyping language without requiring excessive algorithmic detail. CAPS should provide knowledge base support for the following functions:

Design — The CAPS system should contain models of common design activities and common classes of design decisions, to allow prototypes to be expressed in the conceptual framework of the designer rather than that of the machine. If the system is aware of the choices faced by a designer at each point in the design, it can present compact representations of the choices using menus. Such alternatives should have corresponding representations in the prototyping language.

Managing reusable components — The environment should contain a large software base with reusable components. This software base should be coupled with a set of rules for tailoring and combining available components to fulfill queries that do not exactly match any of the components explicitly stored in the software base. This allows the system to find algorithms and data structures without imposing all of the details of the designer.

High level debugging — Errors and failures during prototype execution should be mapped from the programming language level to the level of the prototyping language, to keep programming details from intruding when the designer tests and demonstrates the prototype.

Optimization — The transformations for optimizing a prototype version of a system to produce a production version should be performed with minimum interaction with the designer. CAPS should keep track of optimization decisions made for previous versions of the system, determine which of those decisions are valid for later versions, and automatically apply the ones that are still valid. While it is not currently feasible to produce highly optimized implementations without human help, it is possible to automate routine decisions and rely on the designer for only the difficult decisions.

Explanations — Justifications for decisions made by CAPS should be available to provide feedback to the designer in cases where automated design completion procedures fail. Such a facility is needed to support systematic computer-aided design in situations where complete automation is not possible. This requires an expert system with a substantial knowledge base.

It is natural to consider the execution aspect of a prototyping language in terms of compiler technology. Unfortunately, ordinary compiler technology is insufficient for execution of a rapid prototyping language. The reasons are:

Flexibility — The need for flexibility and run-time handling of newly created types and procedures to support expert systems provides challenges for efficient implementation techniques.

Real-time constraints — Conventional translation techniques must be coupled with facilities for scheduling to meet hard real-time constraints, transformations to allow the execution of incompletely specified processes, and access to an interpreter or an incremental compiler at run-time.

Missing details — An issue that must be faced by an execution support system for a prototyping language is providing missing details. One of the goals of a rapid prototyping system is to execute prototype descriptions that do not contain details of algorithms and data structures [33]. This has to be handled by combining program transformations and specialized schedulers with a knowledge base containing programming and problem domain knowledge.

Transformations are needed to execute incompletely specified components. Such transformations should supply reasonable default values for attributes necessary for execution if the designer does not explicitly specify them. Different choices for these attributes can be explicitly specified to produce a more accurate model of the system or to improve its performance. In particular, default algorithms for unspecified or partially specified component should be supplied. Key problems are finding systematic ways of developing such transformation and determining reasonable default values based on models of the application domain. It is essential to automatically generate stubs for components that are unavailable in the software base and have not yet been designed to allow testing and demonstrating partially completed systems. Such stubs can be created by simple or increasingly sophisticated techniques, such as asking the user to supply values, using random selections from a fixed set of responses, using logic programming to simulate black-box specifications, or using transformation techniques to generate efficient implementations from the black-box descriptions. Other example include assignment of tasks to physical processors and choosing display formats for outputs and error messages.

5. Semantics of a Prototyping Language

The key to computer-aided prototyping is finding simple formal models that can express the range of expected applications and effectively support automated processing. The desire for extensive automated processing in a CAPS system argues for Spartan simplicity in the design of the prototyping language: new language features should be resisted whenever it is possible to cover all required functionality without introducing new primitives. This section examines some likely application areas for rapid prototyping and some of the implications for the design of a common prototyping language.

5.1. *Supporting real-time systems*

The language and the CAPS knowledge base should support representations for timing constraints and overload resolution policies. Scheduling is a difficult issue for real-time systems. High level representations of timing constraints and overload resolution policies are essential to allow the prototype to express the necessary constraints on the scheduling of different tasks at a level matching the problem rather than at the level of the underlying run-time support system. Timing constraints on communications primitives are needed to handle distributed real-time systems.

5.2. *Modeling parallel systems*

High-level mechanisms for coordinating independent activities [12] and primitives for defining independent activities that are guaranteed not to interfere with each other are needed to simplify and speed up the construction of parallel systems. Localized modules with limited data access are essential for this purpose. Message passing, dataflow, and object-oriented ideas have been proposed to address this problem. Another consideration is avoidance of deadlock. It is useful to have a syntactically recognizable subset of the language that is capable of describing concurrent computations and carries a uniform guarantee of freedom from deadlock. Such a guarantee is possible if a suitable computational model is chosen. This kind of restricted subset is sufficient for many applications, and it can be augmented with facilities for adding additional constraints on global orderings of events, which are known to be potentially unsafe and are designed together with tools for checking safety of particular designs. For example, atomic transactions can simplify the design of distributed systems, although they introduce the potential for deadlocks.

5.3. *Designing distributed systems*

A prototyping language should provide a high level means for describing

1. constraints on communication time,
2. the granularity of atomic transactions,
3. standard protocols for achieving reliability despite processing and communications failures, and
4. constraints on the assignment of software tasks to physical processors.

This information should be optional, and the default should be the safest option rather than the most efficient one.

5.4. *Prototyping knowledge-based systems*

CAPS can provide generic predefined software components to realize many of the common building blocks for knowledge-based systems. These include facts, rules, patterns, frames, context, constraints, demons, instance generators, pattern matchers, unification mechanisms, constraint propagation mechanisms, and inference engines. Thus the prototyping language does not appear to require special features beyond the flexibility described in Subsec. 4.1 to provide these facilities. However, standardization of these building blocks requires careful analysis and specification of their required properties.

An open issue is whether current mechanisms for defining generic components are flexible enough to adequately capture the range of behavior required for these kinds of components, and if not, what extensions are required. A solution to this general problem that has been applied successfully in other contexts such as parsing context free languages is meta-programming: a family of reusable components is defined implicity via a special purpose problem definition language and a program generator that tailors a known general solution strategy to the particular problem represented by a statement in the problem definition language. The program generator creates instances of the component family based on statements in the problem definition language. The components created by the program generator can be represented in the prototyping language or in a conventional programming language. In the context of parsing, an example of problem definition language is a grammar notation such as BNF, which defines the source language to be parsed, and an example of a corresponding program generator is an LALR parser generator such as the UNIX yacc tool, which creates a parsing program corresponding to the given grammar. Other examples include tools for generating user interface software [14, 23]. Thus, in addition to a prototyping language, a CAPS system may need a meta-programming language for specifying computed families of reusable components in the software base. A meta-programming language and families of reusable software components could also provide a means for conveniently defining problem-specific external representations and input facilities for the knowledge in the knowledge base.

To support rapid construction of expert systems, a prototyping language should provide:

1. A means for conveniently defining external representations and input facilities for the knowledge in the knowledge base,
2. Unrestricted higher order objects such as types, functions, tasks, and generators, and
3. Control mechanisms such as state-triggered demons, backtracking, run-time control over task priorities, and temporal events.

Several of these features are needed to support flexible prototypes for other kinds of systems as well.

The presence of real-time constraints severely restricts the kinds of computations a system may perform and, in the case of expert systems, limits the amount of logical inference that can be performed. The design of expert systems that operate within real-time constraints is a largely unexplored area, and significant research progress is needed in this area to fully realize the goals of a rapid prototyping language.

6. Conclusions

Prototyping languages are designed based on knowledge and experience from all levels of the computer language hierarchy since they address functions from all of the levels. Studying the relevant aspects of specification, design, and programming languages is helpful in the design of prototyping languages.

The purpose of prototyping languages is to define an executable model of a system. The language is used to create specifications, express designs, and execute prototypes. Prototyping languages are used in requirements analysis for the purpose of requirements validation via early demonstrations to the customer. They are also useful for evaluating competing design alternatives, validating system structures, and exploring feasibility. In contrast, specification languages are used for defining external interfaces in the functional specification stage and for defining internal interfaces during architectural design at the highest levels of abstraction. They are also used for verifying the correctness and completeness of a design or implementation. Design languages are used for recording conventions and interconnections during architectural design and module design.

The difference between specification and design languages is the difference between interface and mechanism: a specification says what is to be done, and a design says how to do it. The main evaluation criterion for both specification and design languages is the ability to express simple, concise, and humanly understandable descriptions of complex behavior. It is useful for specification and design languages to be executable, but simplicity and ease of expression takes precedence when the considerations conflict. Computer aid is desirable for determining the properties of a specification and certifying that a design realizes a specification. An execution capability can contribute to these goals, but other types of mechanical analysis may turn out to be more useful for this purpose.

The difference between a design and a program is the difference between a plan and a finished product: a design records the early decisions that determine an implementation strategy, while a program contains all the details necessary to get an efficiently executable system. The primary goal of a design is documentation rather than execution, while the primary goal of a program is usually efficient execution.

A prototyping language aims at validating specifications and designs mainly via an execution facility. Prototyping languages can benefit from mechanisms developed to increase the expressiveness of specification and design languages, but must accept some restrictions to support execution. The execution mechanisms of a prototyping language should draw on programming language technology, but must accept some inefficiencies to support flexibility and ease of expression. The constructs of a prototyping language should be chosen to allow generation of efficient implementations by smoothly adding information and constraints.

Since completely automatic and totally correct implementation of powerful specification languages is an algorithmically unsolvable problem, research on rapid prototyping should explore human interactions for effectively guiding computer-aided implementation tools. A promising approach is augmenting abstract specifications with annotations or pragmas giving advice about implementation strategies. An important problem is finding concepts and notations that can naturally express such advice in an abstract and orthogonal way. It is desirable to keep the abstract specification separate or easily mechanically separable from the annotations to provide simplified views of large system models.

Providing execution capability for high level prototype descriptions requires a knowledge based approach. The required knowledge bases grows with the problem domain the language addresses. A substantial part of the knowledge in the knowledge base consists of reusable software components augmented with descriptions of their properties. Other kinds of relevant knowledge include methods for adapting and combining the components in the software base, properties of application domains, and the CAPS tools. Progress on rapid prototyping languages depends on solutions to open research problems in areas including semantic modeling, real-time scheduling, program transformations, version control in prototype databases, and retrieval of reusable software components.

References

1. C. Altizer, "Implementation of a language translator for computer aided prototyping system," M. S. Thesis, Computer Science, Naval Postgraduate School, Monterey, CA (December 1988).
2. F. Bauer, B. Moller, H. Partsch and P. Pepper, "Formal program construction by transformations — computer-aided, intuition-guided programming," *IEEE Trans. Soft. Eng.* **15**, 2 (1989) 165–180.
3. V. Berzins and Luqi, *Software Engineering with Abstractions: An Integrated Approach to Software Development Using Ada* (Addison-Wesley, 1991).
4. V. Berzins, Luqi and A. Yehudai, "Using transformations in specification-based prototyping," *IEEE Trans. Softw. Eng.* **18**, 7 (1982).
5. A. Berztiss, "The specification and prototyping language SF," Report 78, Systems Development and Artificial Intelligence Laboratory, Department of Computer and Systems Sciences, Stockholm Unviersity (1990).
6. E. Borison, "Program changes and the cost of selective recompilation," Technical Report CMU-CS-89-205, Computer Science Department, CMU, Pittsburgh, PA (July 1989).
7. D. Cohen, "Symbolic execution of the Gist specification language," in *Proc. Eight International Joint Conference on Artificial Intelligence*, (1983) pp. 17–20.
8. R. Gabriel, ed., *Draft Report on Requirements for a Common Prototyping System*,

DARPA Information Science and Technology Office, Arlington, VA (November, 1988).
9. D. Good, R. Cohen and J. Keeton-Williams, "Principles of proving concurrent programs in Gypsy," in *Proc. 6th Annual Symp. on Principles of Programming Languages*, ACM (1979) pp. 42–52.
10. R. Herndon and V. Berzins, "The realizable benefits of language prototype language," *IEEE Trans. Softw. Eng.* **SE-14**, 6 (1988) 803–809.
11. M. Ketabchi, V. Berzins and S. March, "ODM: An object-oriented data model for design databases," in *Proc. ACM Computer Science Conference* (February 1986) pp. 261–269.
12. B. Kraemer, "SEGRAS—a formal language combining petri nets and abstract data types for specifying distributed systems," in *Proc. 9th Int. Conf. Software Engineering* (March 1987) pp. 116–125.
13. B. Kraemer, Luqi and V. Berzins, "Compositional semantics of a real-time prototyping language," *IEEE Trans. Softw. Eng.* **18**, 9 (1992).
14. T. Lewis, F. Handlosser, S. Bose and S. Yang, "Prototypes from standard user interface management systems," *IEEE Computer* **22**, 5 (1989) 51–60.
15. B. Liskov, "Distributed programming in Argus," *Commun. ACM* **31**, 3 (1988) 300–312.
16. Luqi and V. Berzins, "Rapidly prototyping real-time systems," *IEEE Softw.* **5**, 5 (March 1988) 25–36.
17. Luqi and M. Ketabchi, "A computer aided prototyping system," *IEEE Softw.* **5**, 2 (1988) 66–72.
18. Luqi, V. Berzins and R. Yeh, "A prototyping language for real-time software," *IEEE Trans. Softw. Eng.* **14**, 10 (1988) 1409–1423.
19. Luqi, "A graph model for software evolution," *IEEE Trans. Softw. Eng.* **16**, 8 (1990) 917–927.
20. Luqi, "Real-time constraints in a rapid prototyping language," *IEEE Computer* **24**, 9 (1991) 111–112.
21. Luqi, "Real-time constraints in a rapid prototyping language," *J. Computer Languages* (Spring 1992).
22. A. Mok, "A systematic approach to the design of hard real-time systems," in *Proc. ONR Workshop Foundations of Real-Time Computing*, Office of Naval Research, Falls Church, VA (November 1988) pp. 47–51.
23. B. Myers, "User interface tools," in *Milestone in Software Evolution*, ed. P. Oman and T. Lewis (IEEE Computer Society 1990) pp. 261–270.
24. J. Neighbors, "Draco: a method for engineering reusable software systems," in *Software Reusability*, eds. T. Biggerstaff and A. Perlis (ACM Press, 1989) pp. 295–320.
25. J. Nestor, "Toward persistent object base," in *Advanced Programming Environments*, Vol. 244 (Springer-Verlag, 1986) pp. 372–394.
26. *Refine User's Guide*, Reasoning Systems Inc., Palo Alto, CA (1988).
27. T. Reps and A. Demers, "Sublinear-space evaluation algorithms for attribute grammars," *Trans. Prog. Lang. and Syst.* **9**, 4 (1987) 408–440.

28. E. Schonberg, J. Schwartz and M. Sharir, "An automatic technique for the selection of data representations in SETL programs," *Trans. Prog. Lang. and Syst.* **3**, 2 (April, 1981) 126–143.
29. J. Schwartz, "Board agency announcement for new language in rapid construction of software prototypes," *Commerce Business Daily*, Arlington, VA (February 1989).
30. W. Swartout, "GIST english generator," in *Proc. Nat. Conf. Artifical Intelligence* (AAAI, 1982).
31. M. Tanik and R. Yeh, "The role of rapid prototyping in software development," in *Proc. 22nd Hawaii Int. Conf. System Science*, Kona, Hawaii (January 1989) pp. 337–338.
32. R. Terwilliger and R. Campbell, "PLEASE: executable specifications for incremental software development," *J. Syst. Softw.* **10** (1989) 97–112.
33. J. Tsai, M. Aoyama and Y. Chang, "Rapid prototyping using FRORL language," in *Proc. COMPSAC 88* (October 1988) pp. 410–417.
34. R. Yeh, N. Roussopoulos, Luqi and etc., "Research in software reusability," Final Report, Tech. Rep.-p106/83/0004-3, Ballistic Missile Defense Advanced Technology Center, Huntsville, Alabama (July 1985).
35. A. Yehudai and S. Tyszberowicz, "OBSERV—a prototyping language and environment combining object-oriented approach, state machines, and logic programming," in *Proc. 23rd Annual Hawaii Int. Conf. on System Science* (IEEE Computer Society, January 1990) pp. 247–256.

INTEGRATING USER INTERFACE DEVELOPMENT AND MODERN SOFTWARE DEVELOPMENT

W. DAVID HURLEY
Department of Computer Science, University of Pittsburgh, Pittsburgh, PA 15260, USA

ABSTRACT

A long term goal for software engineers is integrating the separate processes of user interface development and modern software development. With emergent CASE technology, software engineers can begin to explore ways to achieve this integration. Exploration involves investigating candidate methodologies that let developers apply different development strategies to different parts of an interactive system. Disciplined long-term investigation requires that the fundamental principles governing each process be fixed and that evolving development methods comprising each process be accommodated. This paper proposes a computer-based process model that fixes the principles and accommodates evolving methods. Model features include a collection of software engineering and knowledge engineering techniques that supports a development organization of human and computer-based agents, a coordination activity that supports opportunistic behavior of developers, a unifying representation that leads to mutually consistent results from developers, and an extendable topology that enhances collaboration among developers while reducing their communications burden.

1. Introduction

A fundamental difference in orientation between user interface design and software design has driven user interface developers to establish their own methodologies. These methodologies do not fit into mainstream software engineering processes and consequently have reached their limits in terms of successfully addressing certain issues critical to the development of interactive systems.

To successfully address these issues, software engineers have long proposed integrating user interface development and modern software development into the same development process. With emergent CASE technology, software engineers will have the means to accomplish this integration, as evidenced in part by the current efforts of user interface developers to integrate their specialized tools into CASE tools [1]. But software engineers must go beyond integrating tools with specialized capabilities. For interactive systems, the critical development issues can be addressed only by systematic treatment throughout development, which means within the context of a unified methodology, that is, a collection of methods unified by some general philosophical approach to development. Although unified, the methodology must let developers apply different development strategies to different parts of an interactive system.

The task of investigating candidate methodologies will require a disciplined approach applied over a long period of time. The fundamental principles that govern the user interface development process and the modern software development process must be fixed. Evolving methods that comprise each process must be accommodated. Requirements for CASE capabilities that will enable the integration of these processes must be evaluated continually.

This paper proposes a computer-based process model to support this task. The model's components and their interrelationships reflect the fundamental principles governing each development process. Its extendable topology provides a foundation for evolving methods. Its inherent tool orientation reflects the advances in CASE capabilities that will enable the integration of the two processes.

Section 2 gives additional background and motivation. Section 3 examines the strengths and weaknesses of existing process models. Section 4 describes a new process model. Section 5 discusses the advantages and disadvantages of the proposed model. Section 6 presents conclusions and suggests directions for future work.

2. Integrating User Interface Development and Modern Software Development

User interface development differs from mainstream software development. In particular, the orientation of user interface design differs from the orientation of software design. User interface design concerns the design of human-computer dialogues and the design of presentations of information as text, graphics, animation, or sound [2]. It considers the behavior of user and user interface while they interact [3]. In contrast, software design considers the behavior and interactions of software components [4]. Thus, user interface design is user-centered while software design is system-centered [3].

The difference in orientation has led to different underlying concepts and governing principles for user interface development. The key concept is separation, the notion of partitioning an interactive system into an iterative user interface and a noninteractive application to achieve dialogue independence and weak coupling. The principle of dialogue independence says to isolate design decisions about human-computer interaction from design decisions about the application [5]. The principle of weak coupling calls for a small software interface between the user interface and application (henceforth, the UI-AP interface). A third governing principle says that user interface design precedes and provides inputs to user interface software design [3].

The orientation and governing principles of user interface development necessitate a variety of roles for user interface developers, each role requiring specialized skills, involving different responsibilities, and needing specialized representations. *Cognitive scientist* investigate user behaviors and produce user model [6]. *Human factors experts* and *domain experts* study domain tasks and produced task models [6].

Dialogue authors write human-computer interactive dialogues, *dialogue evaluators* appraise the dialogues, and *graphic designers* specify presentation of information, for example, the visual appearance of textual and graphic information [2]. Dialogue authors and dialogue evaluators work with user interface models, which describe user interactions with a computer in terms of elements of a user interface. *Tool builders* build specialized tools for the dialogue author, dialogue evaluator, and graphic designer. *User interface software designers* and *programmers* provide run time environments that support execution of the interactive dialogues and mediate the interactions between user interface software and application software. They work with UI-AP models for architectural and detailed design [7].

User interface development also involves certain critical issues. The dominant issues concern the separation problem: how to achieve the highest degree of separation possible while still satisfying customer needs, system-level constraints, and principles of good user interface design. To achieve this optimal separation, developers need to be able to resolve, early in development, the conflicting implications of decisions made by user interface designers and software designers. For example, say a customer needs to run the same application on both graphical workstations and text-only terminals. How would a dialogue author's choice of interaction techniques (ways to interact with the user, e.g., menus, scroll bars, and dragging images) impact a software designer's ability to satisfy the system-level requirement for interchangeable user interfaces. Methods for addressing this issue have been proposed only recently [8, 9].

Other critical issues concern creating a methodology appropriate for the behavior of user interface developers. Empirical studies of real-life development projects find that user interface development naturally occurs in alternating waves of bottom-up (empirical, user-centered synthesis) and top-down (structuring, system-centered analysis) activities [10]. Small localized mini-cycles of activities are crucial.

To successfully address these issues, software engineers have long proposed integrating user interface development and modern software development into the same development process [5, 11, 12]. With emergent capabilities of CASE tools, software engineers can begin exploring ways to achieve this integration. For modern software development, much progress already has been made in enhancing CASE tool capabilities [13] and in understanding their impact on the software process [14]. For user interface development, similar progress has been made in enhancing the corresponding category of development tools, called user interface management systems (UIMS). Researchers are now trying to integrate UIMSs into CASE tools [1]. Some advanced environments apply knowledge-based systems techniques and transformation technology to user interface development [15].

But integrating user interface development and modern software development involves more than integrating UIMSs into CASE tools. Software engineers must integrate user interface development and modern software development within the context of a unified methodology. Issues concerning separation require systematic treatment throughout the development process. Other issues inherently are process issues and apply to both developments. These issues concern accommodating the behavior of individual developers; actively supporting the communication, coordination, and collaboration (henceforth C^3) among developers with different roles; and ensuring that these developers produce mutually consistent results.

Thus software engineers are faced with the task of taking advantage of emergent tool capabilities to create new methods and organizing them into a single methodology, unified by some general philosophical approach to interactive systems development. This unified methodology must integrate the fundamental principles governing user interface development and modern software development, let developers apply different development strategies to different parts of an interactive system, enforce systematic resolution of conflicting implications of decisions made by developers, actively support C^3, and ensure mutually consistent results.

Disciplined investigation of candidate methodologies requires a project-independent framework that fixes the fundamental principles, accommodates evolving development methods and their tools, and explicitly calls on CASE technology to provide the necessary capabilities of a methodology. This disciplined investigation calls for a new kind of process model.

3. Existing Process Models

Software process models have evolved from reflecting traditional engineering principles to reflecting principles modified and refined to address the unique nature of software. A number of insights have driven this evolution, including the following: requirements change throughout development [16]; continuous evaluation throughout development is essential [16]; specification and implementation are inevitably intertwined [17]; system decomposition should begin during specification [18]; and individual designers exhibit opportunistic decision-making behavior [19].

This section examines process models from mainstream software engineering, from user interface development, and from a relatively new category, called enactable models. Each model or category of models is briefly described and its features evaluated at the architectural, or project-independent, level of abstraction.

3.1. *Phased models*

Phased models partition the software process into a fixed sequence of distinct phases. Variations include the classic waterfall model [20], which permits iteration back to the immediately preceding phase only; the early prototyping model, which introduces prototype development and evaluation in the requirements definition phase [21]; and iterative models, such as iterative enhancement [22] and successive versions [23], which close the loop from the last phase of the process to the first. The most recent well-known phased model is the spiral model, in which each of the standard development phases is carried out in one or more cycles, each cycle beginning with a risk assessment and including a prototype to provide insight into the risk issues [24].

Phased models are in general inadequate. They reflect only an activity perspective on the software process, while artifact perspectives are at least necessary and possibly more useful [25–27]. Distinct phases lead to single development strategies, generally top-down. For example, iterative enhancement accommodates only top-down stepwise refinement, and the spiral model promotes the same sequence of steps for all parts of a software system. C^3 support is limited to early and iterative prototyping. Identifying and resolving conflicting implications of design decisions, such as those made by the dialogue designer and software designer, is hindered because the decisions are made in different phases. Phased models promote no technology, such as extending the scope of formalism, to address mutual consistency among artifacts. The only expressed relationship among process elements is the unrealistic temporal ordering of phases. Lacking any motion of explicit representation other than code, any inherent notion of tool orientation is absent also. Although phased models are meant to be elaborated into detailed process plans for specific projects, they have no inherent extendability at the project-independent level of abstraction, i.e., a given model is considered to be complete.

3.2 *Specifications-based models*

In contrast to phased models, which view the development process as a sequence of phases, specification-based models view the process as a sequence of specifications, each an "implementation" of some other higher-level specification [17]. The motivation for these models is twofold: (1) ensure consistency between specification and production code, and (2) provide not only early and iterative prototyping, but also rapid prototyping, i.e., the accelerated production of prototypes. One variation is the specification-based prototyping model [28], Fig. 1, which employs a formal specification language for creating a specification that can be machine-translated into an executable specification, or prototype. Another variation is the rapid prototyping model, which employs a rapid prototyping language for writing a directly executable specification [29]. Both of these models support continuous evaluation of specification, prototype, and production code. Also, in both of these models, a transformation system, possibly automated, transforms a specification into production code. Partsch [30] gives a current account of transformation systems. Specification-based models have significant advantages over phased models. They integrate two perspectives, activity and artifact. Because they neither recognize distinct phases nor impose a temporal ordering on activities, they accommodate a wide range of development strategies. Rapid prototyping and continuous evaluation are much more effective than just early or iterative prototyping in reducing communication and coordination breakdowns among participants. They are also vital for user interface design because they allow

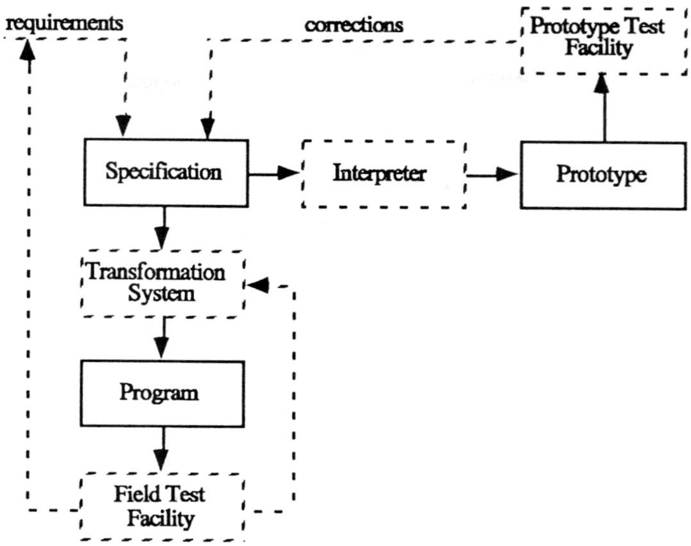

Fig. 1. Specification-based prototyping model (adapted from Berztiss [1990]). (Solid boxes are products, dashed boxes are development facilities.)

experimenting with alternative designs and promptly observing the effects of changes [5]. The process structure (Fig. 1) promotes mutually consistent artifacts by blurring the distinction between requirements specification and design, supporting continuous evaluation, and extending the scope of formalness. The expressed relationship among process elements is the evolution of representations from requirements to formal specification to production code. Tool orientation is inherent in the transformation system, with its potential automation and accommodation of knowledge-based systems techniques. This is valuable to user interface design, where application of knowledge-based transformations have already proved beneficial [15], and to modern software development, e.g., Luqi [31] describes a knowledge-based transformation system that combines reusable components.

These models have two deficiencies. First, they lack a mechanism for ensuring consistency between the customer's needs and the formal specification. Second, although these models accommodate technological evolution, in particular enhancing the transformation system, they have no inherent extendability.

3.3. *User interface development models*

The notion of integrating user interface design software engineering has been considered for some time. Draper and Norman [11] advocated extending software engineering to deal with issues raised by a systematic approach to user interface design, which they said should be pursued through an iterative process. Wasserman [12] defined a software development methodology with an underlying process model consisting of distinct phases but with rapid prototyping of the user interface design. Two models discussed below reflect more recent thinking.

3.3.1. *Knowledge-based specification model*

Cabral *et al.* [32] define a process model that establishes a methodological framework for a knowledge-based development system (MIDAS) that lets designers develop an application-specific user interface while refining the application specification. MIDAS also assists in defining the UI-AP interface. The model is a phased model that accommodates a series of small prototyping subprocesses similar to the spiral model. The prototyping is specification-based, but implementation occurs in a distinctly separate phase that follows. This model falls somewhere between phased models and specification-based models with respect to suitability for integrating user interface development and modern software development, and therefore is not considered further.

3.3.2. *Star model*

The purpose of the star model, Fig. 2, is to emphasize user interface usability [10]. It is intended to reflect three principles: (1) treat user interface development as an integral part of the software engineering process, (2) perform continuous evaluation, and (3) let user interface developers alternate rapidly between analytical and "synthetic" modes of mental activity. The model is evaluation-centered, which encourages continuous evaluation of the user interface throughout development. It imposes no temporal constraints on activities, which accommodates the behavior of user interface developers discussed earlier.

The star model gives a behavior-oriented view of user interface development based on three protocol-gathering case studies involving subjects producing different kinds of interactive systems [10]. It is part of the DMS methodology, which includes a set of representation techniques for capturing outputs of each

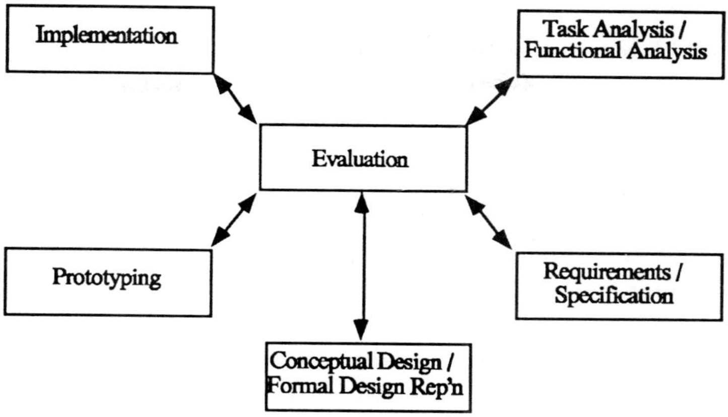

Fig. 2. Star model (adapted from Hartson and Hix [1989]).

activity in the star model [10]. Urlocker [33] presents a strikingly similar testing-centered model to describe the behavior of an individual developer working on an evolutionary development project. However, in this model, peripheral activities are directly connected.

Although the star model has an activity perspective with which to express the behavior of developers, it lacks an artifact perspective with which to express the evolution of representations. Like the models discussed earlier, the star model lacks an agent perspective to express the distribution and sharing of expertise and responsibility. With its arrangement of temporally unconstrained activities, it accommodates the widest range of development strategies of all the models discussed so far. More importantly, it accommodates a methodology that could apply different strategies to different parts of a system. C^3 support consists of rapid prototyping (claimed by the model's authors [10], but not expressed in the model) and continuous evaluation, which is expressed in the model, and which promotes mutually consistent artifacts. The expressed relationship among process elements is the rapid alternation among activities. Tool orientation is not inherent; however, the similarity between the model's topology and the blackboard architecture of knowledge-based systems is suggestive. The model has one degree of inherent extendability — adding peripheral activities.

3.4. *Enactable models*

Contemporary research addresses three aspects of model representation: (1) explicitness is the degree to which a model can be directly examined or manipulated [34]; (2) formalness refers to the precision, lack of ambiguity, and analyzable semantics of the representation scheme with which a model is constructed [34]; and enactablity is the degree to which a model provides humans with computer guidance and assistance [35]. Enactable processes take the form of programs used on-line, while the processes are being carried out, to direct, control, monitor, and instrument them [35].

Researchers on enactable models have demonstrated the following capabilities: to explicitly represent activity, artifact, and agent perspectives; to provide active mechanisms, such as blackboard structures, for supporting C^3; and to promote mutually consistent artifacts by extending the scope of formal methods [25, 26, 35–39]. Enactable models are inherently tool-oriented, which leads to applying AI languages and problem-solving techniques in order to integrate knowledge management and software development. Scacchi [40] surveys the state of the art and current trends in this area. Enactable models, as programs, are inherently extendable.

3.5. *Summary of existing process models*

Table 1 summarizes the software process models. It shows each category collectively except for user interface development models, for which the star model is the sole representative. For enactable models, the table shows only features related to representation.

The following points motivate aspects of the new model proposed in this paper: only the star model attempts to integrate user interface development and modern software development; only the star model accommodates a methodology that could apply different strategies to different parts of a system, but it lacks the constructs with which to express such a methodology; only enactable models can provide active mechanisms for supporting C^3; the specification-based models and the enactable models expressly apply formal methods to promote mutually consistent artifacts; and the star model and the enactable models are inherently extendable.

Table 1. Summary of process models.

Feature	Phased Models	Specification-Based Models	Star Model	Enactable Models
Integration of the two developments	none	none	partial	—
Process perspectives modeled	activity	artifact activity	activity	artifact activity agent
Development strategies accommodated	single strategies, generally top-down	wide range	very wide range	—
C^3 Support	early or iterative prototyping	rapid prototyping & continuous evaluation	rapid prototyping & continuous evaluation	active mechanisms
Features promoting mutually consistent results	none	blurring of specification & design, continuous evaluation, & formal methods	continuous evaluation	formal methods
Process relationships expressed	temporal ordering of activities	evolution of representations	rapid alternation among activities	—
Inherent tool-orientation	none	transformation systems	none	as programs
Extendability	none	none	adding peripheral activities	inherently extendable

4. A New Process Model

The model introduced here results from a project directed towards applying systems science principles to the separation problem. The model fixes an expressly defined philosophical position on developing highly interactive software systems and reflects a set of process principles that integrate established principles from systems science, user interface development, and modern software development.

The computer-based model differs from previous models in two significant ways. First, it expresses a principle-driven integration of user interface development and modern software development. Second, it supports not only explicit representation of a methodology that applies different strategies to different parts of a system but also disciplined investigation of alternative methodologies.

Principle features of the model include the following: an inherently extendable topology enhances collaboration among developers while reducing their communication burden, a unifying representation lets different developers produce mutually consistent artifacts, a coordination activity supports opportunistic behavior of individual developers while enforcing a disciplined resolution of conflicts among them, and an integration of software engineering and knowledge engineering techniques supports an organization consisting of human and computer-based agents.

4.1. *Underlying philosophy and process principles*

The model reflects a specific philosophical position on the development of interactive systems. This position is defined in terms of three areas of philosophical debate that arise when systems science theory is applied to deal with complex situations: ontology, epistemology, and methodology [41]. The ontological debate concerns the nature of reality of a problem or situation. The position of this paper is that the software process for an arbitrary project has an objective reality independent of the perspective of the individuals involved. Thus, mapping between multiple perspectives and a representation of the objective reality is critical. The epistemological debate concerns the nature of the knowledge about solving a problem. The position here is that this knowledge about the software process can be represented in a tangible form to be reused and distributed to others. Thus, explicit representation of process knowledge is critical also. The methodological debate concerns the nature of our attempts to acquire problem solving knowledge. The position here is that process knowledge can result from explicit representation, disciplined investigation, and continuous refinement of principles that we propose to govern the software process. Thus, identifying, modeling, and analyzing process elements and their relationships, and then refining or extending the model based on the findings are important considerations.

In general, process principles address problem structure and govern problem solving strategy. Here, process principles address the structure of a software process model and govern its evolution. We derive these principles two ways: (1) refining the principles that define the philosophical position stated above, and (2) finding common generalizations of established principles in user interface development and modern software development. Refining the philosophical principles produces the following process principles:

- Include, as core elements, objective representations of a domain problem, its software solution, and the process knowledge.
- Support multiple perspectives on the core elements.
- Express the connections between or among its core elements.
- Support mappings between each perspective and its objective reality.
- Support the highest degree of formalness practicable for each representation.
- Include built-in mechanisms for refinement and extension.

Finding common generalizations of principles from user interface development and modern software development produces the following process principles:

- Support decomposing development activities based on goals and independent of temporal ordering.
- Support temporal constraints on activities, sometimes necessary to express more specialized principles or to account for limitations of current technology. For example, one principle of architectural design states that the nature of interactions that need to take place among subsystems should be explored before committing to interfaces [4].
- Define agents in terms of well-defined roles and responsibilities based on skills and knowledge.
- Express the sharing and distribution of expertise and responsibilities among agents.
- Let agents move rapidly and opportunistically between activities and across levels of abstraction, e.g., from domain issues to detailed design and coding issues.

- Enforce systematic comparison of the implications of decisions made by the same developer or by different developers, at the same level of abstraction or at different levels of abstraction.
- Enforce systematic resolution of conflicting implications of decisions.

The proposed model reflects these process principles in three fully integrated perspectives on the software process, as described below.

4.2. *Artifact perspective*

Figure 3 shows the basic artifact perspective. It consists of a unifying representation of a problem and its software solution linked to a set of peripheral representations. The unifying representation reflects the objective reality of problem and solution. The peripheral representations reflect different perspectives on the objective reality. The links reflect the mappings between perspectives and objective reality. All of these representations are explicit and at an appropriate level of formalness.

The role of the unifying representation is to unify the software process by serving as a central repository for all information about a proposed software system. It lets different agents produce mutually consistent results while working in different representations, each suitable for a particular view of a system. It is the key to enforcing systematic comparison of the implications of decisions made by the same developer or by different developers, at the same level of abstraction or at different levels of abstraction. The unifying representation can be machine-analyzed to detect conflicts and inconsistencies, such as the inability of a software designer's choice of data structures to support a dialogue author's choice of interaction techniques.

The artifact perspective supports indirect collaboration among agents through controlled transmission of changes made in one representation to other representations. The links in Fig. 3 represent transformations between the unifying representation and the peripheral representations. The structure defined by these links restricts all transmissions between peripheral representations to be through the unifying representation. This restriction is the key to reliably consistent artifacts. It lets us detect inconsistencies generated in a peripheral representation and prevent their propagation to other representations.

The particular set of peripheral representations used in a project depends on both the nature of the project and the development methodology applied.

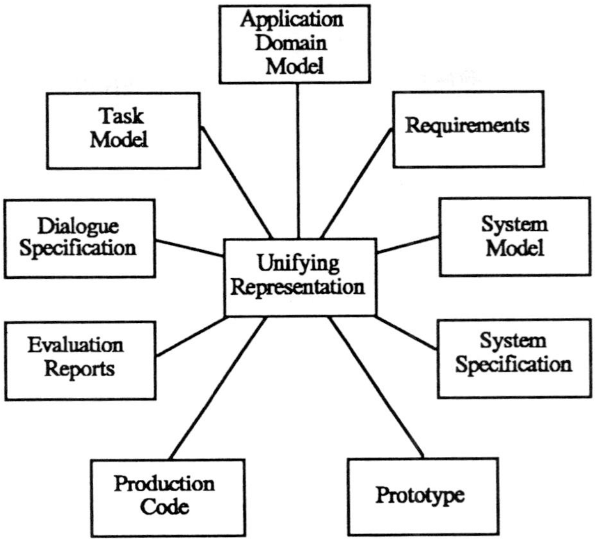

Fig. 3. Basic artifact perspective.

The set shown in Fig. 3 is a superset of the representations associated with the specification-based prototyping model (Fig. 1) and the star model (Fig. 2).

Several candidate unifying representations will be discussed in Subsec. 5.2, along with a unifying representation, peripheral representations, and associated transformations implemented by the author.

We can extend the basic artifact perspective of Fig. 3 two ways. First, we can connect additional peripheral representations directly to the unifying representation. For example, we might add a user model to support the development of adaptive user interfaces. Second, in order to provide multiple perspectives on any individual artifact, a capability dictated by our process principles, we can designate a peripheral representation as a "local" unifying representation with its own set of peripheral representations. Figure 4 shows the system specification of Fig. 3 as a local unifying representation with three peripheral representations: user interface software specification, UI-AP specification, and application specification.

The artifact perspective supports investigating alternative development methods and methodologies. Its highly extendable architecture lets us define

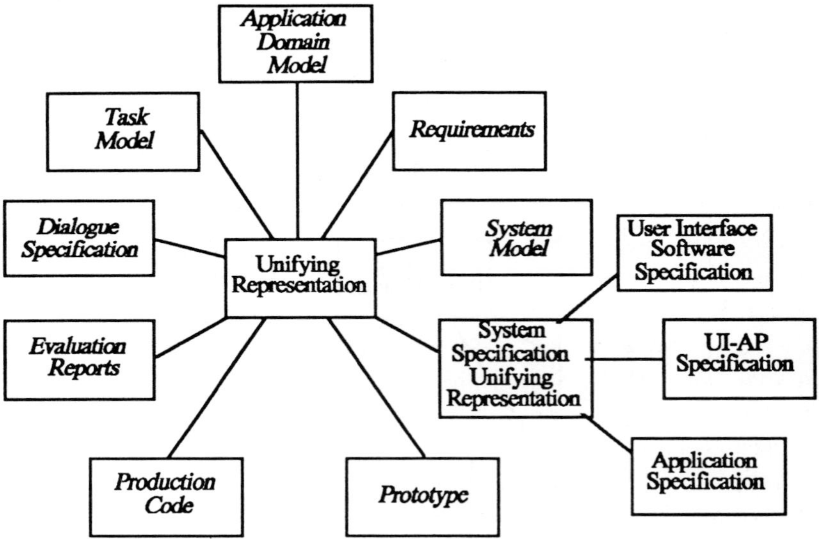

Fig. 4. Extended artifact perspective.

alternative representations. The perspective implies no fixed progression or phased development of artifacts. They could evolve simultaneously or in an order set by the activity perspective, discussed below.

4.3. *Activity perspective*

Figure 5 shows the basic activity perspective. It consists of a central coordination activity for the development process linked to a set of peripheral activities. The central coordination activity incorporates general process principles and high level process knowledge. The peripheral activities reflect a decomposition of the development process based on goals and independent of temporal ordering. Each peripheral activity incorporates specialized principles and process knowledge. The links indicate flows of control and coordination information.

The role of the central coordination activity is to coordinate the development process. The coordination activity is the key to enforcing systematic resolution of conflicting implications of decisions made by the same developer or by different developers, at the same level of abstraction or at different levels of abstraction. The coordination activity maintains an agenda of the following: items that need to be addressed, such as artifact inconsistencies and unresolved conflicts between decision decisions; temporal constraints on the order in which items can be addressed; and the resources required to address each item. The coordination activity integrates knowledge management and software construction by explicitly representing process principles and process knowledge as plans, goals, and procedures, say for adjusting the agenda. A potential implementation for the coordination activity will be discussed in Subsec. 5.3.

The activity perspective coordinates the opportunistic behavior of individual agents through transmission of control and coordination information. The links in Fig. 5 represent two-way flows of this information. Flow out includes information about items maintained by the agenda. Flow in includes notification that an existing agenda item has been addressed or that a new item has been raised. For example, an inconsistency identified as a result of evaluation of the unifying representation is posted on the agenda and at the appropriate time the responsible agent(s) are asked to resolve it.

Each peripheral activity explicitly represents specialized process principles and detailed process knowledge as specialized plans, goals, and procedures for

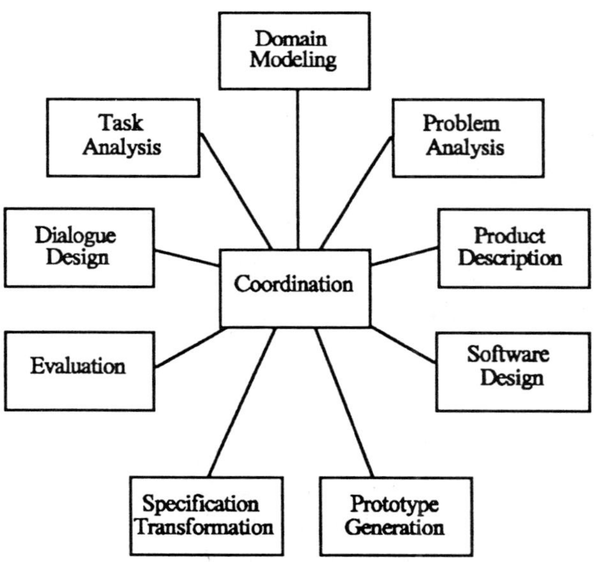

Fig. 5. Basic activity perspective.

accomplishing goals. These plans, goals, and procedures identify required resources and the peripheral artifact representations accessed or modified. The ultimate effect of an activity is manifested when a change or addition to a peripheral representation is transmitted to and recorded in the unifying representation.

The particular set of activities performed in a project depends on both the nature of the project and the methodology applied. The set shown in Fig. 5 is based on producing the artifact representations of Fig. 3.

Candidate implementations for a coordination activity will be discussed in Subsec. 5.3, along with a coordination activity implemented by the author.

We can extend the basic activity perspective of Fig. 5 two ways. First, we can connect additional peripheral activities directly to the central coordination activity. For example, we might add user modeling in order to produce a user model. Second, in order to provide multiple perspectives on any individual activity, a capability dictated by our process principles, we can designate any peripheral activity as a "local" coordination activity with its own set of peripheral activities. Figure 6 shows the software design activity of Fig. 5 as a local coordination activity with peripheral activities for user interface software design, UI-AP design, and application design coordination, which in turn has its own peripheral activities for logical design and physical design.

The activity perspective supports investigating alternative development methods and methodologies. Its highly extendable architecture lets us define alternative activities and decompositions of activities. Like the star model, the lack of inherent temporal ordering accommodates rapid alternation between activities and the opportunistic behavior of individual developers. But unlike the star model, the activity perspective in the proposed model has built-in mechanisms for dictating specific behaviors. For example, by scheduling (via the agenda) an evaluation activity after each activity that impacts an artifact representation, the activity perspective exhibits the evaluation-centered behavior of the star model.

4.4. *Agent perspective*

Figure 7 illustrates the agent perspective. The front plane is the basic activity perspective of Fig. 5 and the rear plane is the basic artifact perspective of Fig. 3. Each agent role is defined as a set of directed mappings between artifact representations and development activities. A mapping into an activity from an artifact representation indicates an input while a mapping out of an

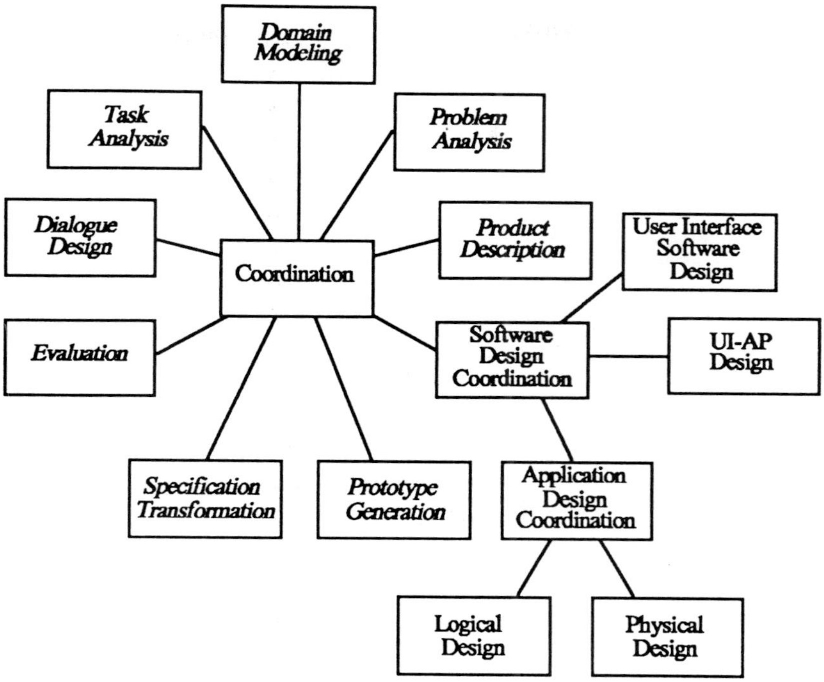

Fig. 6. Extended activity perspective.

activity to an artifact representation indicates possible modification of that representation. Figure 7 shows two mappings, as directed lines, that define a software designer. Both lines point to the software design activity, one from the dialogue specification and the other from the system specification. The latter line is bidirectional, indicating that the system specification is modified by the software designer.

A set of agent definitions establishes distribution and sharing of expertise and responsibility among agents. Expertise corresponds to the activities performed and responsibility corresponds to the artifact representations affected. Different activities and artifacts indicate distribution, while common activities or artifacts indicate sharing. The granularity with which distribution and sharing of expertise and responsibility can be expressed depends on the granularity of the activity and artifact perspectives.

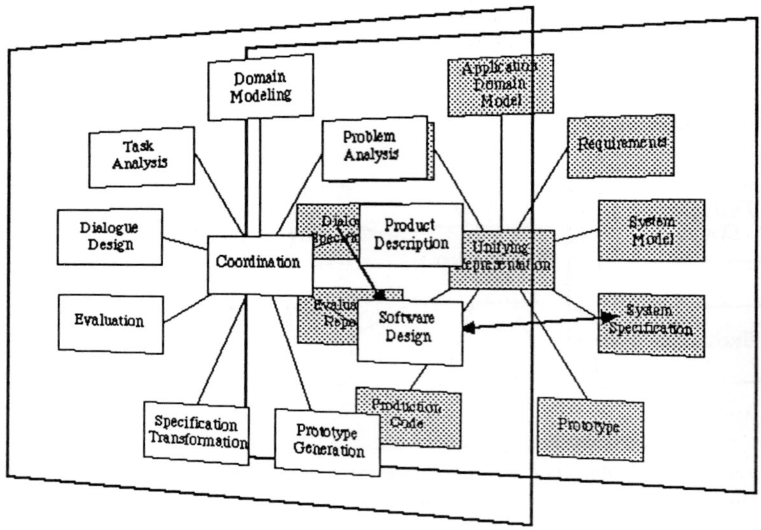

Fig. 7. Agent perspective for software design. (Front plane is activity perspective, back plane is artifact perspective).

The agent perspective supports investigating alternative development methods and methodologies. The agent definitions impose no temporal constraints, new agents can be added easily, and agent definitions can be modified to reflect different division and sharing of expertise and responsibilities.

5. Advantages and Disadvantages of the Proposed Model

The model proposed in this paper has yet to be applied to any real-life software development project. Admittedly, the importance of a process model is limited without empirical evidence to demonstrate its superiority over existing models. Nevertheless, the following features of the proposed model demonstrate its feasibility and worthiness for further consideration.

5.1. *Hyperstar topology*

In network theory, the star topology connects all stations to a central node which sets up a dedicated communication path between any two stations that wish to communicate [42]. This topology is good for station-intensive situations because it imposes the communication processing burden on the central node, which must support multiple concurrent communication paths, rather than on the stations, which employ simple point-to-point communications. A disadvantage is that the central node is the Achilles' heel of network reliability [42].

Also in network theory, when several stations are close to one another, the hyperstar topology connects them to concentrators or multiplexers. These devices connect to a central node [43]. The result is increased efficiency of link use at the expense of an occasional delay in response time.

The proposed model reflects a hyperstar topology. In the artifact perspective, Fig. 4, the local unifying representations are the concentrators, and the global unifying representation is the central node. Here, controlled propagation of changes enhances collaboration among agents. In the activity perspective, the local coordination activities are the concentrators, and the global coordination activity is the central node. Here, controlled information flow reduces the communication burden of individual agents. Although the unifying representation and the coordination activity are potential Achilles' heels, they are also keystones for reliably and mutually consistent artifacts and for reliably effective coordination.

Finally, the hyperstar topology of the proposed model is a logical extension of the topology of the star model, for which substantiating empirical evidence from real-life development projects does exist, as mentioned earlier and discussed further elsewhere [10].

5.2. *Unifying representation*

Researchers have suggested the desirability of developing a representation that would unify a development process. The Computer Science and Technology Board (CSTB) hypothesized a unifying representation that would let different designers produce mutually consistent results while working in a range of languages, each suitable for a particular view of a software system [44]. The architects of the DMS user interface development methodology hypothesized a common representation for communication among individuals in different roles. Filters on the common representation would produce suitable working views for each role [5].

The proposed model uses the notion of a unifying representation two ways. A local unifying representation, such as the *System Specification Unifying*

Representation in Fig. 4, would support mutually consistent results among developers with shared (overlapping) responsibilities, while the global unifying representation, the *Unifying Representation* in Fig. 4, would support mutually consistent results among developers with distinctly different responsibilities.

Considerable research on unifying representations is underway. Meyers [45] presents a survey of current approaches. One promising approach is a formal canonical representation from which others are generated through a series of transformations. Partsch [30] sees this approach as the modern role of formality. Another approach is an object management system (OMS), used for CASE tool integration and communication [46].

The author has implemented an abstract system model with potential as a unifying representation. The model is intended to support a transformational approach in which a sequence of models, from a conceptual model of a proposed model to a final production system, is produced. The abstract system model consists of a set of system-theoretic abstractions for modeling at the architectural level and at the component level. These abstractions have been used by dialogue authors to generate, using software tools, specific system models (see the box labeled *System Model* in Fig. 3) that describe the intended relationships between user interface components and application components. This work is discussed in more detail elsewhere [9].

Kinawi and the author [47] have implemented transformations and peripheral representations based on the abstract system model. Transformations convert, via a unifying representation, between a semiformal representation of a proposed system in an object-oriented analysis notation and a formal specification of that system in a specification-based prototyping language.

5.3. *Coordination activity*

Research areas concerned with activity coordination include computer supported cooperative work [48], planning [49], and design decision making [19, 27, 50]. The blackboard architecture is frequently proposed for supporting and coordinating the opportunistic behavior of individual developers. Opportunistic behavior is characteristic of processes observed in the cognitive literature on planning and is modeled in blackboard architectures of knowledge-based systems [19]. Coordination of individual behaviors is the function of the control component of blackboard architectures [51, 52].

The proposed model uses the notion of a coordination activity two ways. A local coordination activity, such as the *Software Design Coordination Activity* in Fig. 6, would support and coordinate the opportunistic behavior of developers with shared roles, while the global coordination activity, the *Coordination* activity in Fig. 6, would support and coordinate the behavior of developers with distinctly different roles.

The major features of a coordination activity are its agenda and its links to other activities. An agenda corresponds to the control component of a blackboard architecture and its links represent the information flows in a blackboard system.

The author has implemented a major component of the *Software Design Coordination* activity (see Fig. 6). A software designer can invoke a fully automated procedure that analyzes a system model, discussed in Subsec. 5.2, to predict the impact of a proposed user interface design on the software design of the UI-AP interface. For example, the procedure can determine the software mechanisms required in the UI-AP interface to support a given interaction technique, such as dragging one graphical object over another one, for a given application. This work and its validation in a set of real-life situations are discussed in more detail elsewhere [9].

5.4. *Integrating software engineering and knowledge engineering*

The proposed model integrates software engineering and knowledge engineering techniques in the context of an organization (for interactive software development) consisting of both human and computer-based agents. For success in this context, Bobrow [53] identifies five issues that must be addressed: (1) common grounding and shared vocabulary; (2) impedance matching between agents, i.e., optimal undistorted transfer of information; (3) resource management; (4) coordinating goals and actions; and (5) integration with work practice, i.e., local policies, procedures, and work customs. The proposed model addresses all five issues.

First, common grounding and shared vocabulary is necessary because subgroups of developers with common or overlapping roles use languages that share partial vocabularies and abstractions. The model's local unifying representations (Fig. 4) and local coordination activities (Fig. 6) provide the common grounding and capture the shared vocabulary.

Second, impedance matching among developers is necessary to compensate for their different concerns about and views of an interactive system. A local unifying representation, its transformations, and its peripheral representations provide impedance matching for developers with overlapping roles. The global unifying representation, its transformations, and its peripheral representations provide impedance matching for developers with significantly different roles. Third, resource management requires explicit identification of resource use. In the proposed model, activities identify necessary resources and the artifacts they access or modify.

Fourth, the global coordination activity coordinates general goals and actions, while the local coordination activities coordinate more specialized goals and actions. The activity perspective (see Fig. 6) captures the tension between centralized coordination and allocation of subgoals on one hand, and local goal-setting on the other. This tension is another feature of the activity perspective that resembles the blackboard architecture of knowledge-based systems. And fifth, the activities integrate human and computer-based agents with work practice by providing mechanisms for explicitly representing local policy, procedures, and work customs as plans, goals, and procedures.

5.5. *Explicitness, scalability, utility*

Explicitness is the degree to which a model can be directly examined or manipulated [34]. One aspect of explicitness is the degree to which relationships among process elements are expressed, as opposed to implied. In the proposed model, the artifact perspective contains transformations that relate, directly or indirectly, artifact representations, the activity perspective contains information and control flows that relate activities, each activity identifies necessary resources and the artifact representations accessed or modified, and agent definitions express distribution and sharing of expertise and responsibilities in terms of activities performed and artifact representations accessed or modified.

Scalability is the degree to which a model applies to different levels of organization [54]. In the proposed model, the built-in mechanisms for extending the artifact, activity, and agent perspectives, plus the hyperstar topology of the activity perspective provides considerable scalability. The following simplified example illustrates. The terminal nodes of an extended hyperstar activity perspective, such as the one shown in Fig. 6, represent the activities of individual agents. These terminal nodes are connected to local coordination nodes representing the coordination of a team or group of agents. These local coordination nodes are connected to other coordination nodes representing coordination at a higher level of organization, say a collection of teams, possibly dispersed, working on subprojects, and so forth, ultimately to a central node presenting the global coordination activity of corporate management.

In the next context of this paper, utility is the degree to which a model supports disciplined investigation of alternative methodologies, each of which lets developers with different roles apply different development strategies to different parts of a system. The two prerequisites of utility are flexibility and expressiveness. As noted earlier, the star model has flexibility but lacks sufficient expressiveness. The proposed model, however, has both flexibility and expressiveness.

For instance, the proposed model can simultaneously and explicitly represent both an alternating waves strategy for user interface developers and a specification-based transformation strategy for mainstream software developers. For user interface developers, the agent definitions can include user interface development activities and related artifact representations. As mentioned earlier, to express the evaluation-centered behavior of the star model, the agenda can schedule an evaluation activity after each activity performed by a user interface developer. For software developers, the agent definitions can relate activities and artifact representations in a way that reflect the flow relationships between system facilities and product forms defined in the specification-based prototyping model (see Fig. 1). To illustrate just one of these relationships, the production of source code from specification by the transformation system can be described by two directed mappings in the agent perspective (see Fig. 7): (1) from the specification to the transformation activity and (2) from the transformation activity to the production code.

6. Conclusions and Future Work

The proposed computer-based process model supports disciplined investigation of candidate methodologies for integrating the processes of user interface development and modern software development. The model's components and their interrelationships reflect the principles governing the two processes. Its extendable topology provides a foundation for evolving methods and their tools. Its inherent tool orientation reflects the advances in the CASE capabilities that will enable the integration of the two development processes.

The model captures artifact, activity, and agent perspectives on the software process and provides built-in mechanisms for integrating, refining and extending all three. The model includes mechanisms for ensuring mutually consistent artifacts and for actively supporting collaboration, coordination, and communication among human and computer-based agents. Its inherently extendable topology enhances collaboration among developers while reducing their communication burden. The coordination activity supports the opportunistic behavior of individual agents while enforcing a disciplined resolution of conflicting implications of decisions made by these agents. The unifying representation leads to different agents producing mutually consistent results while working in different representations.

Several factors suggest that the model is feasible. Its topology is a logical extension of the topology of the star process model, for which substantiating empirical evidence from real-life development projects exists. Several representations of the artifact perspective, along with associated transformations, have been implemented, including a unifying representation and peripheral representations for a domain model, a system model, and a system specification. The activity perspective is suited to the established blackboard architecture of knowledge-based systems. Also, a component of the software design coordination activity has been implemented. This component predicts the impact of user interface design on the software design of the UI-AP interface, and has been validated against a set of real-life situations [9].

Planned future work includes enhancing the software design coordination activity to predict the impact of system-level constraints on user interface design and adding transformations that generate UI-AP interface software components from a system specification. Representing software development knowledge as machine-manipulable plans, goals, and procedures supports active guidance, natural language explanation, and documentation generation, capabilities which are also planned.

Acknowledgments

My thanks to Siegfried Treu for his thoughtful comments and helpful suggestions on earlier drafts and to Lucy Moran for her editorial assistance.

References

1. D. Hix, "Generations of user-interface management systems," *IEEE Softw.* **7**, 5 (1990) 77–87.
2. D. R. Olsen, Jr. *et al.*, "A context for user interface management," *ACM Comp. Graph. & App.* **4**, 12 (1984) 33–41.
3. H. R. Hartson, A. C. Siochi and D. Hix, "The UAN: A user-oriented representation for direct manipulation interface designs," *ACM Trans. Inf. Syst.* **8**, 3 (1990) 181–203.
4. R. J. A. Buhr, *Practical Visual Techniques in System Design: With Applications to Ada*, (Prentice-Hall, 1990).

5. H. R. Hartson and D. Hix, "Human-computer interface development: concepts and systems for its management," *ACM Comput. Surv.* **21**, 1 (1989) 5–92.
6. S. Card, T. Moran and A. Newell, *The Psychology of Human-Computer Interaction* (Lawrence Erlbaum, 1983).
7. W. D. Hurley and J. L. Sibert, "Modeling user interface-application interactions," *IEEE Softw.* **6**, 1 (1989) 71–77.
8. J. Coutaz and S. Balbo, "Applications: A dimension space for user interface management systems," *CHI'91 Conf. Proc.* (May 1991) pp. 27–32.
9. W. D. Hurley, "Predicting the impact of user interface design on software design," in *Proc. IFIP TC2\WG2.7 Working Conf. on Engineering for Human-Computer Interaction* (August 1992) pp. 349–362.
10. R. Hartson and D. Hix, "Toward empirically derived methodologies and tools for human-computer interface development," *Int. J. Man-Mach. Stud.* **31** (1989) 477–494.
11. S. W. Draper and D. A. Norman, "Software engineering for user interfaces," *IEEE Trans. Softw. Eng.* **SE-11**, 3 (1985) 252–258.
12. A. I. Wasserman, *el al.*, "Developing interactive information systems with the User Software Engineering Methodology," *IEEE Trans. Softw. Eng.* **SE-12**, 2 (1986) 326–345.
13. V. -P. Tahvanainen and K. Smolander, "An annotated CASE bibliography," *ACM Soft. Eng. Nts.* **15**, 1 (1990) 79–92.
14. D. E. Cooke, "Special Issue: The Impact of CASE Technology on Software Processes," *Int. J. Softw. Eng. Know. Eng.* **1**, 2 (1991).
15. J. Foley, *et al.*, "A knowledge-based user interface management system," *CHI'88 Conference Proceedings* (May 1988) pp. 67–72.
16. B. W. Boehm, "Seven basic principles of software engineering," *J. Sys. & Softw.* **3** (1983) 3–24.
17. W. Swartout and R. Balzer, "On the inevitable interwining of specification and implementation," *Commun. ACM* **25**, 7 (1982) 438–440.
18. M. S. Feather, "Language support for the specification and development of composite systems," *ACM Trans. Prog. Lang. & Sys.* **9**, 2 (1987) 198–234.
19. R. Guindon and B. Curtis, "Control of cognitive processes during software design: what tools are needed," *CHI' 88 Conf. Proc.* (May 1988) pp. 263–268.
20. W. Royce, "Managing the development of large software systems: concepts and techniques," *Proc. WESCON* (August 1970).
21. H. Gomaa and D. Scott, "Prototyping as a tool in the specification of user requirements," *Proc. 5th IEEE Int. Conf. Software Eng.*, (March 1981).
22. V. R. Basili and A. J. Turner, "Iterative enhancement: a practical technique for software development," *IEEE Trans. Softw. Eng.* **SE-1**, 4 (1975) 390–396.
23. R. Fairley, *Software Engineering Concepts* (McGraw-Hill, 1985).
24. B. Boehm, "A spiral model of software development and enhancement," *IEEE Comput.* **21**, 5 (1988) 61–72.
25. W. S. Humphrey and M. I. Kellner, "Software process modeling: principles of entity process models," *Proc. 11th Int. Conf. Software Engineering* (May 1989) pp. 331–342.

26. A. T. Nakagawa and K. Futatsugi, "Software processes a la algebra: OBJ for OBJ," *12th Int. Conf. Software Engineering* (March 1990) pp. 12–23.
27. D. Steier, "Creating a scientific community at the interface between engineering design and AI," *AI Mag.* **11**, 4 (1990) 18–22.
28. A. Berztiss, "Formal specification methods and visualization," in *Principles of Visual Programming Systems*, ed. S. K. Chang (Prentice-Hall, 1990) pp. 231–290.
29. Luqi, "The role of prototyping languages in CASE," *J. Softw. Eng. Know. Eng.* **1**, 2 (1991) 131–149.
30. H. A. Partsch, *Specification and Transformation of Programs. A Formal Approach to Software Development* (Springer-Verlag, 1990).
31. Luqi, "Knowledge-based support for rapid software prototyping," *IEEE Exp.* **3**, 4 (1988) 9–18.
32. R. H. Cabral, I. M. Campos and C. J. Cowan, "Interfaces as specifications in the MIDAS user interface development system," *ACM Softw. Eng. Nts.* **15**, 2 (1990) 55–69.
33. Urlocker, "A methodology for the real world," *Comp. Lang.* **6**, 1 (1989) 47–58.
34. A. Finkelstein, "Not waving but drowning: representation schemes for modelling software development," *Proc. 11th Int. Conf. Software Engineering* (May 1989) pp. 402–404.
35. C. Tully, *Proc. 4th Int. Software Process Workshop* (ACM Press, 1989).
36. Y. Bernard and P. Lavency, "A process-oriented approach to configuration management," *11th Int. Conf. Software Engineering* (May 1989) pp. 320–330.
37. T. Katayama, "A hierarchical and functional software process description and its enaction," *11th Int. Conf. Software Engineering* (May 1989) pp. 343–352.
38. M. I. Kellner, "Representation formalisms for software process modeling," *Proc. 4th Int. Software Process Workshop* (May 1988) pp. 93–96.
39. C. Roberts, "Describing and acting process models with PML," *Proc. 4th Int. Software Process Workshop* (May 1988) pp. 136–141.
40. W. Scacchi, "Understanding software productivity: towards a knowledge-based approach," *Int. J. Softw. Eng. Know. Eng.* **1**, 3 (1991).
41. R. L. Flood and E. R. Carson, *Dealing with Complexity: An Introduction to the Theory and Application of Systems Science* (Plenum 1988).
42. W. Stallings, *Local Networks* (Macmillan Publishing Company, 1984).
43. M. Abrams and I. Cotton, *Computer Networks: A Tutorial* (IEEE Computer Society Press, 1984).
44. CSTB, *Scaling Up: A Research Agenda for Software Engineering*, Computer Science and Technology Board Report (National Academy Press, 1990).
45. S. Meyers, "Difficulties in integrating multiview development systems," *IEEE Softw.* **8**, 1 (1991) 49–57.
46. M. P. Papazoglou, L. Marinos and N. G. Bourbakis, "The organizational impact of integrating multiple tools," *Int. J. Softw. Eng. Know. Eng.* **1**, 2 (1991) 165–188.

47. O. Kinawi and D. Hurley, "A unifying conceptual model for information-control systems," Technical Report 91–10, Department of Computer Science, University of Pittsburg (1991).
48. T. K. Bikson, *CSCW'90: Proc. Conf. Computer-Supported Cooperative Work* (ACM Press, 1990).
49. J. Hendler, A. Tate and M. Drummond, "AI planning: systems and techniques," *AI Mag.* **11** 2 (1990) 61–77.
50. M. L. Maher, "Process models for design synthesis," *AI Mag.* **11**, 4 (1990) 49–58.
51. H. P. Nii, "Blackboard systems," *AI Mag.* **7**, 2 (1987) 38–53.
52. H. P. Nii, "Blackboard systems," *AI Mag.* **7**, 3 (1987) 82–106.
53. B. Chandrasekaran, "AAAI '90," *IEEE Exp.* **5**, 5 (1990) 10–12.
54. D. E. Perry, "Problems of scale and process models," *Proc. 4th Int. Software Process Workshop* (May 1988) pp. 126–128.

TEXPROS: AN INTELLIGENT DOCUMENT PROCESSING SYSTEM*

JASON T. L. WANG and PETER A. NG
Institute for Integrated Systems Research, Department of Computer and Information Science, New Jersey Institute of Technology, Newark, NJ 07102, USA

ABSTRACT
This paper presents the design of an intelligent document processing system, called TEXPROS. The system is a combination of filing and retrieval systems, which supports storing, extracting, classifying, categorizing, retrieving and browsing information from a variety of documents. TEXPROS is built based on object-oriented programming and rule-based specification techniques. In this paper, we describe main design goals of the system, its data model, logical file structure, and strategies for document classification and categorization. We also illustrate various retrieval methods and query processing techniques through examples. Finally applications of TEXPROS are presented, where we suggest ways in which the use of the system may alter the software process model.

1. Introduction

The purpose of document processing systems (DPSs) is to support users (e.g., office workers) to manage their documents and to assist them in their work. We envision that DPSs of the future will be a complex, yet an integrated system. They will contain components for transforming original documents to computer-readable ASCII representations (e.g., Optical Character Recognizers (OCRs)), components for document classification, components for intelligent information retrieval, and components for image, information and knowledge base management. A possible architecture that interconnects these components is shown in Fig. 1.

*This work is supported, in part, by the New Jersey Institute of Technology under Grant No. 421280 and by an equipment grant from AT&T Foundation.

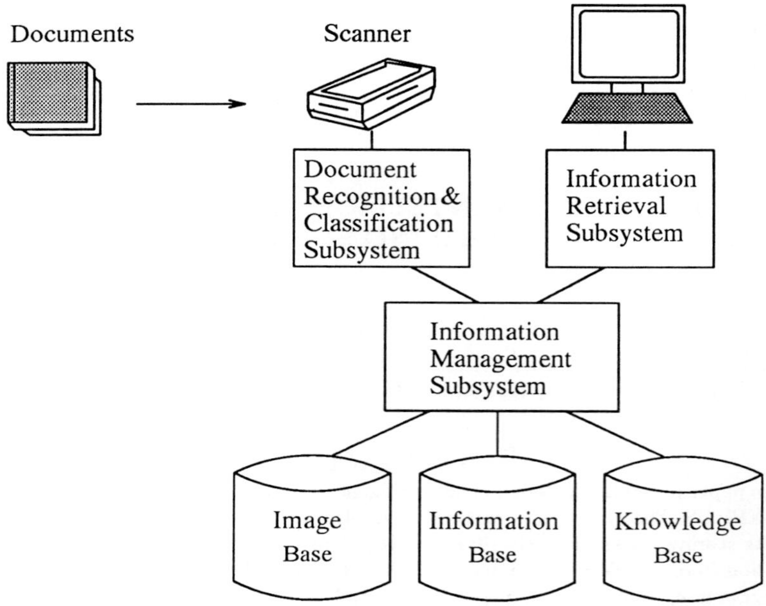

Fig. 1. Architecture of an integrated document processing system.

These systems should have functional capabilities of automating (or semi-automating) the following activities:

- *Document classification.* A user may need to deal with many kinds of documents. These include paper documents (e.g., books, reports, memos, letters, etc.), electronic documents (e.g., electronic mails, messages, fax), form documents [36, 44], voice documents [26], and more complicated multimedia documents [5]. By performing the content analysis of a document, the DPSs should be able to identify automatically the types or classes to which the document belongs (e.g., is the document a memo, a report, a book, an electronic message, or others?).
- *Document categorization.* Consider how a user, say a university professor, may organize his paper documents in the cabinet. He may group students' grades, class notes, and research papers in separate folders. He may further categorize the research papers according to their subjects or years of

publication. Documents in the same folder satisfy the same categorization criterion. By matching the content of a newly coming document against these criteria, the DPSs should be able to insert the document into an appropriate folder (e.g., store a paper published in 1990 in the folder of that year if all the papers are categorized based on publication years).

- *Information extraction.* Often, different users are concerned with different pieces of information in a document. For example, when receiving a conference proceedings, a secretary may record its publisher, date and the conference title. On the other hand, a researcher may be interested in certain papers related to his field and make short notes about these papers' abstracts. When retrieving a document, such piece of information (or the synopsis of the document) is often sufficient to satisfy the user's need. The DPSs must provide tools to help users extract and organize the synopses they are particularly interested in.

- *Information retrieval.* One of the major tasks of DPSs is to support information retrieval. The systems should allow users to input keywords (possibly connected with boolean operators such as AND, OR, NOT) and return documents that contain exactly those words. When users do not have a clear idea of finding documents relevant to a given subject, these systems should allow them to specify words that characterize, in their opinion, the subject. (A subject can be a topic as handled by most intelligent retrieval systems [32, 38], or can be very general such as a picture, a logo, etc., contained in a document). The DPSs then rank documents according to their degrees of relevance to the subject, and return the most relevant documents' list to the users.

- *Information browsing.* The result of a query might be a collection of documents or their synopses. It would be an extremely laborious task for users to read sequentially all the information in these documents. Instead, the DPSs should present different options to allow the users to determine which pieces of information to be read when browsing the documents. This means that the systems should set up a number of alternatives for users to explore rather than a single stream of information.

- *Information synthesizing.* At times, users might want to synthesize information from existing documents. For example, a course supervisor may need to prepare an annual report, summarizing the number of students registering each course, withdrawing from each course, and failed in each course. Such information may come from different documents, including registration forms, course withdrawn forms and transcripts. The report can be physically produced or stored merely as a view [8]. The DPSs must provide tools to facilitate both operations.

- *Document reproduction.* In a paperless environment, all the documents are eventually scanned and stored in the computer. The DPSs should be able to reproduce the original documents from the database. This capability is particularly important for certain types of documents (e.g., those involving legal issues) for which the initiators' signatures are sometimes needed to verify their originality.

When these DPSs are used in a distributed, cooperative environment (where the most common documents are perhaps electronic messages [23]), they must also support information sharing and exchange. These generally include the following activities: (1) composing messages to be sent, (2) selecting, filing and prioritizing messages that are received, (3) responding to some urgent messages, and (4) suggesting likely responses to other messages [23].

We have initiated a project, called TEXPROS (TEXt PROcessing System), which is intended to meet the above functional requirements. Our research is directed towards producing a document processing system which can be used in many different domains, and which combines innovative technologies of various disciplines, such as image processing, software engineering, rule-based specifications, hypertext, and information retrieval systems.

1.1. *Related work*

Many document processing systems have been developed in the past. They basically fall into four categories.

1. The first group deals with multimedia information including text, form, image and voice data. Diamond [41], for example, allows users to create, edit, and transmit multimedia documents. However, it does not explore in depth the retrieving methods. MULTOS [2], on the other hand, supports a well-defined query language and many query processing techniques. MINOS [5] provides integrated facilities for creating complex document objects, and for extracting and formulating new information from existing documents.

There are also various data models proposed for multimedia documents, spanning from relational [39, 50], semantic [7, 31] to object-oriented ones [12, 16, 51].

2. The second group deals with bibliographic information retrieval. A typical example is SMART [32], which supports keyword based retrieval for bibliographic databases. There are also intelligent systems built based on AI techniques. EX-P [38], for example, is an expert system supporting information retrieval from documents concerning environmental pollution. Relevant work includes RUBRIC [43], THOMAS [28], and the systems proposed by Pollitt [29] and Shoval [35].
3. The third group is concerned with intelligent document categorization. Resumix [42] is one of such systems. It reads applicants' resumes, creates a resume summary, matches candidates to job openings, generates reports, and prints applicant acknowledgement letters with a bitmap signature from the appropriate hiring manager. Other systems, such as the news story categorization system [13], also provide similar functions.
4. The fourth group is concerned with message exchanging and filtering. The goal of such systems is to help users filter, sort, and prioritize messages that are already addressed to them, and also help them find useful messages they would not otherwise have received. One most successful example is the INFORMATION LENS system [23]. Relevant work includes ISCREEN [30], MAFIA [22], and the system described by Chang and Leung [3].

While these systems appear successful in their own domains, their functional capabilities are generally limited. Also, most of these systems only handle a special type of document. In contrast, our system is designed to deal with a variety of documents. Furthermore, there are three key aspects that distinguish our system from the existing systems, and that make our approach a promising one.

First, unlike the multimedia information systems, most of which have a complex data model, TEXPROS employs a simple, yet powerful model to specify documents. Each document is divided into textual and non-textual parts. (The latter includes logos, drawings, graphics, pictures, images, etc.) The system permits users to capture the meaning and synopsis of both parts and organize them into a semistructured form (which we call a frame instance). When retrieval occurs, the system often returns the frame instances, rather than the original documents, to the user. (In most cases, the user should content with the information in the frame instances.) By doing so, it speeds up the information retrieval considerably. In addition, the system exploits many AI techniques (e.g., organizing the knowledge base as a three dimensional semantic network) to support intelligent retrieval, which is absent in the previous multimedia document systems.

Second, most of the existing systems have a monolithic design; it is difficult, though not impossible, to replace their components or to improve their functions. In contrast, TEXPROS is designed as an "open system". It can be customized to have different functional capabilities that meet different user's need. The system can be used in many ways, for example, as a personal system, a multi-user bibliography retrieval system or a group communication and coordination system. When data communication and sharing are necessary, the system provides mechanisms for users to specify protocols for extracting, transmitting and exchanging information.

Third, we employ a toolkit approach to accomplishing the open design. The system encompasses various tools, generators and programming modules, which interact with each other through well-defined interfaces. These modules and tools are "glued" together and can be easily modified or replaced.

This paper presents an overview of the TEXPROS system, and proposes solutions to several issues in the design phase. We concentrate on using TEXPROS as a personal system, and mainly discuss the data definition and manipulation aspects of the system. Other aspects, such as image processing and storage, will be treated in subsequent reports. In Sec. 2, we describe the data model. Section 3 discusses techniques used for document classification. Section 4 describes the agent based implementation supporting document categorization and file reorganization. Section 5 illustrates queries provided by TEXPROS and discusses some query processing tactics. In Sec. 6, we present applications of TEXPROS, discussing how the system may support the manipulation of documents used in developing software. We conclude the paper in Sec. 7.

2. The Data Model

We use an object-oriented approach to specifying documents. A (DAG-structured) type hierarchy is employed to describe the properties of documents. We allow users to define *folders*, which are logical repositories of the documents. The folders constitute the user's logical file structure; they are connected via various relationships.

2.1. *Document types*

We classify documents that are similar in properties into a document class. Each class is associated with a type, which describes the properties for the class of documents [25]. For example, we can define the type for the *Memo* class as

```
Define type for Memo begin
  subtype of Document;
   attributes:
     Sender: string(30);
     Receiver: string(30);
     Date: string(20);
     Content: TEXT;
     Remark: TEXT;
end;
```

The type definition indicates that each memo has five attributes (slots), which are of types string and TEXT respectively. (TEXT is strings of arbitrary length.) We group these attributes into a tabular form (which we call a *frame template*). Each object (memo) in the *Memo* class is associated with a frame instance (reminiscent of the document surrogate used in bibliographic information retrieval [38], or the frame used in knowledge representation [11]). Figure 2 illustrates a memo and its corresponding frame instance.[a]

Frame template

Each frame template is divided into two parts: *structured* and *unstructured* parts. Fields belonging to the former have types of strings while the latter have types of free text.[b] In the above frame template, the content slot contains

[a]The procedure of converting a document into its frame instance is called *information extraction*. We discuss the procedure in Sec. 3.

[b]Clifton [6] and Malone *et al.* [23] proposed similar ideas in representing documents as partially structured information, though the documents they considered are very special.

New Jersey Institute of Technology

Computer & Information Science

Ext. ________

MEMORANDUM

To : Chairpersons
From : Gary Thomas, Provost
Date : April 16, 1991

****

A meeting has been set up to discuss the interdisciplinary programs on Monday, April 29, 1991, from 1 pm till 2:30 pm in the Alumni Center Board Room. The focus of this meeting will be on the curriculum of the programs.

(a)

Sender	Gary Thomas
Receiver	Chairpersons
Date	April 16, 1991
Content	Interdisciplinary Programs Meeting. Monday, April 29, 91, 1:00 ~ 2:30. Alumni Center Board Room. Meeting will focus on program curriculum.
Remark	

(b)

Fig. 2. (a) A memo sent from the Provost to departmental chairpersons; (b) the memo's frame instance.

the synopsis of the document. The remark slot contains supplementary information (i.e., those that are relevant, but not specified in the document).[c]

In general, a frame template may contain a variety of slots. Consider, for example, the template for a book. It may have a "title" slot, composed of several subslots such as "book title", "chapter title", and "section title". These slots contain information concerning various titles in a book. There may be a "picture" slot that contains the descriptions for all the pictures in the book.[d] Besides, the user is allowed to add additional slots to a frame instance. Thus, our data model basically uses a weak typing system [2]. (A type that completely specifies the structure of its instance is called a strong type. For example, in the relational model, a relation definition completely specifies the structure of its tuples. A weak type, on the contrary, only partially specifies the structure of its instance.)

[c]For example, after the chairperson receives the memo in Fig. 2(a), he may call the Provost, inquiring the details about it. Through the phone conversation, he realizes that this memo is concerned with the development of the *research* curriculum. He may then add such information into the remark slot.

[d]We separate the textual part from the nontextual part (including pictures, images and graphics) of a document. The original pictures are stored in the image base. In the frame instance, we only keep their descriptions.

Frame instance

Each document corresponds to a unique frame instance. Each frame instance has a unique identification (internal id). The frame instance has the following properties:

- *Completeness.* A frame instance is said to be *complete* if every keyword [32] that appears in the original document also appears in it. In TEXPROS, we do not require a frame instance to be complete. Rather, a user may type whatever is interesting or important to him in the frame instance. The information contained in the frame instance governs the scope of subsequent queries (see Sec. 5).
- *Time-dependence.* A frame instance may vary as the time passes. For example, after certain days, the chairperson may receive another amendment memo which says the meeting specified in the memo of Fig. 2(a) will be delayed. In this case, the user may retrieve the frame instance in Fig. 2(b) and modify its contents accordingly.
- *User-dependence.* The contents in a frame instance are often user-dependent. For example, as discussed in Sec. 1, for the same conference proceedings, the information interests of a secretary can be very different from a researcher. As a result, these users may store different information in the frame instance. When TEXPROS is used as a personal system, this discrepancy usually causes no problems. On the other hand, when it is used as a multi-user system, a set of protocols needs to be provided to guide the information extraction.

It should be pointed out that our typing system differs in spirit from that proposed in the ODA (Office Document Architecture) standard [14]. ODA is part of the standards for document interchange being developed by ISO (International Standardization Organization) and ECMA (European Computer Manufacturers Association). It distinguishes between the logical and layout structures of a document.

The logical structure associates the content of the document with a hierarchy of *logical objects.* Examples of logical objects are summaries, titles, sections, paragraphs, figures, tables, etc. These objects are classified according to their types, which are either *composite* or *basic.* Basic logical objects (e.g., paragraphs) are at the lowest hierarchical levels. They are associated with *content portions*, which contain the content of the document. Composite logical objects (e.g., sections) consist of components that may be other composite objects and/or basic objects.

The layout structure associates the same content with a hierarchy of *layout objects*. Examples of layout objects are pages, columns, and footnote areas. Layout objects are also classified according to their types, which include *page set*, *composite page*, *basic page*, *frame* and *block*. Basic pages or blocks are directly associated with content portions of a document.

Figure 3 illustrates how the memo in Fig. 2(a) may be modeled using the ODA standard. In this example, the highest level of the logical structure consists of three basic objects ("Sender", "Receiver", "Date") and a composite object "Memo-Body". The "Memo-Body" in turn consists of a basic object "Paragraph".

The layout structure consists of three levels. At the highest level, there are two composite pages: "First Page" and "Second Page". The former contains three frames ("Sender", "Receiver", "Date") and the latter contains a "Body" frame. Each frame in turn consists of a block, which is directly associated with content portions.

Thus, instead of distinguishing the logical and layout structures of a document, we combine both structures and incorporate them into the frame template.[e] Moreover, we store the synopses for both textual and nontextual parts of a document, rather than the original contents, in the frame instance. There are several reasons for doing so. First, by separating the textual from nontextual parts, and keeping only the synopses for both parts in the frame instance, we can describe a document in a very succinct manner. Second, in practice, a user may not be concerned with all the information in a document. (In fact, a large body of contents in a document, say a memo, often contain "junk" information.) When retrieval occurs, the synopsis suffices to satisfy the user's need. (The synopsis contained in the frame instance in Fig. 2(b), for example, suffices to remind the user what actions he must take corresponding to that memo.) Third, frame instances have a rather structured form, which makes it easy to store and manipulate them. Retrieving and browsing such a small piece of information require much less time than retrieving the original document. The cost saved may improve the overall performance dramatically.

[e]Gibbs and Tsichritzis [12] mentioned similar template concepts, though they use that for the layout purpose only.

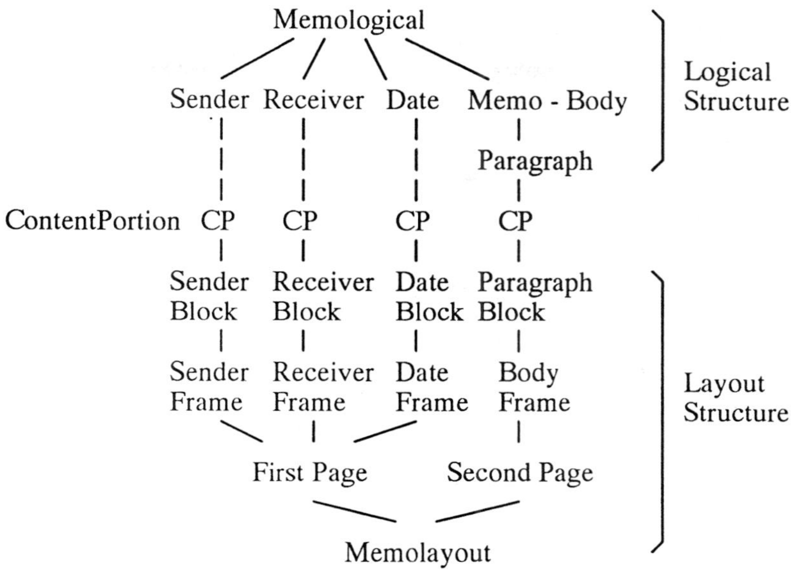

Fig. 3. Modeling the memo in Fig. 2(a) using the ODA standard.

2.2. *Type hierarchy*

Document types (and classes) are related by specialization and generalization [37]. For example, in the type definition in Subsec. 2.1, the reserved word **subtype of** indicates that *Memo* is a specialization of *Document* (they are connected through the **is-a** relationship). Instances of *Memo* also belong to *Document* and have all attributes for *Document* (inheritance property [12]). The **is-a** relationship generally forms a directed acyclic graph. Figure 4 illustrates one such case.

2.3. *Folders and views*

TEXPROS provides facilities to define *folders*, which are repositories of documents. For example, we can define the folder for graduate students as

Define folder Graduate-Student
  with polymorphism

relationship:
  depends on Student
categorization criterion:
  based on Name: string(30);

This statement creates a folder labeled Graduate-Student; it contains the frame instances for all graduate students' documents. The folder is a logical repository; it does not physically exist in the database (reminiscent of the views discussed in relational database systems [8]).

The reserved word **with polymorphism** indicates that `Graduate-Student` is heterogeneous (i.e., the constituent frame instances have different types).[f] A folder is homogeneous if all its frame instances are of the same type. An example would be a folder that contains technical reports produced by some university (cf. Fig. 4).

The relationship **depends on** indicates that `Graduate-Student` is a subfolder in (or child of) `Student`. Intuitively, when a folder is removed, its dependent subfolders are also removed. The **categorization** clause is optional. When it is present, the folder is further categorized based on the specified criterion. For example, in Fig. 5, the `Graduate-Student` folder is categorized based on the attribute "Name". Note that each student folder may contain a number of different frame instances. Some graduate students have financial support, and we may keep the notes concerning the status and stipend in their folders. The categorization criterion can be modified dynamically. For example, the user may recategorize the graduate students' documents according to their entrance year.

Not only attributes, but also the *concept* (or *topic*) can be used as a criterion for categorization. For example, a professor may categorize his database research papers based on the topic they discuss. TEXPROS allows users to define criteria using rules. The rules are both user-readable and computable. For example, a folder holding papers concerning the transaction management may require all papers in the folder to have keywords `logging`, `crash`, `recovery`, `concurrency` and so on.

TEXPROS also allows users to synthesize information from existing documents. For example, in creating a summary note that includes all

[f]Each graduate student, for example, may have two types of documents, *admission-letter* and *transcript*, associated with him/her.

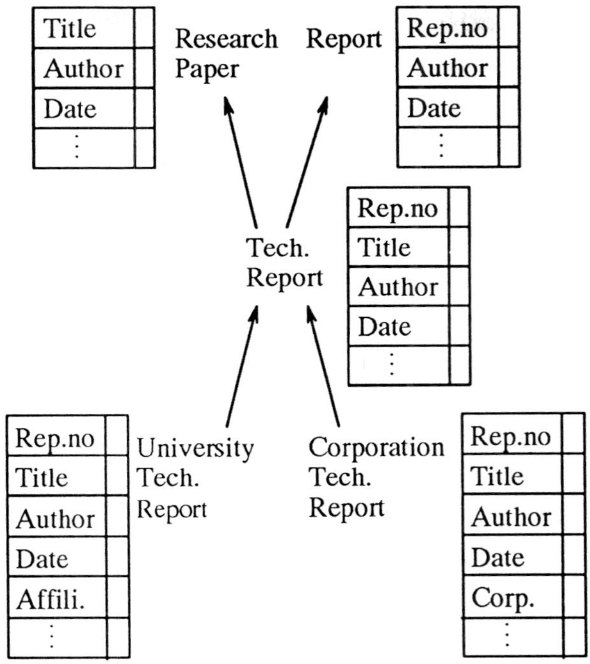

Fig. 4. **A type graph with the frame template associated with each type.**

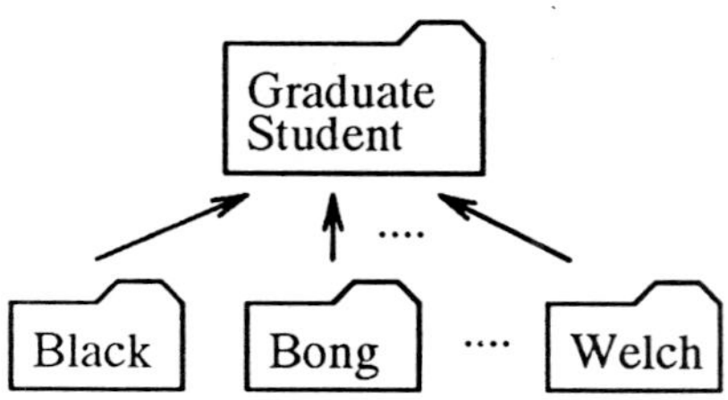

Fig. 5. The **`Graduate-Student`** folder is categorized based on the attribute "Name".

Ph.D. students' names who have passed the qualifying examination, one may issue[g]

> **Define view** *summary note*
> **set of** s
> **where**
> s = t.name;
> t is **an instance of** *qualifying-exam-pass-letter*;

Like frame instances, views can also be grouped into a folder.

2.4. *Logical file structure*

TEXPROS provides users with a logical file structure that mimics their filing systems. The logical file structure is made up of folders, which are linked via various relationships. The folders can be added, deleted and modified by the user.

Figure 6 shows a (partial) file structure describing a university departmental chairperson's filing system. Here, the entire Document folder is categorized into subfolders Research-Paper, Departmental-Affairs, Personnel-Information based on the concept criterion. Each subfolder is further categorized based on another criterion. The criteria can be distinct at different places.

A folder is *concrete* if it does not contain any subfolders; otherwise it is *abstract*. Intuitively, a concrete folder actually contains frame instances, whereas an abstract folder is a repository of folders. For example, Smith is concrete while Personnel-Information is abstract. Note that an abstract folder may also contain frame instances. For example, the chairperson may place documents for all non-Ph.D. students indistinguishably in the Student folder. A concrete folder will become an abstract one if it is further categorized.

A folder may be contained in more than one folder. For example, Lecturer is contained in both PhD-Student and Faculty (they are connected through the "depend on" relationship). A folder may also contain views produced by other frame instances. For example, Annual-Report contains views produced by frame instances in Promotion-Tenure, Faculty, Student and Staff (they are connected through the "synthesize from" relationship). The arrow pointing

[g]At times, users may wish to create a note (or report) that physically exists in the database. We provide tools to help users clip and move text segments between documents. The tools facilitate considerably the task of information synthesizing.

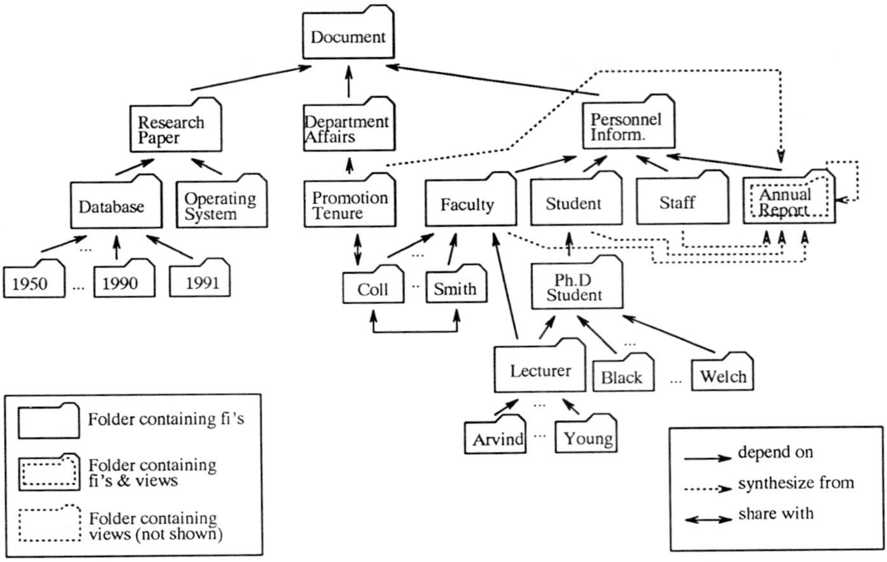

Fig. 6. An example logical file structure; the string on each folder represents the label of that folder.

back to Annual-Report indicates that the folder also contains views produced by frame instances in itself.

In reality, it is possible that copies of a frame instance are stored in several different folders. For example, the departmental chairperson may keep two copies of the same promotion letter for the faculty member Coll—one is in Coll's folder, and the other is in Promotion-Tenure. In this case, we say that the two concrete folders share each other, and they are connected through the "share with" relationship.

2.5 *Operations on logical file structure*

As a personal filing system, the logical file structure is dynamic and evolving. Some common operations that can change the file structure include the following (all examples here refer to the departmental chairperson's file structure in Fig. 6):

- *Decomposing.* This operation decomposes a folder into subfolders based on a new criterion (e.g., categorize the folder **Operating-System**, which contains all papers discussing operating systems, according to their publication years).

- *Merging.* This operation combines two or more folders into a new one (e.g., combine all database papers that were published before 1970 into a folder *Old-Database*).
- *Inserting.* This operation adds a new folder into the file (e.g., create a folder **Post-Qualified-Student**, which is a subcateogry of **PhD-Student** and contains documents for all Ph.D. students who have passed the qualifying examination).
- *Deleting.* This operation removes a folder in the file (e.g., remove the folder for a staff member who is unemployed).
- *Pruning.* This operation erases the descendants of a folder;[h] the folder itself remains in the file (e.g., delete all the subfolders labeled by years and put all database papers indistinguishably in the **Database** folder).
- *Moving.* This operation moves a folder from one category to another (e.g., move a Ph.D. student's folder, who has graduated and has been hired as an adjunct professor, from **PhD-Student** to **Faculty**).
- *Modifying criteria.* This operation changes an existing categorization criterion (e.g., recategorize papers in **Database** based on topics, rather than years).

For a filing system such as TEXPROS, we believe that keeping both document type definitions and logical file structure is better than just keeping type definitions as adopted in others' work [2, 51]. The reasons are twofold. First, as can be seen above, the filing system is dynamic and file reorganization may occur frequently. The logical file structure provides users with an intuitively clear view, which shows how their filing system currently is. Second, since the logical file structure is composed of folders, it is easy for users to perform folder-at-a-time operations. By using these operations, users can query, create, remove an entire folder, rather than perform many separate retrieve/insert/delete operations on frame instances.

3. Document Classification

After scanning a document, TEXPROS's document recognition subsystem

[h] A folder A is called a descendant of folder B if there is a path of "depend on" edges going from A to B.

separates its textual part from the nontextual part, and converts the document into an encoded form (cf. Fig. 1). The encoded document consists of the ASCII representation of the textual part and simplified symbols for the nontextual part.[i] The system then classifies the encoded document. Documents not in paper form do not pass through the recognition subsystem and are classified directly.

The classification procedure often includes two parts:

1. Identify the type of the document and locate the corresponding frame template;
2. Extract the contents from the document and construct a frame instance.

We discuss each part in turn.

3.1. *Type identification*

Identifying the type for a document often entails the automatic recognition of the document contents. Obviously, the best approach would be full-text understanding. But existing natural language approaches only work in very limited domains. The wider the coverage, the less robust they tend to be. This makes them unsuitable candidates for handling the wide range and large quantities of documents [9].

We feel that a more promising solution is to use a knowledge-base generator, which accepts the format description and domain knowledge for the documents, and produces a custom classification subsystem. There have been several attempts in developing customizable classification units [9, 22, 24, 42]. A most successful example is the integrated document handling project developed by Eirund *et al.* [9]. They employ *a priori* defined type hierarchy to perform logical and content analysis of documents. While our work has been inspired by Eirund *et al.*'s, our approach bases largely on image analysis on page layouts of encoded documents [49]. We elaborate the techniques in the following paragraphs.

Consider again the memo in Fig. 2(a). It can be represented as a collection of "blocks" as shown in Fig. 7(a). Each block is a minimum rectangle or square enclosing an area of text satisfying certain conditions (e.g., the distance between certain pixels in a block must be bounded by some constant). We

[i]For example, a university logo may be represented by the university name. When the user wishes to see the original picture, he clicks on the symbol. The system will display the image of the picture on the screen.

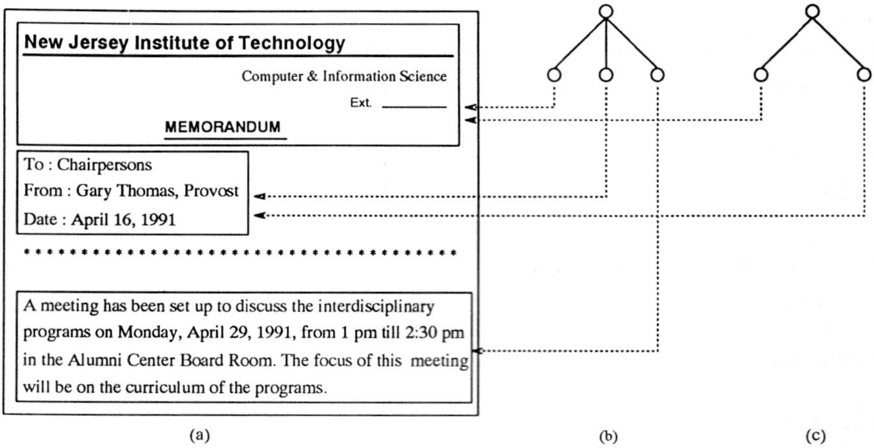

Fig. 7. Mapping a document into an ordered tree.

provide a set of rules to convert the block representation to an ordered tree given in Fig. 7(b). The tree structure describes the spatial relationship among blocks in the memo.

In the knowledge base, we maintain a set of trees that correspond to the known types in the system. Suppose T is the type tree for a class C of documents. T contains nodes corresponding to common blocks shared by all documents in C (the contents in these blocks are immaterial). Figure 7(c) shows the type tree for the memo in Fig. 2(a).

TEXPROS uses our previously developed tree pattern matcher [45–48] to compare the tree structure for a newly coming encoded document against those in the knowledge base. An operation which is supported by the pattern matcher is to compare two trees A and B, allowing arbitrary subtrees to be removed from B.

Often, there may exist a number of type trees that match the document's tree (i.e., these documents have similar page layouts). We then refine solutions by performing the textual analysis on the block contents using a capable string pattern matcher. Part of the textual analysis would include searching for keywords such as `To`, `From`, `Memorandum`, etc., in the blocks. In this way, the system can identify the type for the document.

It is likely that a new document does not match any type tree in the knowledge base. In this case, the user needs to input the format description, the frame template, and the corresponding type tree for this new class of documents through the knowledge acquisition tool [3] provided by the system.

3.2. *Information extraction*

If the type is identified and the corresponding frame template is found, the system extracts and fills in the information in slots belonging to the structured part, which includes fields of fixed length strings. The user can verify the extracted information against the image of the encoded document on the screen, and correct any wrong information that is not extracted properly. He then fills in descriptive terms and comments (if any) in the unstructured part (cf. Subsec. 2.1).

Automatic information extraction for the structured part entails identifying content portions relevant for an attribute. A set of rules is used to describe the "relevant content". For example, a rule associated with the memo in Fig. 2(a) may state that the document portion following "From" represents the sender of the memo. These rules are also input through the system's knowledge acquisition tool.

4. Agent-based Categorization Subsystem

Given a frame instance, TEXPROS needs to identify a folder and place it in the folder. This procedure is called *document categorization*. Similarly, in reorganizing files (cf. Subsec. 2.5), the system needs to place all the involving frame instances in appropriate folders. To automate these operations, we adopt an agent-based architecture to implement TEXPROS's categorization subsystem (reminiscent of Shoham's agent oriented language [34]).

Each folder is associated with a filing agent. Each agent has its private data structures and methods for manipulating these data structures. The agents communicate with each other through message passing. The implementation is data driven in the sense that the agents operate concurrently and the frame instances flow around among these agents [33].

In the next subsections, we discuss in turn how this implementation supports both document categorization and file reorganization.

4.1. *Document categorization*

The criteria used to categorize documents are defined in terms of attribute values and rules. Each filing agent (or folder) is associated with a criterion. By comparing the contents in a newly generated frame instance against the criterion, the agent is able to distribute the instance to its children.[j] If the frame instance satisfies categorization rules for many children, copies are made and sent to each of these children. Doing so recursively will place the frame instance in appropriate folders.

As an example, consider again the file structure in Fig. 6. The following describes part of the rules associated with folders on the path from Document to 1990:

- A document is a research paper if it has attributes "title", "author", and "date", which is part of the criterion used for categorizing generic documents.
- A research paper is concerned with databases if it has keywords **database**, **query processing**, **transaction management**, etc., which is part of the criterion used for categorizing research papers.
- A database paper is in the folder labeled X year if it is published in that year, which is part of the criterion used for categorizing database papers.

Based on these criteria, TEXPROS is able to insert a database paper (more precisely, its frame instance) published in 1990 into the correct folder.

In practice, it is likely that a frame instance is inserted into several different folders. Also, a frame instance may remain at certain point during categorization. We call such a frame instance a *transient*. A buffer is maintained at each agent to keep the transients.

We say a frame instance f is inserted *unsuccessfully* if the folders into which f is inserted do not coincide with what the user wants. Such a situation may happen when the criteria are too misleading, too restrict or too coarse. We define the *successful rate* of inserting a frame instance as

$$\left(1 - \frac{n}{N}\right) \times 100\%$$

[j]Agent A is said to be a child of agent B if the folder associated with A is a child of that associated with B (cf. Subsec. 2.3).

where n is the number of frame instances inserted unsuccessfully, and N is the total number of frame instances inserted. Clearly, the higher the successful rate, the better the performance of the categorization subsystem will be.

For an information retrieval system such as TEXPROS, guaranteeing that frame instances are inserted successfully in a proper location is important. Otherwise, the user may get wrong information when retrieving frame instances from a folder. However, it is unlikely to have a fully automatic categorization subsystem which always inserts frame instances successfully. As a consequence, we adopt a semi-automatic, but practical approach for TEXPROS. Each time after a frame instance is categorized, the result will be displayed on the screen. If the resulting folders are not exactly what the user wants, he can correct them manually. This includes the case in which the user wishes to place copies of a frame instance in different folders but the system only inserts it into one of them (cf. Subsec. 2.4). In situations where the successful rate tends to be unacceptable, the user may need to redefine the criteria, which are both user-readable and computable. We expect that when the system first runs, the successful rate may be low. However, as more interactive modifications on the criteria are made, the overall performance including the successful rate can be improved.

One interesting issue here is concerned with the integrity of the filing system. Consider again the memo in Fig. 2. Suppose the chairperson receives an amendment memo on April 17, saying that the meeting originally scheduled on April 29 will be delayed to May 6. Under this circumstance, what is stated in that memo is no longer true. This may cause the system to return incorrect results to the user. For example, if the chairperson wishes to see all meetings on April 29, he would get wrong information. To assure the integrity of the filing system, TEXPROS maintains a set of alerters [20, 40] which will give the user the warning about inconsistent information when the amendment memo is inserted into the system. The development of alerters involves extracting facts from frame instances [19] and is a major topic of current research.

4.2. *File reorganization*

As discussed in Subsec. 2.5, many operations may be applied to the logical file structure. Most of the operations can be implemented by using two primitive operations.

- agent attachment — agent A (cf. Sec. 4) is said to be attached to agent B

if A becomes a child of B.[k]

- agent detachment — agent A is said to be detached from agent B if A was B's child but is not any more.

When a folder F_1 is defined as a child of F_2 (cf. Subsec. 2.3), F_1's agent A_1 is attached to F_2's agent A_2 automatically. The user must specify rules for distributing frame instances from A_2 to A_1. These rules become part of the criterion used to categorize F_2. A procedure, called frame instance *re-distribution*, is activated spontaneously which sends frame instances currently in A_2's buffer satisfying the rules to A_1. As elaborated below, these frame instances may be accumulated due to the agent detachment.

When folder F_1 is removed from the children of F_2, its agent A_1 is detached from A_2. The categorization rules for A_1 are deleted. A procedure, called frame instances *re-collection*, is activated spontaneously which collects frame instances from A_1 and keeps them in A_2's buffer.

We illustrate these techniques by considering two operations in Subsec. 2.5.

- Suppose the user wants to decompose Operating System based on years. In this case, agents representing different publication years are attached to the agent A for Operating System. Categorizing rules are defined (by the user) and the frame instances which are originally in A's buffer are distributed into A's children according to the rules.
- Suppose the user wants to recategorize the database papers based on topics. In this case, categorizing rules associated with the folder Database must be updated and the frame instances that were originally in the children folders are recollected and redistributed based on the new rules.

Just as document categorization, file reorganization may render frame instances accumulated in buffers due to poor categorization criteria. TEXPROS will display the results for each file reorganization and the user can verify them on the screen.

It is interesting to note that file reorganization may also cause duplicate frame instances to be placed in the same folder. For example, merging two folders F_1 and F_2 into F causes two copies of a frame instance which were originally placed in F_1 and F_2, respectively, to be placed in F. While the duplicates may be harmless, the system's alerters will still notify the user of this situation.

[k] We use the term "attachment" and "inserting as a child" indistinctively in the paper.

5. Information Retrieval

As discussed in Sec. 1, one major requirement for document processing systems is to support information retrieval. This often involves three areas:

- the query language;
- the access methods and storage structure, and
- the query processing techniques.

In the following subsections, we discuss each area in turn and describe our approaches used in TEXPROS.

5.1. *Types of queries*

We support three types of query methods. These include querying by classes, by folders, and by attributes with values. The results of all these queries are a collection of frame instances.

Querying by classes

If the user memorizes the classes (types) of documents he is searching for, he can query the system by explicitly specifying these classes. An example would be "Find all memos sent from the Provost on April 16, 1991". A query may involve more than one class. For example, assume both *transcript* and *qualifying-exam-pass-letter* are existing types in the system. A user may want to find the transcripts for those students who passed the qualifying examinations. In this case, the system may first identify the persons who received the letter confirming their success in passing the qualifying examinations, and then locate their transcripts. It is likely that the user misspells the type names, or he only has a vague idea about the types of documents he is interested in. In this case, the system will guide the user to refine his query by displaying the portion of the type hierarchy that is most relevant to the class specified in the query.

Querying by folders

If the user is interested in information stored in folders, he may query by specifying the folders' labels (recalling that each folder has a label). For example, consider again the file structure in Fig. 6. The folder of database papers is categorized based on publication years. A user may retrieve information from the concrete folders; for instance, "Find all database papers in the folder 1990". At times, the user may be interested in information coming from different folders. An example would be "Find all database papers published between 1980 and 1990". As in querying by classes, if the user misspells the folder names or only has a rough idea about the folders he intends to search for, TEXPROS allows him to browse the most relevant folders and dynamically reformulate queries as he proceeds.

Querying by attributes with values

It is likely that the frame instances the user is interested in belong to different types and are placed in different folders. It would be very inconvenient, or in fact may be unlikely, to memorize and specify all these types or folders. In this case, the user may query by attributes and/or their values. An example would be "Find all documents dated on April 16, 1991 whose sender is Provost". The resulting frame instances may have types of *memo*, *letter*, *notice* and so on.

A query may contain string matching operators. For example, if the user wants to find all meetings held on April 29, 1991, he can issue "Find all documents whose content slot contains April 29, 1991". A query may also involve topic (concept) searching. An example would be "Find database papers discussing the transaction management". In answering this query, the frame instances whose content slots contain the keywords **transaction management**, **logging**, **crash recovery**, **concurrency**, etc., are returned as the result of the query. This is under the assumption that all frame instances for papers have such a slot in which the user describes the contents of the papers. In addition, those whose keywords match the query partially are also returned. These may include frame instances having only the keyword **transaction** or **management** but not both.

At times, the user may not even memorize the attributes used in different types of frame instances. In this case, the querying by values method can be used, in which he may query by simply entering certain keywords describing what he wants. Also, it is likely that what impresses the user is a picture in the document, in which case he may type in words (i.e., query) depicting the picture, since TEXPROS allows users to describe pictures in a document's frame instance. Because it's likely that the input query differs from the descriptions previously stored in the frame instances, the system returns all those whose picture descriptions match partially with the query.[1] When desired, the system can display the images of the pictures on the screen.

Combination of queries

Any of the queries described above can be combined to create a complex query. An example is the query "Find all memos from the Provost that are in the meeting folder and that are concerned with the interdisciplinary research curriculum". This query combines a number of sub-queries. The performance of the execution of the query may be dependent on the order in which the individual subqueries are executed. One sequence of execution is to first find the memos whose sender is the Provost, then focus on those in the meeting folder, and finally display those which have keywords **interdisciplinary research curriculum**. Other sequences of subquery execution are possible and may result in different performance.

We note that, because TEXPROS searches and returns frame instances, rather than the original documents, to the user, the information contained in the frame instance (i.e., attributes, values, etc.) governs the scope of the above queries. Note also that when these queries are concerned with topics or pictures, there is no clear distinction between frame instances that qualify the specified conceptual descriptions and those that do not; some instances are more relevant, while others are less so. As a result, TEXPROS always returns a list of frame instances, ranked according to the degree of their relevance to the query.

5.2. *Access methods and storage structures*

We maintain pointers that link documents and frame instances. These pointers allow the system to locate and return original documents to the user when necessary. Also, we maintain tables that map the logical file structure to the physical storage. Entries in the tables are pointers from folders (more precisely, the buffers associated with the agents of the folders) to their component frame instances on disk.

Two kinds of access methods are used for storing the frame instances: indexing the structured data (B^+ tree) and storing the unstructured data

[1] As an example, consider finding the documents that have a horse picture. Suppose that the user queries by describing the horse as an animal having four legs. The system may present frame instances having a horse, a cow, or arbitrary four-legged animal description.

using the signature file [2], or the inverted file [6]. Each of the access methods has pros and cons. Faloutsos [10] points out that inverted files are easy to implement and fast, but suffer from two shortcomings: (1) the storage overhead (50–300 per cent of the original file size, if word-level indexing is used); (2) the high cost of updating and reorganizing the index. On the other hand, the signature file yields a slower response time, but has many advantages such as efficiency in handling insertions, ability to support a growing file, and tolerance for typing and spelling errors. The trade-offs and the relative performance of these access methods are examined in current research.

5.3. *Query processing tactics*

One key aspect that distinguishes TEXPROS from existing document processing systems is that it supports concept-based retrieval. In performing such kind of retrieval, it is necessary for the system to guide or assist the user to gradually refine his query. In order to make the system "intelligent" and active in assisting search, we need the help of the knowledge base.

There have been numerous techniques proposed for organizing the knowledge base to support intelligent retrieval, mostly for bibliography database systems. We comment on some of the techniques below. In RUBRIC [43], Tong and Shapiro organize knowledge as "rule evaluation trees" represented as production rules. To determine the relevance of a document to a topic (the root of the tree), RUBRIC matches the document's keywords to triggering phrases (leaf nodes). Each edge is associated with a relevance score. By propagating up the tree and applying a collection of predetermined formulae, one can calculate the relevance score to the topic for the document. The system then presents to the user the documents in the database ranked according to their relevance scores.

In THOMAS [28], Oddy created a network of associations among concepts or keywords. The system plays a passive role in answering queries. The user is presented with documents retrieved by the initial query, along with associated concepts or keywords. The user then makes judgement of relevance and indicates which associated terms (keywords) are important. This new input serves to define the subsequently retrieved set of documents.

Shoval [35] also proposes the use of an unlabeled set of associations among concepts. He describes a system that is much more active in seeking related concepts and documents. Shoval employs a two-stage process based on spreading activation through the semantic network. During the "search" stage, relevant knowledge in the network is activated, and search and evaluation rules are applied in order to find appropriate vocabulary terms to represent the user's query. During the "suggest" stage, those terms are further evaluated, dynamically rank-ordered according to relevance, and suggested to the user. More recently, Chen and Dhar [4] described a similar document retrieval system. They developed several heuristics to direct the system's spreading activation effort.

We feel that organizing the knowledge base as a semantic network is a promising approach. However, unlike THOMAS, our system has capabilities of spreading activation through the network. On the other hand, unlike Chen *et al.*'s system, we allow users to modify the flow of the spreading activation freely. We organize the semantic network as a three dimensional hypergraph. Each edge is associated with dynamically adjustable weights that indicate the relative relevance of the concepts. Each node contains additional information (e.g., a node for the keyword **university** may contain some names of the universities in the country). The user is allowed to zoom in each node for the information during the spreading activation.

We also keep a class of knowledge that captures the mapping of words to semantic primitives (e.g., July 2, 7/2, and Jul. 2nd trigger the same semantic primitive). Such information helps locate frame instances whose terms do not match those specified in a query, though they are semantically equivalent.

Another area we are currently examining is query optimization. Observe that different frame templates may have radically different slots. For example, a frame instance of the *book* class can have slots "chapter titles" and "author" but never contain the slots "sender" or "receiver". Thus, in processing a query such as "Find memos whose sender is John Smith", the query processor can eliminate a large amount of frame instances that lack the sender slot, thereby reducing the search space considerably.

Another technique for query optimization is to let the query processor "learn" from the history and store certain frame instances in the cache. The underlying reason is that "documents that were accessed most frequently in the past should also be the ones that are most likely accessed in the near future". For example, a researcher whose expertise is the transaction management may access papers of that topic most frequently. Therefore, storing *those* "hot spot" papers in the cache should speed up information retrieval.

6. Impact of TEXPROS on Software Development

Having described the capabilities of TEXPROS, we now turn to its applications. TEXPROS is intended to be used in many domains. One application of the system is in the office automation area. As illustrated by the various examples in the previous sections, the system helps office workers considerably in managing their documents. Another important application is in the software development process, where TEXPROS can be used to manage and control the configurations of software systems throughout their life cycles.

A software configuration is a collection of documents, called software configuration items (SCIs), which are related to one another in a predefined way described with respect to a particular phase of a software system life cycle (SSLC). Table 1 lists some common documents produced during each phase of the SSLC [16].

Table 1. Documents produced during each phase of SSLC (*Source*: Horowitz and Williamson [16]).

SSLC phase	Documents produced
Requirement Analysis	Requirement Document
Functional Analysis	Functional Specification
Design Analysis	Design Document
Implementation	Implementation Notebook and Source Codes
Test	Test Plans, Procedures and Data
Integration	Integration Document

There have been a number of systems proposed to support SSLC document production through the application of database technology [15–18, 27]; however, their functional capabilities are limited. Applying TEXPROS to software development would help decrease software life-cycle costs significantly. For example, the system can help classify software configurations according to software baselines/updates which are the arrangements of related SCIs. Important information can be extracted from these SCIs (including SCIs of various software systems) and then be categorized and stored in the computer. The configuration of a system can be identified at times for the purposes of systematically controlling changes to this configuration and maintaining traceability of this configuration throughout the life cycle of the system [1], thus facilitating the test and maintenance phases. Information pertinent to the significance of the users (i.e., the software developers) can be retrieved and browsed. Finally, in preparing reports, information can be synthesized from various existing documents (SCIs), rather than be generated from scratch.

7. Conclusions

In this paper, we have described the design of an intelligent document processing system. We discussed approaches to addressing various issues concerning the data model, document classification, document categorization, file reorganization, and information retrieval. We also discussed applications of TEXPROS, and described how it may be used to manage the configurations of software systems through their life cycles.

There are several other issues which are also important, though we do not address here. One of them is concerned with information sharing and exchange. As discussed in the beginning of this paper, TEXPROS will also be used in a multi-user distributed environment. In such an environment, one needs to specify protocols to govern frame template definitions. For example, when using TEXPROS as a library bibliographic retrieval system, one may need to stipulate that all frame instances for books in the library contain attributes "authors", "affiliation", "subject", "title", "abstraction", "category", "classification" and so on. Another relevant issue is concerned with transaction management. Clifton *et al.* [6] suggested that documents may require new types of transactions: serializability may not be appropriate. Some form of locking must be done, and that could be based on an explicit check-out mechanism. Since transactions involved often have long duration, the shadow/versioning mechanisms described by Lorie and Plouffe [21] appear also a good alternative.

As a first step of this research project, we have built a personal prototype system using C and X windows. The hardware platforms utilized include several SUN and SPARC workstations. The current system allows the user to perform document classification, information extraction and document categorization manually by employing an interactive graphical editor. The user can query by classes. The system stores frame instances using the B tree and inverted file. In the near future, we plan to incorporate the knowledge-based techniques described here into the prototype, and extend the system into a multi-user one.

Acknowledgments

TEXPROS is a group research effort. Wen-Chung Shang, Fortune Mhlanga, and Ching-Song Wei have contributed to the design of data model, document classification and categorization. The following individuals have also contributed: T. H. Shiau, Frank Shih, Dan Benanav, D. C. Douglas Hung, Wilhelm Rossak, Steve Chiang, Shun-Chih Chen and Tamar Zemel. Finally, we would like to thank Yoav Shoham for drawing our attention to the paper concerning the agent-oriented programming [34], the anonymous referees and the editor, Dan Cooke, for their excellent comments, which have greatly improved the presentation and quality of this paper.

References

1. E. H. Bersoff, V. D. Henderson and S. G. Siegel, *Software Configuration Management, An Investment in Product Integrity* (Prentice-Hall, 1980).
2. E. Bertino, F. Rabitti and S. Gibbs, "Query processing in a multimedia document system," *ACM Trans. Office Inf. Syst.* **6**, 1 (1988) 1–41.
3. S. K. Chang and L. Leung, "A knowledge-based message management system," *ACM Trans. Office Inf. Syst.* **5**, 3 (1987) 213–236.
4. H. Chen and V. Dhar, "A knowledge-based approach to the design of document-based retrieval systems," in *Proc. ACM Conf. on Office Information Systems*, Cambridge, Massachusetts (April 1990) pp. 281–290.
5. S. Christodoulakis, M. Theodoridou, F. Ho, M. Papa, and A. Pathria, "Multimedia document presentation, information extraction, and document formation in MINOS: A model and system," *ACM Trans. Office Inf. Syst.* **4**, 4 (1986) 345–383.
6. C. Clifton, H. Garcia-Molina, and R. Hagmann, "The design of a document database," in *Proc. ACM Conf. on Document Processing Systems*, Santa Fe, New Mexico (December 1988) pp. 125–134.
7. W. B. Croft and D. W. Stemple, "Supporting office document architectures with constrained types", in *Proc. ACM SIGMOD Int. Conf. on Management of Data*, San Francisco, CA (May 1987) pp. 504–509.
8. U. Dayal and P. A. Bernstein, "On the correct translation of update operations on relational views," *ACM Trans. Database Syst.* **7**, 3 (1982) 381–416.
9. H. Eirund and K. Kreplin, "Knowledge based document classification supporting integrated document handling," in *Proc. ACM Conf. on Office Information Systems*, Palo Alto, CA (March 1988) pp. 189–196.
10. C. Faloutsos, "Access methods for text," *ACM Comput. Surveys* **17**, 1 (1985) 49–74.
11. R. Fikes and T. Kehler, "The role of frame-based representation in reasoning," *Commun. ACM* **28**, 9 (1985) 904–920.
12. S. Gibbs and D. Tsichritzis, "A data modeling approach for office information systems," *ACM Trans. Office Inf. Syst.* **1**, 4 (1983) 299–319.

13. P. J. Hayes and S. P. Weinstein, "CONSTRUE/TIS: A system for content-based indexing of a database of news stories," in *AAAI Proc. 2nd Annual Conf. on Innovative Applications of Artificial Intelligence*, Washington, D.C. (May 1990) pp. 1–5.
14. W. Horak, "Office document architecture and office document interchange formats — current status of international standardization," *IEEE Comput.* **18**, 10 (1985) 50–60.
15. E. Horowitz and R. C. Williamson, "SODOS: A software documentation support environment — Its definition," *IEEE Trans. Softw. Eng.* **12**, 8 (1986) 849–859.
16. E. Horowitz and R. C. Williamson, "SODOS: A software documentation support environment — Its use," *IEEE Trans. Softw. Eng.* **12**, 11 (1986) 1076–1087.
17. W. E. Howden, "Contemporary software development environments," *Commun. ACM* **25**, 5 (1982) 318–329.
18. S. E. Hudson and R. King, "The Cactis project: Database support for software environments," *IEEE Trans. Softw. Eng.* **14**, 6 (1988) 709–719.
19. J. L. Kolodner, "Indexing and retrieval strategies for natural language fact retrieval," *ACM Trans. Database Syst.* **8**, 3 (1983) 434–464.
20. G. M. Lohman, B. Lindsay, H. Pirahesh, and K. B. Schiefer, "Extensions to STARBURST: objects, types, functions and rules," *Commun. ACM* **34**, 10 (1991) 94–109.
21. R. Lorie and W. Plouffe, "Complex objects and their use in design transactions," in *Proc. IEEE Annual Meeting — Database Week: Engineering Design Applications*, San Jose, CA (May 1983) pp. 115–121.
22. E. Lutz, H. V. Kleist-Retzow, and K. Hoernig, "MAFIA — An active mail-filter-agent for an intelligent document processing support," in *Multi-User Interfaces and Applications*, eds. S. Gibbs and A. A. Verrijn-Stuart (Elsevier, 1990) pp. 16–32.
23. T. W. Malone, K. R. Grant, K. Y. Lai, R. Rao, and D. Rosenblitt, "Semistructured messages are surprisingly useful for computer-supported coordination," *ACM Trans. Office Inf. Syst.* **5**, 2 (1987) pp. 115–131.
24. N. M. Mattos, B. Mitschang, A. Dengel, and R. Bleisinger, "An approach to integrated office document processing and management," in *Proc. ACM Conf. on Office Inf. Syst.* (Cambridge, Massachusetts, April 1990) pp. 118–122.
25. F. Mhlanga, Private communication (March 1991).
26. R. A. Myers, "Trends in office automation technology," Technical Report RC-9321, IBM Watson Research Center, New York (April 1982).
27. P. S. Newman, "Towards an integrated development environment," *IBM Syst. J.* **21**, 1 (1982) 81–107.
28. R. Oddy, "Information retrieval through man-machine dialogue," *J. Doc.* **33** (1977) 1–14.
29. S. Pollitt, "CANSEARCH: An expert system approach to document retrieval," *Inf. Process. Manage.* **23**, 2 (1987) 119–138.
30. S. Pollock, "A rule-based message filtering system," *ACM Trans. Office Inf. Syst.* **6**, 3 (1988) 232–254.

31. F. Rabitti, "A model for multimedia documents," in *Office Automation*, ed. D. Tsichritzis (1985) pp. 227–250.
32. G. Salton, *Automatic Text Processing* (Addison-Wesley, 1989).
33. W. C. Shang, Private communication (June 1991).
34. Y. Shoham, "Agent-oriented programming," Technical Report STAN-CS-90-1335, Stanford University (1990).
35. P. Shoval, "Principles, procedures and rules in an expert system for information retrieval," *Inf. Process. Manage.* **21**, 6 (1985) 475–487.
36. N. C. Shu, F. C. Tung, and C. L. Chang, "Specification of forms processing and business procedures for office automation," *IEEE Trans. Softw. Eng.* **8**, 5 (1982) 499–512.
37. J. M. Smith and D. C. P. Smith, "Database abstractions: aggregation and generalization," *ACM Trans. Database Syst.* **2**, 2 (1977) 105–133.
38. P. J. Smith, S. J. Shute, D. Galdes, and M. H. Chignell, "Knowledge-based search tactics for an intelligent intermediary system," *ACM Trans. Inf. Syst.* **7**, 3 (1989) 246–270.
39. M. Stonebraker, H. Stettner, N. Lynn, J. Kalash, and A. Guttman, "Document processing in a relational database system," *ACM Trans. Office Inf. Syst.* **1**, 2 (1983) 143–158.
40. M. Stonebraker and L. A. Rowe, "The design of POSTGRES," in *Proc. ACM SIGMOD Int. Conf. on Management of Data*, Washington, D.C. (May 1986) pp. 340–355.
41. R. H. Thomas, H. C. Forsdick, T. R. Crowley, R. W. Schaaf, R. S. Thomlinson, V. M. Travers, and G. G. Robertson, "Diamond: A multimedia message system built on a distributed architecture," *IEEE Comput.* **18** 12 (1985) 65–78.
42. L. Tokuda, "Computers assist humans in human resources," in *AAAI Proc. 2nd Annual Conf. on Innovative Applications of Artificial Intelligence* (Washington, D.C., May 1990) pp. 31–35.
43. R. M. Tong and D. G. Shapiro, "Experimental investigations of uncertainty in a rule-based system for information retrieval," *Int. J. Man-Machine Studies* **22** (1985) 265–282.
44. D. Tsichritzis, "Form management," *Commun. ACM* **25**, 7 (1982) 453–477.
45. T. L. Wang and D. Shasha, "Query processing for distance metrics," in *Proc. 16th Int. Conf. on Very Large Data Bases*, Brisbane, Australia (August 1990), pp. 602–613.
46. T. L. Wang, "Query optimization in database and information retrieval system," Ph. D. thesis, Courant Institute of Mathematical Sciences, New York University, New York (1991).
47. J. T. L. Wang, K. Jeong, K. Zhang, and D. Shasha, "Reference manual for ATBE: A tool for approximate tree matching," Technical Report TR-551, Courant Institute of Mathematical Sciences, New York University, New York (1991) pp. 1–57.
48. J. T. L. Wang, K. Zhang, K. Jeong, and D. Shasha, "A tool for tree pattern matching," in *Proc. 3rd IEEE Int. Conf. on Tools for Artificial Intelligence*, San Jose, CA (November 1991) pp. 436–444.

49. C. S. Wei, Private communication (August 1991).
50. K. Y. Whang, A. Ammann, A. Bolmarcich, M. Hanrahan, G. Hochgesang, K. T. Huang, A. Khorasani, R. Krishnamurthy, G. Sockut, P. Sweeney, V. Waddle, and M. Zloof, "Office-by-Example: An integrated office system and database manager," *ACM Trans. Office Inf. Syst.* **5**, 4 (1987) 393–427.
51. D. Woelk, W. Kim, and W. Luther, "An object-oriented approach to multimedia databases," in *Proc. ACM SIGMOD Int. Conf. on Management of Data*, Washington, D.C. (May 1986) pp. 311–325.

SAMEA: OBJECT-ORIENTED SOFTWARE MAINTENANCE ENVIRONMENT FOR ASSEMBLY PROGRAMS

S. CHEN, W. T. TSAI and X. P. CHEN

Department of Computer Science, University of Minnesota, 200 Union Street SE, Minneapolis, MN 55455, USA

ABSTRACT

This paper presents a software maintenance environment for assembly programs, SAMEA. It presents an object-oriented database support for displaying, understanding, modifying and configuring assembly programs for software maintenance. Understanding of assembly programs is based on the theory of explicit representation of various structural and functionality elements of code and multiple relationships among them. Modification of program is based on an object-oriented incremental editor and a set of rules to check the correctness of instruction format.

The characteristics of SAMEA are: integration of multiple tools, on-line information, ease of adoption of new tools, and finally, support of software maintenance activities such as program understanding, ripple effect analysis, and program re-documentation. The ripple effect of a contemplated change is the parts of the code that need to be re-examined for possible modification.

Assembly code elements and relations among code elements are represented as objects in SAMEA which is built on top of an object-oriented database, GemStone. SAMEA consists of 26K lines of C code and 4K lines of GemStone code. We have successfully populated 18K lines of BAL code in SAMEA.

Keywords : Software maintenance, object-oriented database, assembly language programs.

1. Introduction

This paper presents a Software Maintenance Environment for Assembly programs, SAMEA. It presents an object-oriented database support for maintaining assembly programs. The software maintenance process includes problem identification, program understanding, modification, re-validation, and re-documentation. Program understanding is a prerequisite for an effective software maintenance. Program understanding is difficult. Each individual piece of information that contributes to the understanding of software is simple, but the combination of these pieces to form the basis of software understanding is difficult. Thus, it is important to organize and classify information properly, and represent this information *explicitly* for easy access.

The goal of software maintenance is to enhance the existing software by adding new features, or changing existing features [8]. Part of the difficulty in software maintenance comes from the inability to describe effectively the contemplated maintenance activity in terms of software structural and functionality elements. This involves the identification of software structural and functionality elements affected by maintenance activities [10, 24].

The characteristics of SAMEA are: integration of multiple tools, on-line information, ease of adoption of new tools, and finally, support for software maintenance activities such as program understanding, ripple effect analysis, and program re-documentation. The ripple effect of a contemplated change is parts of the code that need to be re-examined for possible modification.

This paper describes a software maintenance environment for assembly language programs based on the code model [3]. It addresses an important issue: Is an object-oriented database suitable for implementing a complex computer-aided environment such as maintaining large-scale assembly language programs? Specifically, we address:

(a) Whether it is possible and desirable to use an object-oriented database to store and manipulate huge number of information objects generated for maintaining large-scale assembly language program development and maintenance.
(b) Whether it is possible to integrate software development and maintenance applications within an object-oriented database to support maintenance activities such as program understanding, incremental program editing, ripple effect analysis, program re-documentation, version control, user interface, and program modification.

This paper gives affirmative answers to the above two questions. The SAMEA environment is built using GemStone (Trademark of Servio Logic) object-oriented database, running a UNIX (Trademark of AT&T) environment, on Sun SPARC Stations. Currently, SAMEA consists of 26K lines of C code, and 4K lines of GemStone kernel language OPAL code. We also experimented multiple tools integrated into SAMEA. It aids program understanding, as it can explicitly show various interconnections among software components. It helps in ripple effect analysis by allowing programmers to trace using these interconnections. It is also useful for program re-documentation because it stores the documentation side-by-side with the code in the database. It stores multiple versions of a source in the database. It also supports incremental change of source code.

The structural and functionality views proposed in the object-oriented model [3, 7] are summarized in Appendix A and B. Readers are encouraged to go over Appendix A and B before proceeding further. Consult the related books [2, 20, 21] for information about GemStone.

Section 2 describes features provided by SAMEA. Section 3 describes characteristics of SAMEA. The description of each component of SAMEA is provided in Sec. 4. Finally, Sec. 5 concludes the paper.

2. Features Provided by SAMEA

SAMEA implements an assembly language model [3]. The model supports both structural and functionality views of the code and can be useful for maintenance activities such as program understanding, ripple effect analysis, and program re-documentation. A parsing technique to extract required elements from assembly code to populate the model is presented in RETA [3].

SAMEA is built on object-oriented database GemStone. It is also designed and implemented in an object-oriented fashion. Software artifacts are complex in nature and object-oriented paradigm is well-known in supporting complex data types. This paradigm also supports strong typing and hierarchical approaches. In relational systems, data information is scattered across different tables. Object-oriented systems have the advantage of organizing information as complex objects. An object-oriented database offers data persistence, and highly extensible schema compared to a relational database. Data persistence is important for large software systems, because it is unwise to generate information needed every time that a maintainer sets to work on the system. Highly extensible data schema allows SAMEA to store different kinds of objects extracted from programs.

Several maintenance tools are integrated seamlessly in SAMEA. The underling object-oriented database allows us to integrate a rich set of software tools into SAMEA. For example, an object-oriented editor is implemented in SAMEA, through it a maintainer can change the software directly. Also a query system supporting program slicing and ripple effect analysis is implemented. The information generated resides within SAMEA, and is available for easy access. New application tools can be added to SAMEA quickly and easily. All the necessary information, such as data definition, data use, data modification, and routine called within a routine, is extracted from the source code and is explicitly stored in GemStone for new applications to use.

SAMEA stores text *documentations*, such as structural and functionality documentations in a central repository. It keeps multiple *versions* of the application on-line for easy access. It provides *multiple views* for the user to view information either from design point-of-view (functionality view) or from implementation point-of-view (structural view). The documentations can be used to *abstract*, i.e., to control the level of details, of various views of the code.

SAMEA recognizes possible branches and calls from a code block. It provides the user information on the branches of the code blocks and call graph, hence, *control flow information* [17]. It also provides data uses and modifies within a code block, hence, *data flow information* [6].

The user can select functionality members from functionality documentation that have a role in the functionality to be changed. An immediate list of variables and code blocks used by selected functionality members can be produced. SAMEA supports *ripple effect analysis* [27]. When the user is contemplating a change to a code block or a variable, a list of functionality members using that code block or variable can be produced to decide which competing options have the least ripple effect. When a change of variable occurs, the maintainer needs to know what code blocks use and modify the variable. When a code block has been changed, the maintainer needs to know what functionality members call this code block. Finally, SAMEA *supports software change.* When there is a change in a routine, a code block or an instruction, SAMEA will verify the correctness of the inserted instruction format, and update the database to ensure the database is still consistent.

The model [3] implemented in SAMEA supports multiple views, structural abstraction, control flow information, data flow information, program slicing [25, 26] and ripple effect. SAMEA has an incremental parser that can support software change. It also has linking capabilities such as those provided in the ESE system [18] which supports version control. Finally, SAMEA has composite object constructor that can be used for documentation and version control. All these features are integrated in an object-oriented design built on top of GemStone.

3. Characteristics of SAMEA

SAMEA consists of several characteristics. They are integration of tools, online documentation and source code, ease of extension and adoption of new tools, and its object-oriented design.

3.1. *Integration of tools*

SAMEA supports necessary tools to extract information from source code. The user can use these tools to query information in one centralized environment, thus releasing burden on the user to go from one system to another of searching information. All information is stored in a centralized repository and all components of SAMEA can access the same data. The data produced by one component can be used and modified by other components. Figure 1 shows the integration of an object-oriented database, and tools that generate, change and display information. The information generated is stored in GemStone. The information can be changed and viewed by the user.

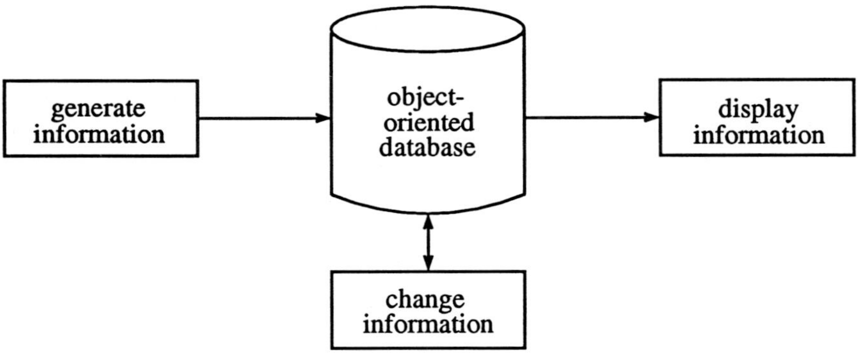

Fig. 1. An example of tool integration.

Integration of tools is achieved by modular design and decomposition. The data and procedures within each component in SAMEA are encapsulated. The layering of component and the boundary between components are clear. Objects created by one component can be used and manipulated by other components by using methods supplied by the component that created those objects. This enforces modularity.

3.2. *On-line documentation*

Documentation represents user requirement, design decisions, and user manual. It is important to keep documents consistent with the state of the application.

SAMEA keeps on-line documentation and source code so that they can be updated whenever there is a change.

Information generated by any component in SAMEA is stored in a central database which provides data persistence. Because documentation is kept in a database, the user can query information concerning any software artifacts interactively, i.e., soft real-time response. Figure 2 shows how structural, functionality and version control objects can be retrieved and manipulated by the user interactively.

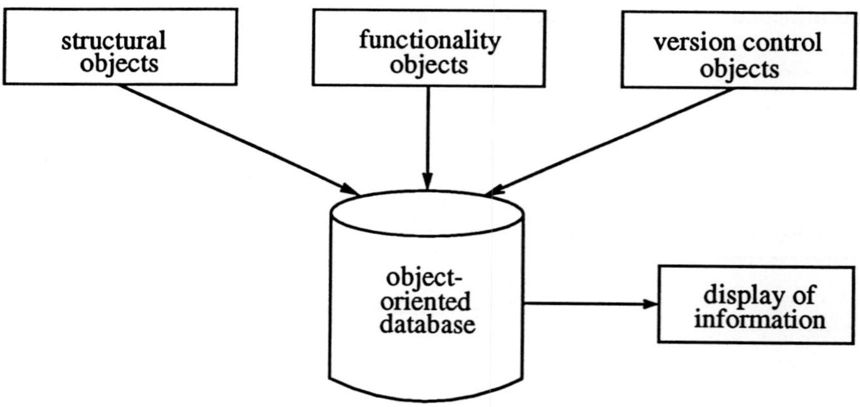

Fig. 2. An example of on-line documentation.

To support on-line operations, SAMEA employs efficient algorithms to insert, delete and search for objects in the database, incremental (real-time) parsing, and object clustering to speed up query processing.

3.3. *Ease of extension*

SAMEA must facilitate extension because new components may be added and old components may be modified to perform new requirements of SAMEA as time evolves. SAMEA is designed using an object-oriented paradigm. Because objects are highly cohesive and loosely coupled, it is easy to add new objects and new tools to SAMEA.

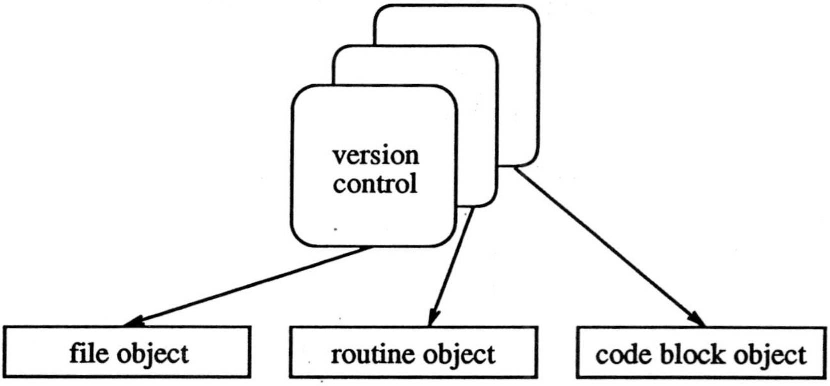

Fig. 3. An example of adaptable environment.

Figure 3 shows how SAMEA can adopt to different functionalities. The version control, described in Subsec. 4.3.3, can be done at different granularities such as at code block, routine, or file level. The user can request version control at different granularities. Extension is supported through object class hierarchy and class inheritance.

3.4. *Object-oriented design*

Object-oriented paradigms support modular design and component reuse [12]. In SAMEA, every piece of information is considered as an object. Each object encapsulates its methods and attributes. Because definition of each piece of information has a clear boundary, it decomposes naturally. In object-oriented paradigm, objects respond to messages, and no outside object can directly access attributes. Other objects cannot interfere with internal structure of an object. Object-oriented paradigms also support flexible extension and reuse. Extending a system can be achieved by reusing existing object definitions.

4. SAMEA Overview

SAMEA consists of five components, Information Generator, Change System, Composite Constructor, Object Query and User Interface as shown in Fig. 4. Information Generator extracts information from source code written in CODEL [15], a variant of BAL. Change System supports program modifica-

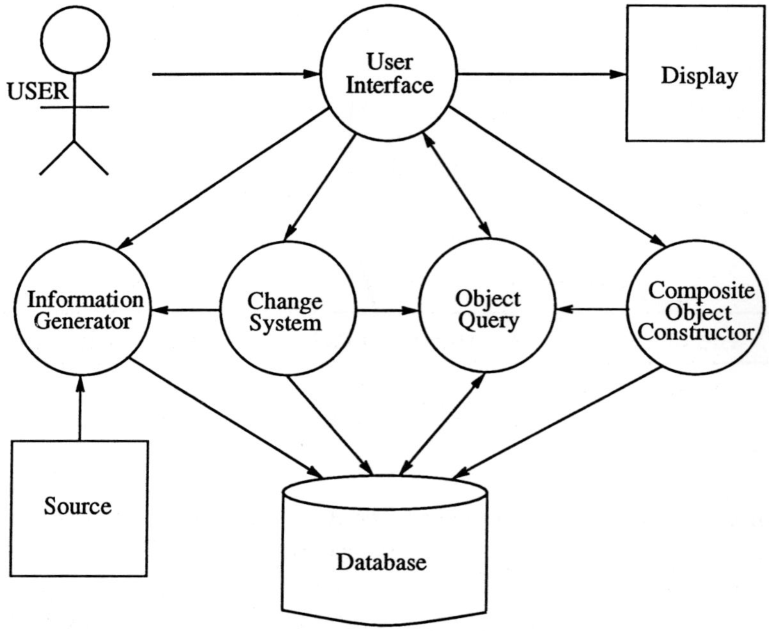

Fig. 4. Main components of SAMEA.

tion, i.e., deletion and insertion. Composite Object Constructor supports both version control and the structural and functionality documentations of the system from application level down to the code block level. Object Query arranges information for querying the database. User Interface takes user command and displays results graphically on the screen.

We built SAMEA incrementally. We first designed Information Generator, and part of Object Query and User Interface. Subsequently, we added Composite Object Constructor, Change System, and User Interface without any major design change. The modularity of SAMEA is preserved and we believe that it can be extended further.

4.1. *Information generator*

Information Generator takes CODEL assembly program as input, and extracts structural information from the code. Structural information, represented as objects, is instantiated and stored in the database. Information Generator is driven from either User Interface or Change System. When it is driven by User Interface, Information Generator takes input from the source file. Otherwise, Information Generator will take input from the standard input stream, i.e., the screen. Figure 5 shows the interface of Information Generator.

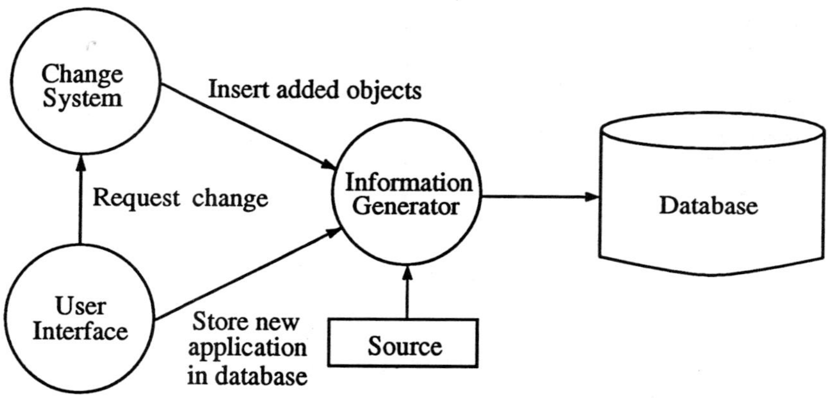

Fig. 5. Information generator.

Structural information is captured by identifying the structural hierarchy [3] (refer to Appendix A), data flow relations such as variable *uses* and *modifies* in code blocks, and control flow information such as branches from code blocks. Data flow and control flow information together with the structural hierarchy can be used to derive control flow and data flow diagrams.

We employed high-level programming language parsing techniques [4, 9]. Specifically, we use syntax tree [1] to represent code. Syntax tree is hierarchical in structure and contains syntactic information from the code. Use of existing tools, such as YACC [11], LEX [13], Make [5], and SED [14], helped in building Information Generator.

By using the C–GemStone interface, the instantiation of GemStone objects is realized. Figure 6 shows the separation of GemStone methods and C functions. The programmer does not need to be concerned with the details of either the OPAL or C language syntax. With each attribute in an object, there is a corresponding attribute access method. Thus, any outside

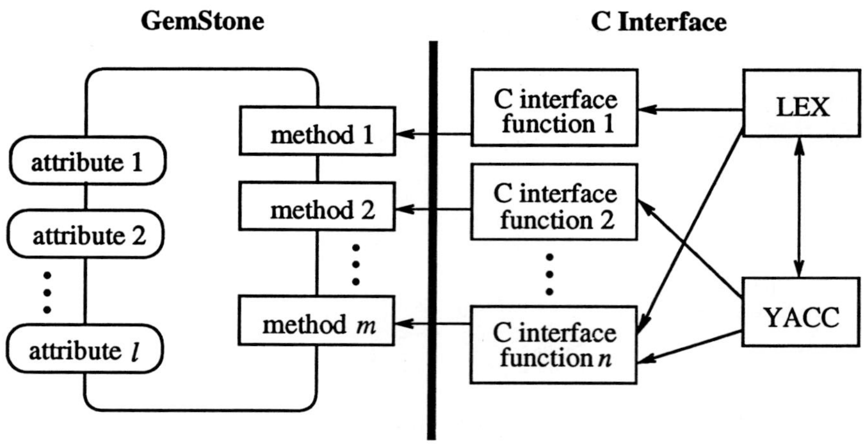

Fig. 6. Separation of GemStone detail from high-level language interface.

function can retrieve the value of an attribute through corresponding method. Besides retrieval methods for attributes, there are higher level methods such as searching methods, which search through object instances with a particular attribute value. Hence, the number of methods is more than the number of attributes. For each method, there is a corresponding C function. Each C function consists of the calling of the corresponding GemStone method and the error trap mechanism, which is supported by GemStone when faults arise. In summary, GemStone object class methods are one-to-one correspondence with C interface functions. In Fig. 6, the thick line indicates the separation of the GemStone and the C parts of the program.

Object class hierarchy for information generator

Because the underlining database is object-oriented, the first step is to create and identify an object class hierarchy [16]. We use the following strategy to create object class definitions.

1. Identify objects and their attributes.
2. Form object classes and an object class hierarchy based on commonalties and differences among objects identified in (1).
3. Decide partitions to store instances of the object classes for efficient retrieval.

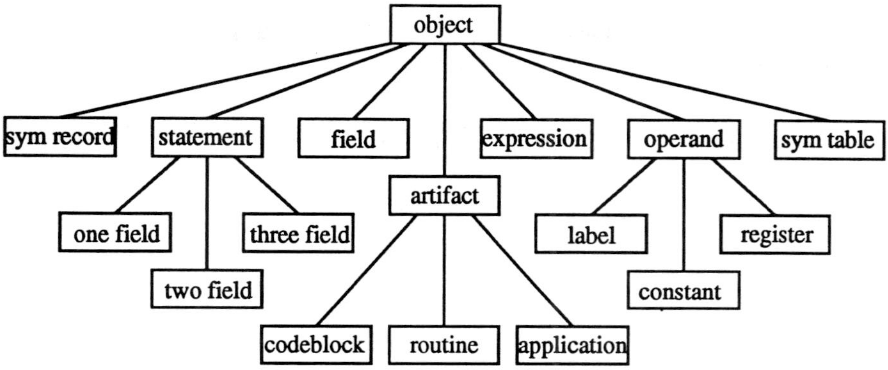

Fig. 7. Object class hierarchy and inheritance for information generator.

4. For each attribute of an object, create an attribute access method.
5. Create higher level searching methods and instance object creation methods associated with objects.

Figure 7 shows the structural object class hierarchy for CODEL programs. In step (1), we identified all objects in a flat hierarchy except One-field, Two-field, Three-field, Label-operand, Constant-operand, Register-operand and Artifact. In step (2), we found that statement objects can either be a zero, one, two, or three-operand instructions. Operand type can be either label, constant, or register type. Thus, these specifics are being created as sub-classes. We also found that Code Block, Routine and Application had the same characteristics. Thus, the class Artifact was created as the parent class of these three classes.

The information stored in the database is partitioned into several storage areas. Application classes represent different software systems, hence they are stored in a set. Within each application, there may be one or more routines; and within each routine, there exists one or more code blocks. The orderings of the routine within an application, and code blocks within a routine are important. These orderings are preserved by arrays. The symbol table is stored as a set in a different area. Because the data occupy large memory space, storage area partition makes database queries efficient. Each time only a particular area must be searched.

Within each code block, there are sequential and branch instructions. A sequential instruction is a series of statement objects (array subclass) that

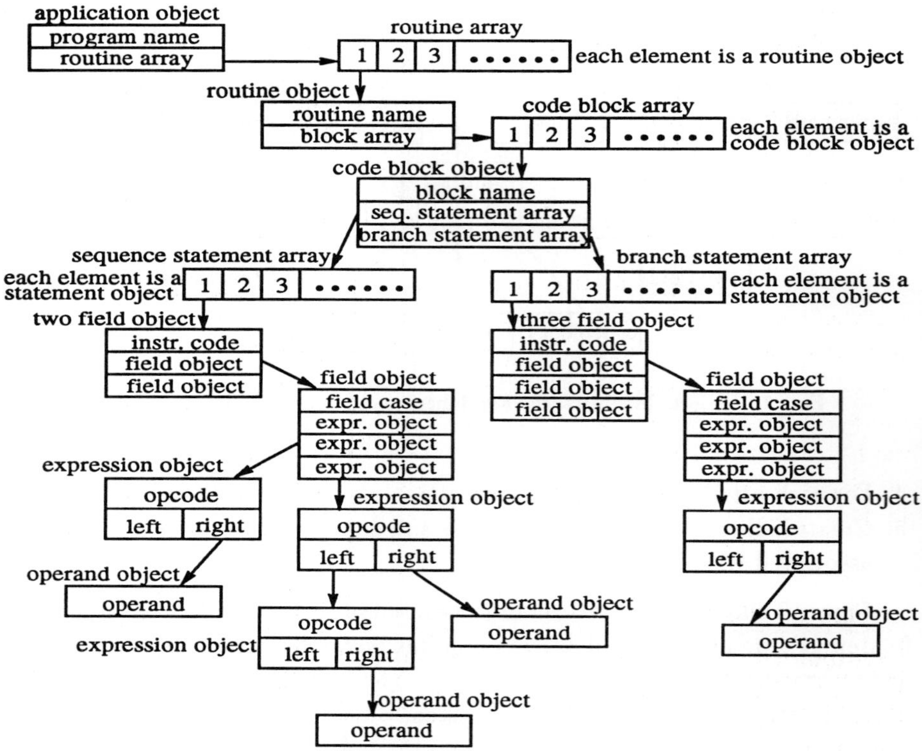

Fig. 8. Syntax tree construction for a structural object.

do not alter the execution sequence of the program. A branch instruction is a series of statement objects that do alter the execution sequence. Each statement is either zero-field, one-field, two-field, or three-field. Each operand field in a statement is either a simple operand or an expression.

Figure 8 shows a possible structural object syntax tree constructions. The first level of an application is the application object. Under the application, there is a sequence of routines. Under each routine, there is a sequence of code blocks. Under each code block, there is a sequence of sequential and branch statements. Because the source code is ordered, the sequence of routines and code blocks is important. The ordering of the code is preserved by arrays. Each statement consists of zero to three operands. The instantiation of *statement object* depends on the type of instruction statement. *Statement object* consists of instruction opcode, and pointers to each of *field objects*. Figure 8 shows a *two-field object* and a *three-field object*. Under each *statement object* are *field objects*. A *field object* consists of its type which is indicated as an integer number, and a pointer to an *expression object*. An expression can be either a simple operand, or an operand consisting of a simple arithmetic, such as "+" and "–". Hence, an *expression object* consists of an opcode field, which is either "+" , "–", or "leaf" to indicate a leaf node, and a pointer to *operand object*.

The symbol table contains symbolic labels appeared in the program. Associated with each symbolic label is a set of symbol records. A symbol record stores the place where the label appears in the program. The place is represented by both routine and code block names. A symbol record also stores the number of times a symbol label is used and its usage status, i.e., use or modification of the symbolic label. A symbol record also keeps symbol scope, i.e., local to one routine versus global. Figure 9 shows architecture for symbol table.

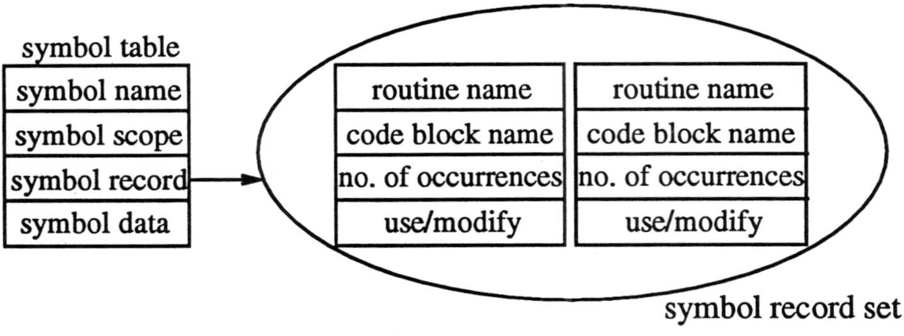

Fig. 9. Architecture for symbol table.

When an object is retrieved from the database, it is copied to a local area, i.e., the change made to the object is local. Once the change is committed, the local copy is copied to a permanent storage area. In GemStone, the new version of the object may not be put back to the original location where it was first retrieved. Thus construction of syntax tree objects must be a bottom-up process because we need to find out the new permanent addresses of lower level objects before higher level objects can link to it.

In RETA [3], we used YACC to specify the grammar of CODEL. We re-use these parts of the code. However, we replace the semantic routines with the instantiation of database objects, and data flow information (such as data uses and modifies) tools. Figure 10 shows the use of LEX and YACC with GemStone.

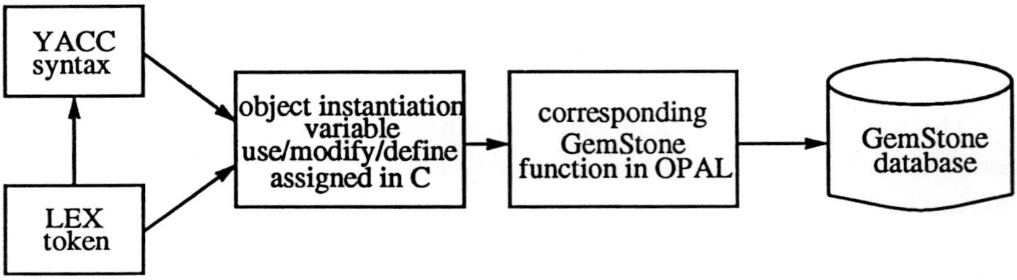

Fig. 10. Object instantiation in information generator.

Information Generator transforms assembly source code to database objects. Database objects instantiated by this component are called *basic* objects. Other SAMEA components will either retrieve, built-on-top-of, or modify these objects. Hence these objects are the input of other components. These objects are on-line and can be retrieved interactively. Other information such as call graphs and control flow diagrams can be constructed and generated using basic objects.

4.2. *Change system*

Change System allows on-line modification of the application stored in the database. After modification, it updates all relevant information such as structural hierarchy in the database immediately. For example, data use and data modify information must be updated when a variable is added or removed from the code. Change System follows an incremental parsing technique to extract information of the change instruction.

Change System is activated when the user requests for an insertion to the given application. The user is prompted for the statement number to insert. The actual instantiation of objects is in Information Generator. When the user requests a deletion, Change System will remove the objects from the database directly. Change System requests Object Query to search relevant objects stored in the database. Figure 11 shows the interface of Change System.

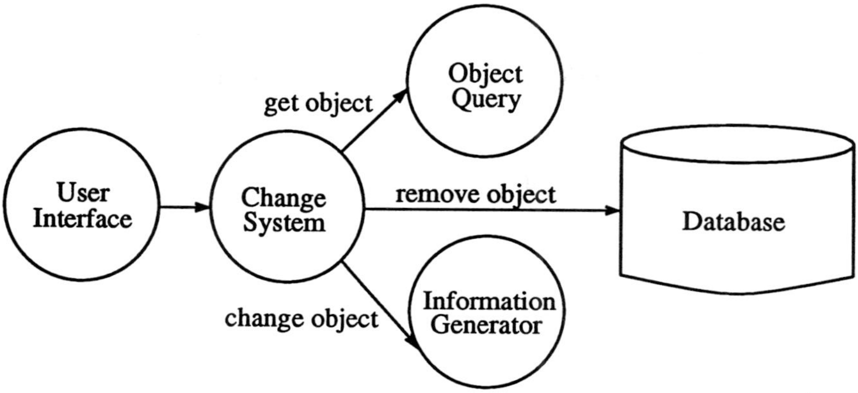

Fig. 11. Change system.

Change System consists of the following components:

1. unit for change system command processing;
2. unit for rules for instruction format;
3. unit for creation of object instances;
4. unit for remove object; and
5. unit for re-organization of code blocks.

Command processing unit of Change System parses user input streams. An input consists of insertion and deletion commands. If the command is an insertion, the input stream also contains the instruction to be inserted.

The rules for instruction-format unit consist of templates for every assembly instruction including the number of operands and the type of each operand. This unit is written in OPAL. We first identify general instruction formats of CODEL (see Table 1). The rows in Table 1 indicate the type of instruction format. The second column indicates how many operands there are. The third column indicates the type of first operand. The fourth column and fifth column indicate the types of the second and third operands respectively, if they are there.

Based on these general instruction formats, we built an object class hierarchy for instruction template in Change System. The number of attributes of

Table 1. Instruction format and operand types.

Instruction format	No. of operands	First operand type	Second operand type	Third operand type
Branch Register to Register	1	register mode		
Branch Register to or from storage	2	register mode	displacement (index, base)	
Register-to-Register	2	register mode	register mode	
#1 Register(s) to or from storage	3	register mode	register mode	displacement (base)
#2 Register(s) to or from storage	3	register mode	mask	displacement (base)
#3 Register to or from storage	2	register mode	displacement (base)	
Register to or from storage	2	register mode	displacement (index, base)	
No Transfer	1	displacement (base)		
Immediate data to or from storage	2	immediate	displacement (base)	
Storage to Storage	3	length	displacement (base)	displacement (base)

these objects depends on the number of operands, and the types of operands determine the constraints of corresponding attributes. Subsequently, for each assembly instruction, we create an instruction template (see Fig. 12). The constraint of the operand attribute is used to check validity of input operand.

If the user wants an insertion, once the instruction is being typed on the screen, the template corresponding to that instruction will appear on the screen. If the operand corresponding to the instruction is invalid, SAMEA will prompt the user to input the operand again until it is of the correct type. In this way, the user can then follow the template to finish the entire instruction. Once all the operands are valid, Change System will call Information Generator to generate objects.

The creation of object instances units takes a validated input from rules for instruction formats and instantiates objects in Information Generator (see Fig. 5). Algorithms C.1 and C.2 in Appendix C show the insertion of instruction statement into the database and the deletion of statement from the database, respectively.

The remove object unit is used to remove objects from the database. This is needed when deletion of an instruction takes place.

Modification is equivalent to a deletion followed by an insertion. When doing either an insertion or deletion, the user needs to specify the place where the change will take place. It can be specified by application name, routine name and code block name.

After series of insertion and deletion, the rules used to built up the structural hierarchy may be violated, e.g., inserting a sequential statement among branch statements. Therefore, there is a need to re-organize code blocks so that the rules are followed faithfully. Algorithm C.3 in Appendix C shows this reorganization of code blocks.

The *current code block* and the *next code block* can be merged only if the *next code block* has a system generated name. Figure 13 shows possible situations for code block re-organization. *S1* and *B1* are the sequential and branch statements of the current code block respectively. *S2* and *B2* are the sequential and branch statements of the next block respectively. If *S1* (*S2*) is missing, the current (next) code block does not contain sequential statement. If *B1* (*B2*) is missing, the current (next) code block does not contain branch statement. By the definition of code block (See Appendix A), merging code blocks is possible only when the current code block contains no branch statements.

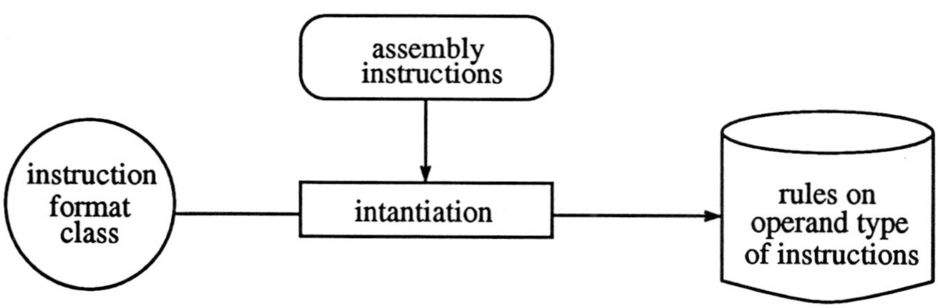

Fig. 12. Implementation of rules.

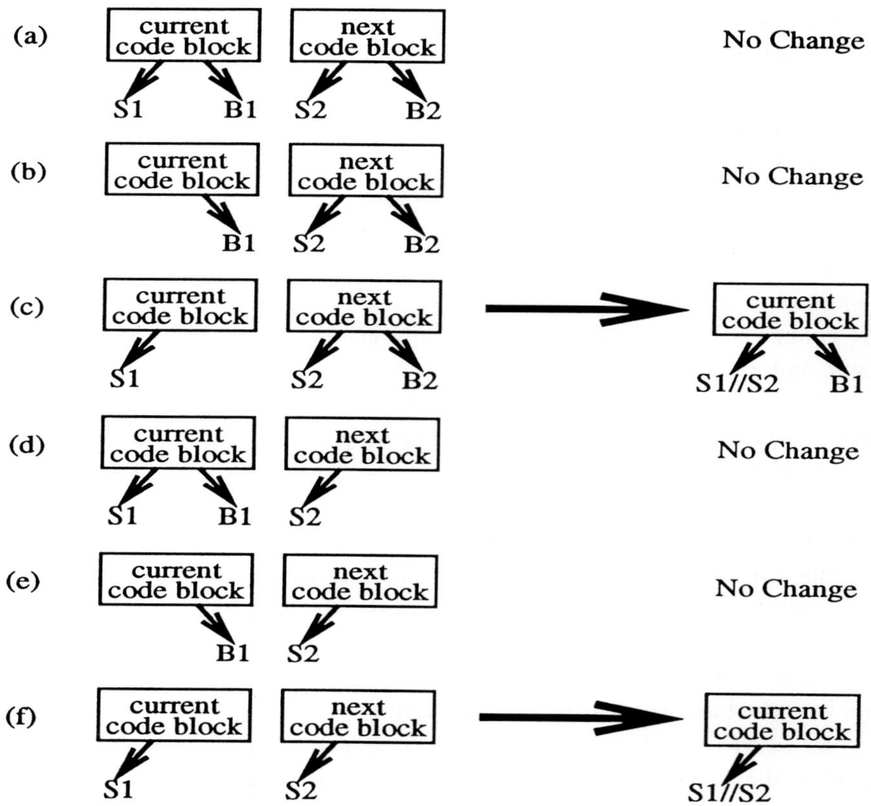

Fig. 13. Situations for code block re-organization.

For example, in Figs. 12(a) and 12(b), the current code block consists of branch statements and the next code block, which has a system generated name, consists of sequential statements. Hence, the two code blocks cannot be merged because branch statements cannot be followed by sequential statements within the same code block. In Fig. 12(c), the current code block contains only sequential statements. Hence the current and next code blocks can be merged together. The current code block will contain block sequential statements from the current and next code blocks and branch statement from the next code block. Because the next code block has a system generated name, after the merge, the name is returned to the system for reuse. The newly merged code block bears the current code block name, which is either a label or system generated name.

Insertion and deletion of statements may change data flow information, i.e., data uses and modifies. During insertion, we may add new symbols to the code. SAMEA must search through the symbol table to find the symbol name. The insertion and deletion may also change the scope of the symbol. Algorithms C.4 and C.5 in Appendix C show the manipulation of the symbol table to maintain consistency and the scope rule.

Example of an insertion

Figure 14 is an example of insertion. Figure 14(a) shows the position of insertion. Because the inserted statement consists of a label and by definition of a code block, a statement with a label is the first statement of the code block. Thus Change System creates a new code block with only this statement, and the label is the name of the code block (see Fig. 14(b)). The code block following the inserted code block is a code block with a system-generated name, which indicates that this code block is being formed because of the branch statements in the previous code block, e.g., code block #1 in Fig. 14(a). Thus, after the insertion of the newly inserted statement, the inserted code block becomes the current code block. We need to merge the inserted code block and the code block following it (see Fig. 14(c)).

If a sequential statement with no label is inserted after a sequence of branch statements in code block #1, the editor will try to find the next code block, i.e., code block #2, automatically. If code block #2 is a named code block, Change System will create a new code block with a system-generated name and insert this statement in the newly created code block. Otherwise, if code block #2 is a code block with a system-generated name, Change System will insert this statement as the first statement of code block #2.

Examples of deletion

If the second sequential or the second branch instruction of code block #1 in Fig. 15 is deleted, we can simply remove this statement. The symbol records associated with symbols appeared in the deleted statements are updated. If the number of occurrences in the symbol record is zero, Change System removes the record associated with this symbol from the symbol table.

If all three branch instructions under code block #1 are deleted, because code block #2 is a code block with a system-generated name, we need to merge the sequential statements of code block #1 and code block #2 and move the branch statements of code block #2 into code block #1. Subsequently, we remove code block #2.

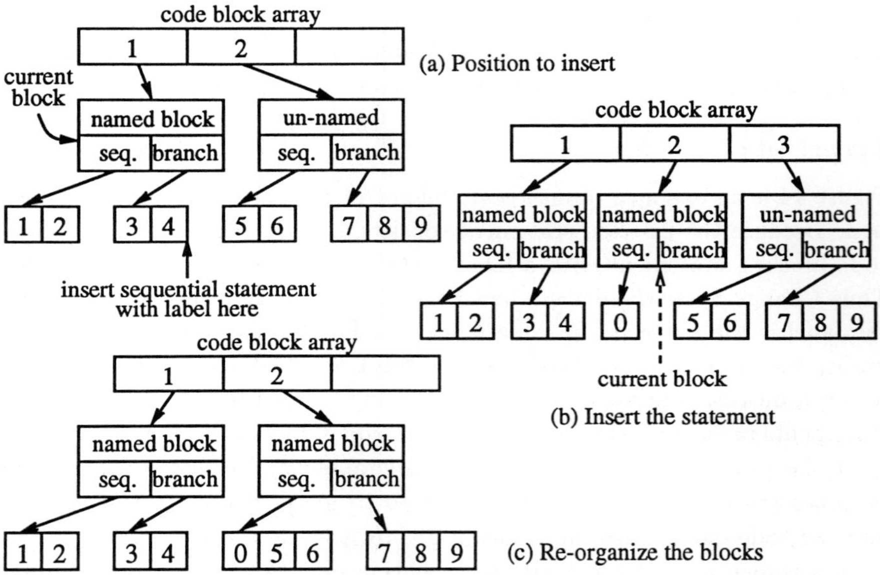

Fig. 14. Scenario for insertion.

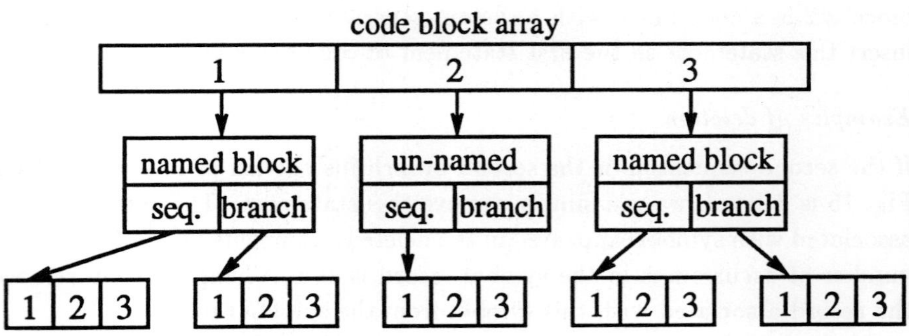

Fig. 15. Snapshot of the system for deletion.

If a code block array is empty, i.e., no code block or instruction exists within the routine, the routine is removed. If a routine array is empty, the whole application is removed from the database. For the symbol table, if both the symbol record array and the symbol data are empty, then this label is no longer in use. Hence, Change System removes this symbol from the database.

Change System ensures that after a change in the code the information stored in the database will be consistent. In other words, all the relevant information concerning the changed parts in the structural hierarchy including data use and data modify will be automatically updated by Change System. Furthermore, the update will be immediately carried out after the user enters the change, so that any subsequent query to SAMEA will produce the latest and correct information.

4.3. *Composite object constructor*

Composite Object Constructor supports documentations and version control. Composite Object Constructor is entered from User Interface when the user wants to built a composite object on-top-of basic objects that are created by Information Generator. Composite Object Constructor requests Object Query to search for the needed basic object. If the basic object is not found, no further action by Composite Object Constructor can take place. Otherwise, Composite Object Constructor will record the information in a composite object. Figure 16 shows the interface of Composite Object Constructor.

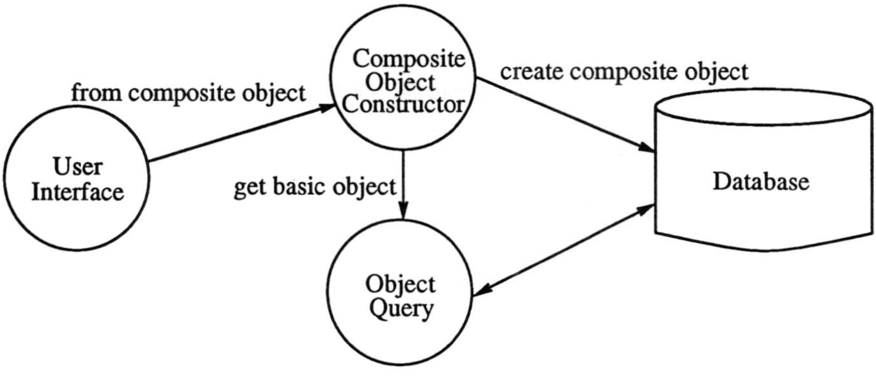

Fig. 16. Composite object constructor.

Composite Object Constructor allows documentations of applications, routines, and code blocks. This helps identifying what application, routine or code blocks are doing. The highest level of documentation is application, the next is routine, and the final is code block.

4.3.1. *Support for structural documentation*

The definition of structural hierarchy is in Appendix A. Documentation of structural hierarchy is done by indicating and searching application, routine and code block names. Documentation of structural hierarchy forms the structural view. From the structural view, the modules of interest can be sliced.

Structural documentation corresponds with the code. It documents the structures and relationships between pieces of code. Because structural hierarchy consists of three layers, structural documentation can go at most three layers. Because structural documentation corresponds with the code, an alternative is to parse the documentation directly from the code by specifying keywords, as is done in RETA [3]. Figure 17 shows the implementation of structural documentation. The object consists of three attributes, i.e., the application name, the document text, and an array of description of the next level of detail. Because we use values to search for objects in the database, we need to store only the names of applications, routines, and code blocks. We do not need to store links to objects.

This design has one advantage. Recall that GemStone makes a local copy of retrieved objects. When a code block object gets changed by Change System, the local copy of the code block object gets modified. The committed code block object's permanent address may be changed. If there is a link to the changed object, the corresponding Composite Object must also be changed. Thus, with each modification, we must search through structural documentation to look for this modified object to change the linking. By storing names, as long as names are not changed, Composite Object Constructor can still find it.

The names of routines within an application, and code blocks within a routine are stored in a sorted order. This helps searching for structural documentation of a particular routine or a code block.

The algorithms for structural documentation are in Appendix D.

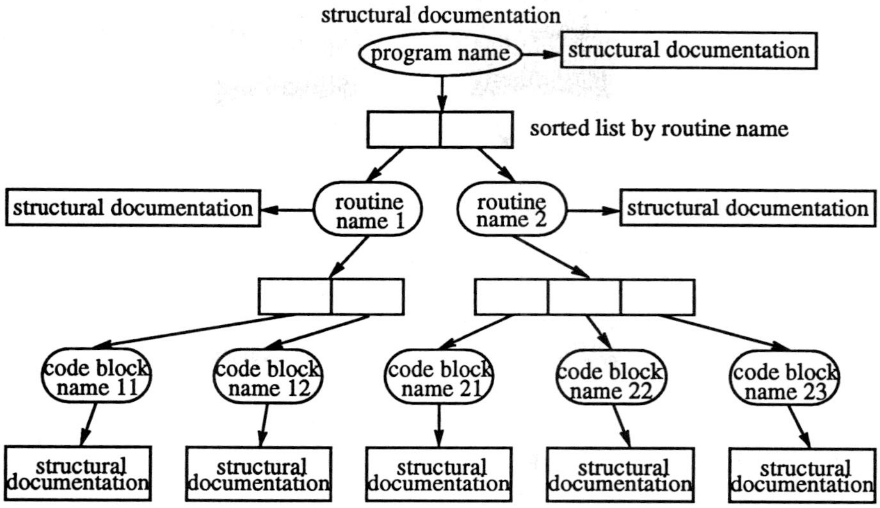

Fig. 17. Structural documentation of code.

4.3.2. *Support for functionality documentation*

The definition of functionality hierarchy is in Appendix B. Documentation of functionality hierarchy, which forms the functionality view, is done by grouping of code blocks and nesting functionality members. The functionality view can be used to slice out appropriate code that performs a certain functionality. Assembly language is flat, in other words all routines are on the same level. Even though for any large application a conceptual hierarchy exists, this hierarchy is lost during coding. Hence, it is important to re-capture the functionality view.

Composite Object Constructor allows grouping of code blocks to form functionality hierarchy: A functionality member is created by grouping code blocks. Functionality hierarchy is represented in the same way as structural hierarchy. The lowest level of functionality hierarchy consists of code blocks. Only code blocks from the same routine can be grouped as the lowest functionality members. Thus, the lowest functionality member corresponds with structural relations. Functionality members can be nested to form higher level functionality members. When doing grouping of functionality members, the user can document functionality members at each level.

Figure 18 shows an implementation of a three-level functionality hierarchy. The root of functionality hierarchy of an application is always the application name. Under the application name is a series of functionality members. Because the step of carrying out actions to achieve a certain feature may be ordered, the functionality members are ordered. Again, the leaves of the hierarchy are code blocks. Because one code block may contribute to different features on the same level, code block names are stored in a Bag [2].

The algorithms for functionality documentation are in Appendix E.

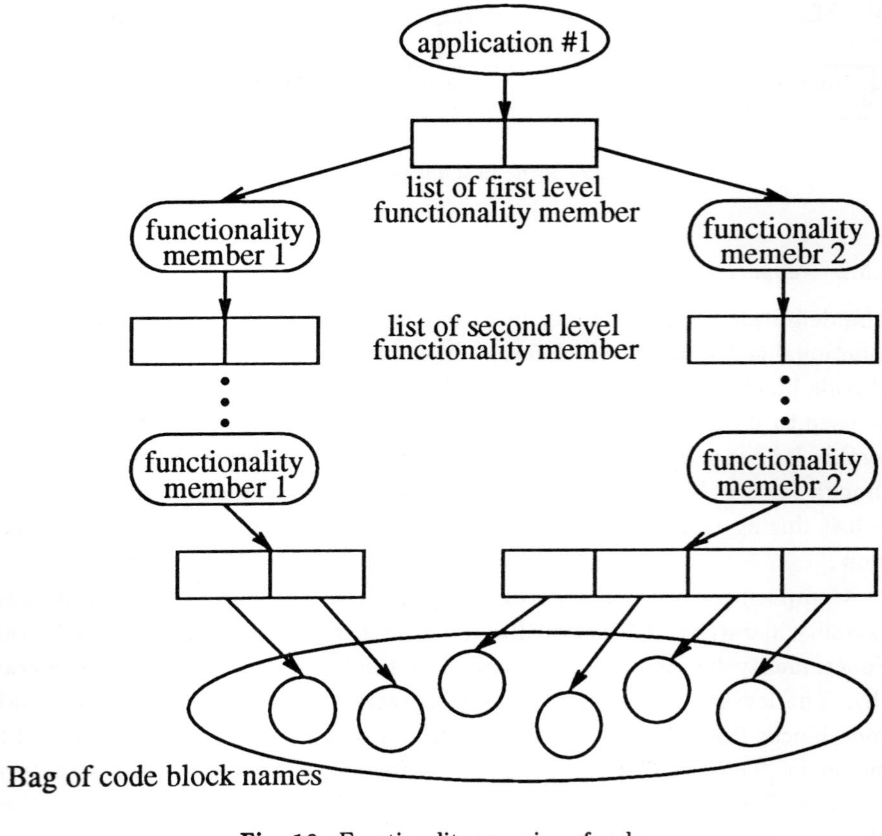

Fig. 18. Functionality grouping of code.

4.3.3. *Support for version control*

Different versions of a software system can make up different configurations of applications. These different configurations can be used concurrently. Thus, it is useful to keep different versions of the system on-line [19, 22, 23]. Unlike traditional version control tools, such as RCS [23], SCCS [19], version control is done at routine level instead of file level. Furthermore, the *granularity in tracking change is at code block level instead of routine level* (see Fig. 19). In Fig. 19, code block #2 has been changed to form a newer version of the routine. Hence the composite object, i.e., the version object, creates a new version, V2, to point to the new sequence of code blocks. The routine now links to the new sequence instead of the old, but the old sequence is still kept by version object. The code block changed is the only code block that is newly created, the rest of the code blocks still remain unchanged. Once the version control mechanism is used, editing of the system must be done within the version control environment. The user will not be allowed to change the application directly.

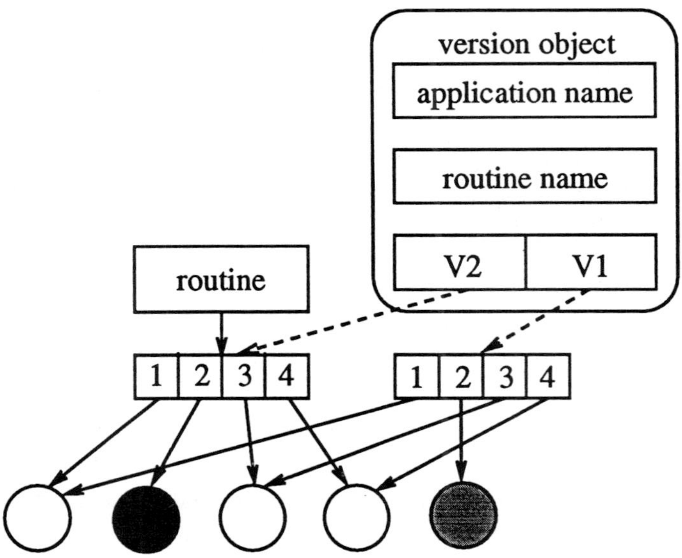

Fig. 19. Scenario for version control.

The version control algorithm is in Appendix F. It supports documentation of information generated by Information Generator and changed by Change System. It also supports version control of the system under change. This component integrated with other tools supported by SAMEA. The information generated by Composite Object Constructor is always on-line, and this component integrates seamlessly with the tools supported by SAMEA. The version control component can be adapted to different levels of granularity. This is done by object inheritance.

4.4. *Object query*

Object Query retrieves all kinds of information that are stored in the database. It takes commands from User Interface, Change System or Composite Object Constructor to search for relevant information. Figure 20 shows the interface of Object Query.

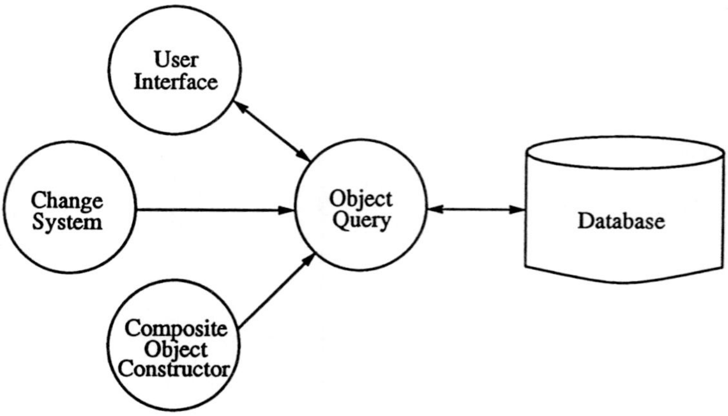

Fig. 20. Object query.

The design of the C–GemStone interface function is the same as mentioned in Information Generator. This component can retrieve data objects, such as variables, code blocks, and documentation in the database through high-level language interface or OPAL query. Object Query is used as query interface. It supplies source code of a given code block; finds the data uses and modifies within code blocks, routines or functionality members; finds branches and calls within a code block, routine, and functionality member; and controls the display detail of applications.

Object Query supports both low-level and high-level access capabilities. Low-level object access involves raw information such as retrieval of object by giving its name. High-level object access involves complex information such as displaying the code of a code block, data uses and modifies within a code block, branches and calls within a code block, functionality members and routines, routines within an application, code blocks within a routine. It may issue a series of object retrievals to perform requests. Figure 21 shows the design of Object Query.

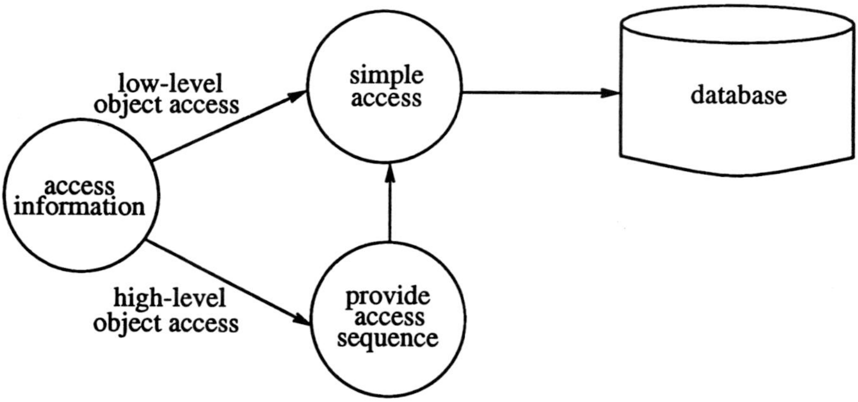

Fig. 21. Design of object query.

Supply source code of a given code block: Once a block within a particular application and particular routine is located, the user can reconstruct the source code from the database. This is done by retrieving the sequential statement and branch statement arrays under the given code block.

Routines with an application: Routines within a particular application are stored in the same partition of the database. Once the application of interest is being located, array of routines can be immediately obtained. Thus, the retrieval of routine name is straightforward.

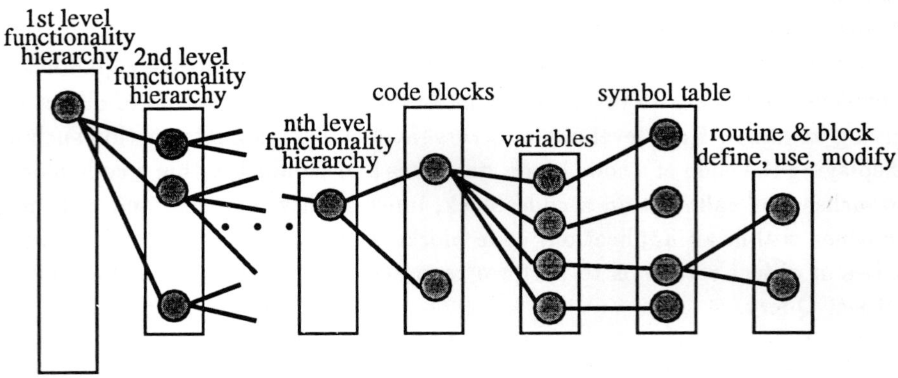

Fig. 22. Information retrieval supported by SAMEA.

Code blocks within a routine: Once the application name and routine name have been specified, the code block array object can be obtained. The sequence of code block name can be displayed too.

Find branches and calls within a code block, routine, and functionality member: The branch of a code block can be queried by specifying routine name and code block name within the routine. The calls within a routine generate information for call graph. For each code block, if it terminated with branch statements, then the branches are indicated by the branch statements. Otherwise, it is assumed that the branch of the code block is the code block immediately following it.

Find data uses and modifies within a code block, routine, and functionality member: Data uses and modifies, and defines can be obtained directly from the symbol set (see Fig. 9). Associated with each symbol object is a symbol record set. Each entry to the symbol record set indicates where this symbol has been used. It also contains the number of occurrences of this symbol used/modified in routines and code blocks. When searching for data uses and modifies information within a functionality member, the user can step through functionality hierarchy (see Fig. 22) and get to code blocks. From code blocks, a list of the variables used and modified can be found.

Functionality view is supported by documentation of functionality hierarchy. *Structural View* is supported by documentation of structural hierarchy.

Abstraction is supported by the number of levels of functionality hierarchy that the user wants to view the application. *Control Flow Information* is provided by branch information within and calls from each code block. *Data Flow Information* is supported by the symbol table.

Slicing is supported by viewing parts of functionality hierarchy, which leads to code blocks, and subsequently variables used and modified, and possible branches and calls from code blocks. Two types of ripple effects are supported. They are namely variable and code ripple effects. *Variable Ripple Effect* is examined by supplying the symbol table, in which each variable has its associated use/modification information. *Code Ripple Effect* is examined by supplying functionality hierarchy.

Object Query serves as the output system of SAMEA. It retrieves information generated by Information Generator and Composite Object Constructor, and changed by Change System. It also organizes information stored in the database into higher level query as queries in this section.

4.5. *User interface*

This component supports graphical multi-window display. It allows the maintainer to send requests for query or modification, and it displays requests on the screen. Figure 23 shows the design of this component. We used X-windows to integrate with Object Query.

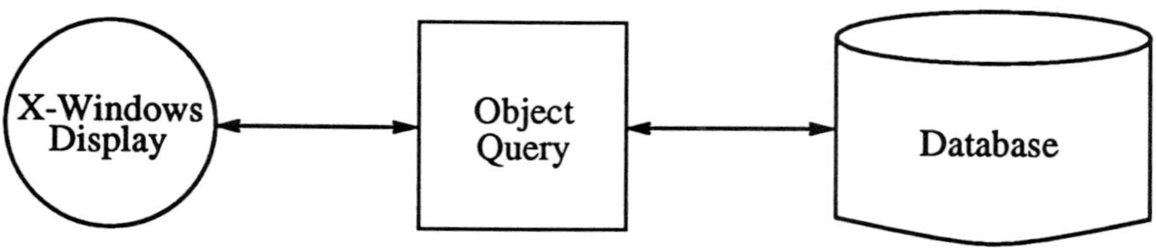

Fig. 23. User interface.

When the user requests information from User Interface, X-windows processes the command and sends the command to relevant components. If the user's request is *display*, the system will display the accessed information on the screen. Figure 24 shows the design of User Interface using X-windows. X-windows uses an event-driven approach and it will call Object Query to access information from the database. After obtaining the information, X-windows will call User Interface to display the accessed information.

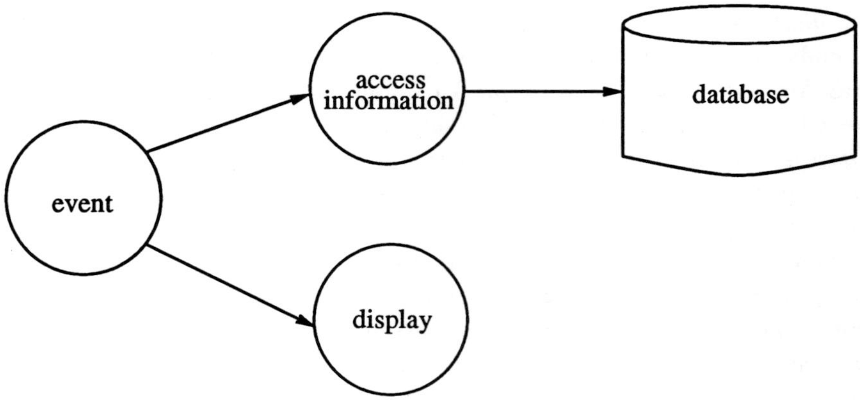

Fig. 24. Design of user interface using X-windows.

5. Conclusion

We presented an object-oriented database support for building a software maintenance environment. Relevant tools, such as Information Generator, Change System, Composite Object Constructor, Object Query, and User Interface are developed to support SAMEA. All these tools are integrated within SAMEA. All the information generated is one-line and stored in GemStone. The information can also be retrieved by the tools in SAMEA when necessary. New tools can be developed and integrated into SAMEA to enhance the power. Finally, SAMEA supports software maintenance activities.

We parsed more than 18,000 lines of CODEL code and had GemStone to store all the relevant information such as variable uses and modifies, calls and branches of code blocks and documentations. It took about 18 hours to parse the 18,000 lines of code. After the initial parsing, it took about 1 minute to store, i.e., commit, the entire generated data into the database. Subsequent queries of the information in the database averaged to about 1 minute depending on the complexity of the queries. A change made to the database requires the initial query of objects and subsequent commit of the changed data. The incremental change supported by Change System requires less time (2 minutes).

We used an iterative object-oriented design method for defining the object classes and object class hierarchy. The definitions of object class, i.e., attributes and methods, are written in OPAL. We found out that GemStone can support this kind of software development.

SAMEA supports maintenance activities such as program understanding, ripple effect analysis, program slicing, re-documentation and version control. We have presented a parsing technique together with the object-oriented database support to populate data elements in SAMEA. Specifically, we used a syntax tree to capture required information from the code.

SAMEA aids in program understanding. The design information is recaptured by entering the documentation in conjunction with the source code. From the application level, we can trace the functionality of the application down to the code blocks that perform the functionality. This functionality is useful for program understanding.

SAMEA helps in performing ripple effect analysis. There are several kinds of ripple effect analysis. We provide variable and code ripple effect analysis. The functionality and structural documentation, variable analysis, and branch/calling information are generated.

SAMEA supports program slicing that the user can select to view a portion of the functionality or structural hierarchy at a time. By viewing a portion, the user can localize the part of the code of interest.

SAMEA also supports change by using an incremental interactive editor. When a change is made, SAMEA provides calls, called-by, jump information. The user can interactively trace and re-trace through the connections to different routines. Because all information is stored in the database, a change of code will be updated in the database, and in turn automatically reflected in the documentation. This facilitates program re-documentation. SAMEA also provides version control by providing linking mechanism.

Many concepts and techniques discussed here can apply to other high-level and assembly languages. Similar data structures and the same parsing technique can be used to generate syntax trees for these languages. The information retrieval tool can be re-used also.

It is easy to tailor applications using GemStone because it can support a wide range of objects and it is flexible. We found it is easy to add new applications by reusing existing objects developed for other applications. Furthermore, in our experience, the old objects did not suffer from undesirable side effects. The object hierarchy remains stable throughout the entire development process. The stable hierarchy allows us to locate proper objects quickly.

Acknowledgments

Special thanks to students who participated in Computer Science 5199, Object-Oriented Databases Class in Spring 1989 at the University of Minnesota; Ronadi Gunawan for implementing part of Composite Object Constructor; Dale Wyttenbach for X-windows display of source code and structural hierarchy, S. Kirani and H. J. Lee for their help in preparing this paper.

References

1. A. V. Aho, R. Sethi, and J. D. Ullman, *Compilers: Principles, Techniques, and Tools* (Addison Wesley, 1986).
2. R. Bretl, D. Maier, A. Otis, J. Penney, B. Schuchardt, J. Stein, E. H. Williams, and M. Williams, "The GemStone data management system," in *Object Oriented Concepts, Databases, and Applications*, ed. W. Kim and F. H. Lochovsky (Addison Wesley, 1989) pp. 283–308.
3. S. Chen, K. G. Heisler, W. T. Tsai, X. Chen, and E. Leung, "A model for assembly program maintenance," *J. Softw. Maintenance: Research and Practice* **2**, 1 (1990) 3–32.
4. S. Chen, K. G. Heisler, Y. Kasho, and W. T. Tsai, "An integrated object-oriented environment for re-engineering for *C* and *BAL* programs," *Proc. Naval Surface Warfare Center Workshop on Re-Engineering* (1990).
5. S. I. Feldman, "Make — a program for maintaining computer programs," *UNIX Programmer's Manual* **2**, (1984) 291–300.
6. M. S. Hecht, *Flow Analysis of Computer Program* (North-Holland, 1977).
7. K. G. Heisler, W. T. Tsai, and P. A. Powell, "An object-oriented maintenance oriented model for software," *Proc. COMPCON* (February, 1989) pp. 248–253.
8. K. G. Heisler, P. Johnson, W. T. Tsai, Y. Kasho, and R. Snyder, "Software representation to support change," *Proc. IEEE Tools for AI* (1990) pp. 593–602.
9. K. G. Heisler, Y. Kasho, and W. T. Tsai, "A reverse engineering model for C programs," to appear in *Inf. Sci.* (1992).
10. P. E. Johnson, W. T. Tsai, K. G. Heisler, Y. Kasho, and R. Synder, "Mental models for software maintenance," *Proc. Naval Surface Warface Center Workshop on Re-Engineering* (1990).
11. S. C. Johnson, "Yacc: yet another compiler-compiler," *UNIX Programmer's Manual* **2** (1984) 353–387.
12. T. Korson and J. D. McGregor, "Understanding object-oriented: a unifying paradigm," *CACM* **33**, 9 (September, 1990) 40–60.

13. M. E. Lesk and E. Schmidt, "LEX—a lexical analyzer generator," *UNIX Programmer's Manual* **2** (1984) 388–400.
14. L. E. McMahon, "SED–a non-interactive text editor," *UNIX Programmer's Manual* **2** (1984) 440–450.
15. NCR COMTEN, *CODEL Communication Definition Language Revision A*, (August, 1986).
16. C. L. Ong and W. T. Tsai, "Class and object extraction from imperative code," to appear in *J. Object-oriented Programming* (1993).
17. R. S. Pressman, *Software Engineering, A Practitioner's Approach*, 2nd edition (McGraw-Hill, 1987).
18. C. V. Ramamoorthy, Y. Usuda, A. Prakash, and W. T. Tsai, "The evolution support environment system," *IEEE Trans. Softw. Eng.* **SE-16**, 11 (1990) 1225–1234.
19. M. J. Rochkind, "The source code control system," *IEEE Trans. on Softw. Eng.* **SE-1**, 4 (1975) 364–370.
20. Servio Logic Corporation, *GemStone C Interface Manual* (April, 1989).
21. Servio Logic Corporation, *Programming in OPAL* (April, 1989).
22. O. Shigo, Y. Wada, Y. Terashima, K. Iwamoto, and T. Nishimura, "Configuration control for evolutionary software production," *Proc. Sixth Int. Conf. Software Engineering* (September, 1982) pp. 68–75.
23. W. F. Tichy, "Design, implementation, and evaluation of a revision control system," *Proc. Int. Conf. Software Engineering* (1982) pp. 58–67.
24. W. T. Tsai, P. E. Johnson, and K. G. Heisler, "Computational theory of software maintenance," *Proc. Naval Surface Warfare Center Workshop on Re-engineering* (1990).
25. M. Weiser, "Programmers use slices when debugging," *CACM* **25** (1982) 446–452.
26. M. Weisner, "Program slicing," *IEEE Trans. Softw. Eng.* **SE-10**, 4 (1986) 353–357.
27. S. S. Yau, J. S. Collofello, and T. MacGrefor, "Ripple effect analysis of software maintenance," *Proc. IEEE COMPSAC* (1978) pp. 60–65.

Appendix A. Code Block and Structural Hierarchy

Structural view

The structural view is presented as a hierarchy of code blocks. It contains various relations within a code block, data flow information such as data use and modify, and control flow information such as exits. The structural view can be derived using a parsing technique.

Definition of code block

A code block is similar to a basic block in compiler theory. A basic block is a contiguous sequence of instructions that are always entered at the beginning and there is no branching within a basic block, i.e., any branching is always to other basic blocks [6]. Furthermore, a call within a basic block is considered as an assignment statement. A code block, however, may have multiple branches placed at the end.

Definition of structural hierarchy

Code blocks and their relative positions in a program form a structural hierarchy. Structural hierarchy consists of three layers:

1. The application, which represents the overall software application.
2. Routines within the application. An application may contain multiple routines.
3. Code blocks within a routine. A code block which is a contiguous sequence of instructions is defined below.
   a. When an instruction starts with a label, it is the first instruction of the code block. The label is the name of the code block.
   b. A code block ends if the next instruction begins with a label or when a sequential instruction follows one or more branch instructions. In the first case, the label will be assigned as the name of the code block, and it is a named code block. In the later case, the newly created code block will be assigned with a system generated name, we consider it as a un-named code block.

Assembly languages are flat in scope, i.e., all routines and variables within routines are global. Thus, the structural hierarchy consists of only three layers, the overall application, routines within applications, and code blocks within a routine. The rules for blocking code blocks are as follows:

Rule 1: The instruction immediately preceding a label is the last instruction of a code block. Labels will be generated for code blocks with no label.

Rule 2: The instruction associated with a label is the first instruction of a code block.

Rule 3: A branch instruction is the last instruction of a code block unless it is followed by another branch instruction.

Rule 4: If the code block ends with a branch instruction (BAL and BALR excepted) then there is no implicit branch to the next code block; otherwise there is.

Data and control flow information

We capture two kinds of information within each code block.

1. Data flow:
   scope of the variable;
   variables referenced but not modified within a code block;
   variables whose value may be modified within a code block.
2. Exits from a code block:
   call to a routine;
   returns;
   explicit branches to another code block;
   implicit exits to the next code block in sequence.

Relations within code block

Code blocks and their associated information establish a hierarchical structure and important relations as follows:

1. The structural hierarchy.
2. A set of relations as follows: (dn = variable; cbn = code block name)
   r1: <dn> defined-in <cbn>
   r2: <dn> referenced-by <cbn>
   r3: <dn> modified-by <cbn>
   r4: <cbn> part-of <cbn>
   r5: <cbn> includes <cbn>
   r6: <cbn> defines <dn>
   r7: <cbn> references <dn>
   r8: <cbn> modifies <dn>
   r9: <cbn> exits-to <cbn>
   r10: <cbn> entered-from <cbn>

The relation "references" implies use but not modification of the variable within a code block. This hierarchical structure and its associated relations constitute the structural view of the model.

Appendix B. Functionality Member and Functionality Hierarchy

Functionality view

The functionality view presents the user's view on the program. The functionality view provides a hierarchical outline describing the functionalities and subfunctionalities carried out by the application. It can be used to slice out appropriate code for software maintenance. Assembly language is flat, thus all routines are on the same level. Even though for any large application a conceptual hierarchy exists, this hierarchy is lost during coding.

The intent of grouping code blocks to form functionality member is to recover missing design. Thus, functionality hierarchy supports design recovery. The maintainer combines code blocks and functionality members to form higher level functionality members. The lowest level of functionality hierachy corresponds to code blocks, information contained in code blocks such as data uses, data modifies, possible branches from a code block, which is inherited by higher level functionality members.

Definition of functionality member

A functionality member is a grouping of code blocks or other functionality members that perform a feature in the application. Functionality members are collections of code blocks, and they automatically inherit relations associated with code blocks. In particular, each functionality member uses certain code blocks and references or modifies certain data. A given code block is used by certain functionality members and a given variable is referenced by or modified by certain functionality members.

Definition of functionality hierarchy

Functionality members can be nested. The lower level functionality members represent sub-features of higher functionality members. The lowest level of functionality member contains code blocks. Hence, the functionality member is hierarchical.

The functionality hierarchy is displayed as a functionality menu. The menu is headed by the functionality associated with the overall application. Within the application, there are entry points to each routine. Within each routine, its functionality can be divided into subfunctionalities. This process can be repeated until the routine call level. A call in the functionality menu leads to the entry point of another routine.

The formation of code blocks into functionality members leads to the formation of a functionality menu, representing a hierachical specification of what the code does. A functionality menu serves as a table of contents and index into the functionality of an application. The functionality menu is closely related to requirement specification. These may stand alone as reconstituted documentation when original documentation is inadequate or may be cross referenced to original specifications and design.

Relations with functionality hierarchy

Each entry in the functionality menu corresponds to a functionality member which is a set of code blocks. Therefore, all relations which hold between code blocks apply equally to functionality members. These include: (fn = functionality member name, dn = variable; cbn = code block name)

r11: < fn > uses < cbn >
r12: < cbn > used-by < fn >
r13: < fn > exits-to < fn >
r14: < fn > entered-from < fn >

There are also two relations that define the functionality hierarchy.

r15: < fn > part-of < fn >
r16: < fn > contains < fn >

Appendix C.

The algorithms for insertion, deletion, code block re-organization, and the update of the symbol table entry in Change System.

Algorithm C.1. This algorithm is used to do insertion of a statement.

```
(1)   Get the position where the instruction is to be inserted by indicating
      (a)   the application name
      (b)   the routine name within the application
      (c)   the code block name within the routine, i.e, the current code block
      (d)   the inserting_position within the code block
(2)   Input the instruction opcode.
(3)   Search for the instruction opcode in the database.
      if ( the instruction opcode not found ) then
            display error message - no such opcode
            exit
      end if
```

```
(4)   Display the instruction template as the guideline to the user.
(5)   more_operand = true
(6)   while ( more_operand) do
          Input operand.
          Check if the operand is in proper mode.
          if ( operand is valid ) then
              instantiate the proper objects
              Check if all operands have been input.
              if ( more operand to come ) then
                  more_operand = true
              else
                  more_operand = false
              end if
          else
              more_operand = true
          end if
      end while
(7)   /* Check if statement consists of label */
      if ( inserted statement is a labelled statement ) then
          (a) put the label in the symbol table
          (b) create a new code block for it
          (c) make new code block as current code block
          (d) the inserting_position = 1
      end if
(8)   /* Insert this statement in the inserting_position of the current code block */
      if ( a sequential statement is inserted at the end of a branch statements ) then
          if ( next code block is not a named code block ) then
              insert this statement as the first statement of the code block
          else
              (a)   create a new code block with system generated name
              (b)   put this statement as the first statement in the code block
              (c)   make new code block as current code block
          end if
      else if ( a sequential statement is inserted among branch statements ) then
          (a)   split the current code block
          (b)   create a new code block with system generated name
          (c)   put this statement as the first statement of the code block
          (d)   move all branch statements following this statement to new code block
          (e)   make new code block as current code block
      else if ( branch statement is inserted among sequential statements ) then
          (a)   split the current code block
          (b)   create a new code block with system generated name
          (c)   move all statements immediately after this statement to new code block
          (d)   make new code block as current code block
      else
          insert statement in the inserting_position of the current code block
      end if
(9)   Re-Organize code blocks.
```

Algorithm C.2. This algorithm is used to delete a statement.

```
(1)   Get the position where the instruction is to be deleted by indicating
      (a)   which application
      (b)   which routine within the application
      (c)   which code block within the routine.
(2)   while ( more fields to remove ) do
            while ( more expression to remove ) do
                  while ( more operand to remove ) do
                        Remove operand object
                  end while
                  Remove expression object
            end while
            Remove field object
      end while
(3)   Remove statement object
(4)   Update current code block
      if ( no more statements in the current code block ) then
            if ( current code block is the first code block within the routine ) then
                  change name of the current routine
            else make previous code block as current code block
            end if
      end if
(5)   Re-Organize code blocks
```

Algorithm C.3. This algorithm is used to decide whether to merge two code blocks.

```
(1)   Check the status of current and next code blocks
      if ( current code block consists of only sequential statements ) then
            if ( next code block has no label ) then
                  merge the current and next code blocks
            end if
      end if
(2)   Remove symbols
```

Algorithm C.4. This algorithm is used to add new records to the symbol table.

```
(1)   Search for the symbol name
      if ( label-operand ) then
            search the label in the symbol table
            if ( label not found ) then
                  abandon insertion
                  print message for inserting the label first
                  exit
            end if
      end if
(2)   Search symbol record from symbol record set associated with the label given
      (a)   the routine name
      (b)   the code block name
(3)   Check symbol record found
      if ( symbol record found and use/modify flag match ) then
            (a)   increment number of occurrence
            (b)   new_record_added = false
      else
            (a)   create a new symbol record object
            (b)   assign the routine and code block names, and the use/modify flag
            (c)   new_record_added = true
      end if
(4)   if ( new_record_added ) then
            if ( routine name ¡¿ symbol scope ) then
                  symbol_scope = global
            end if
      end if
```

Algorithm C.5. This algorithm is used to delete records from the symbol table.

```
(1)  Search for the symbol name given the label
(2)  Search for the symbol record
(3)  Decrement number of occurrence by 1
(4)  if ( number of occurrence = 0 ) then
         remove symbol record from symbol record set associated with the label
     end if
(5)  if ( symbol record set is empty ) then
         if ( symbol data is empty ) then
             remove the symbol from the symbol table
         end if
     end if
```

Appendix D.

The algorithms used to construct the structural documentation of Composite Object Constructor.

Algorithm D.1. This algorithm shows the creation of structural object on top of the application, routine, and code block objects.

```
(1)  Input application name
(2)  if ( application name does not exists ) then
         exit
     end if
(3)  Create structural document object for the given application name
(4)  Input document text for the structural document object
(5)  while ( more routine to document ) do
         Input the routine name
         if ( routine name object exists ) then
             find index in alphabetical order among routines names
             insert routine name in structural document array under application
             while ( more code blocks under routine name to document ) do
                 Input code block name
                 if ( code block name object exists ) then
                     find index in alphabetical order among code block names
                     insert code block name in routine document array
                 end if
             end while
         end if
     end while
```

Algorithm D.2. This algorithm shows the insertion of new routine or code block documentation.

```
(1)  Input application name
(2)  if ( application object name valid ) then
           Array_to_insert = application level structural document array
     end if
(3)  Input routine name
(4)  if ( routine object name provided ) then
           Array_to_insert = routine level structural document array
     end if
(5)  name_found = true
(6)  if ( application object name provided) then
           search for routine object name
           if ( routine object name not found ) then
                 name_found = false
           end if
     else if ( routine object name provided ) then
           search for code block object name
           if ( code block object name not found ) then
                 name_found = false
           end if
     end if
(7)  if ( name_found ) then
     (a)   binary search the Array_to_insert given object name
     (b)   insert in location
end if
```

Algorithm D.3. This algorithm shows the deletion of routine or code block documentation.

```
(1)  if ( application object name provided ) then
           Array_to_insert = application level structural document array
     else if ( routine object name provided ) then
           Array_to_insert = routine level structural document array
     end if
(2)  Binary search Array_to_insert given object name
(3)  Remove the entry to Array_to_insert
```

Appendix E.

The algorithms used to construct the functionality documentation of Composite Object Constructor.

Algorithm E.1. This algorithm creates the initial functionality documentation.

```
(1)  Input application name
(2)  if ( application name not found ) then
         exit
     else
         create new functionality member
         input documentation of the functionality member
         assign application name as the keyword to this functionality member
         work_on_array = new array linked to the functionality member
     end if
(3)  done = false
(4)  while ( not done ) do
         more_functional_level = true
         while ( more_functional_level ) do
             if ( not leaf of functionality hierarchy ) then
                 create new functionality member
                 input documentation of functionality member
                 input the functionality member keyword
                 append functionality member to work_on_array
                 work_on_array = new array linked to functionality member
             else
                 while ( more code blocks to group ) do
                     input code block name
                     search for code block object name
                     if ( code block object name found ) then
                         if ( code block name from the same routine ) then
                             create code block name object
                             store code block name object in Bag
                             append code block object to work_on_array
                         end if
                     end if
                 end while
                 up one level on work_on_array
                 move to the next location of the work_on_array
                 if ( work_on_array is the top most level and
                     no more functionality member to add) then
                     more_functional_level = false
                     done = true
                 end if
             end if
         end while
     end while
```

Algorithm E.2. This algorithm shows the insertion of new code block names to functionality hierarchy.

```
(1)   Input application name
(2)   if ( application name not found ) then
              exit
      end if
(3)   Specify the path to insert the newly created code block
(4)   done = false
(5)   while ( not done ) do
              if ( code block name from the same routine ) then
                      create code block name object
                      store code block name object in Bag
                      insert code block name in the location specify in (3)
                      if ( no more path ) then
                              done = true
                      else
                              specify the path to insert the newly created code block
                              done = false
                      end if
              else specify the path to insert the newly created code block
              end if
      end while
```

Algorithm E.3. This algorithm shows the deletion of code blocks from functionality hierarchy.

```
(1)   Input application name
(2)   if ( application name not found ) then
              exit
      end if
(3)   Input the code block name to delete
(4)   Search the Bag of code block names
(5)   while ( code block name exists ) do
              work_on_array = array that code block name exists
              remove code block name object from array
              while ( work_on_array is empty ) do
                      remove work_on_array
                      work_on_array = up one level
              end while
      end while
```

Appendix F.

The algorithm for version control in Composite Object Constructor.

Algorithm F. The editing through the version control

(1) Input application name
(2) **if** (application name found) **then**
        input routine name
    else
        exit
    end if
(3) **if** (routine name found) **then**
        input code block name, *j*
    else
        exit
    end if
(4) **if** (*j* not found) **then**
        exit
    end if
(5) **if** (code block *j* is being modified) **then**
        create a new version object
        set pointers to the all the unchanged code blocks
        set pointer *j* to the new changed code block
    else if (code block *j* is deleted) **then**
        set pointer *1* to *j-1* to original code blocks *1* through *j-1*
        set pointer *j* to *n-1* to original code blocks *j+1* through *n*
    else if (code block *j* is inserted) **then**
        set pointer *1* to *j-1* to original code blocks *1* through *j-1*
        set pointer *j* to newly created code block
        set pointers *j+1* to *n+1* to original code blocks *j* through *n*
    end if

THE ORGANIZATIONAL IMPACT OF INTEGRATING MULTIPLE TOOLS

MIKE P. PAPAZOGLOU
Queensland University of Technology, Faculty of Information Technology, GPO Box 2434, Brisbane Q4001, Australia

LOUIS MARINOS
Erasmus University Rotterdam, AI Laboratory, Postbus 1738, 3000 DR, Rotterdam, The Netherlands

NICOLAOS G. BOURBAKIS
SUNY Binghamton, Department of Electrical Engineering and Computer Science, Binghamton, NY 13902, USA

ABSTRACT
This paper elaborates on the data modeling and data sharing issues that arise when developing and interconnecting modern software development environments. It primarily focuses on the investigation of adjoined object management issues for tool integration, software development environment extensibility, and interconnectivity.

Keywords : Software engineering, environments, object management, tool integration, interoperability

1. Introduction

Software Engineering Environments (SEEs) aim at providing an integrated and coherent set of tools for managing the design, construction, testing, use, and eventual reuse of software, thereby increasing software productivity and product quality [1, 2]. A key objective of SEEs is to support software projects in the generation, management and control of the volume of data and associated information which is generated and utilized during the software development life-cycle. The term environment is reserved to encompass the entire set of automated facilities, such as a unique linguistic and operating framework, required to support all of the activities of the software life-cycle and allowing to switch smoothly from one task to another. Desirable features of such an environment include: ease of tool integration, reusability of internal components, extensibility, support for prototyping, and automated support for the various tasks performed during the life-cycle of multi-user, multi-version software development projects.

The development of such a complex software system involves the management of a significant volume of diverse kinds of data and associated information (such as data properties, constraints or relationships to other data) which make up a software project. The result of user interaction with an SEE is a number of identifiable complex data entities, called (software) "objects,"[a] which carry information relevant to software development life-cycle at a suitable level of abstraction. Typical examples of objects are constructs generated by a project to support the software under development such as source, object, and executable code objects as well as requirement, specification, schedule, test plan and test data objects.

To reduce the efforts spent in maintaining this enormous and highly interrelated amount of data and at the same time improve the overall productivity for software development, SEEs provide a special component for storing, managing, and manipulating the objects. This component, referred to in the literature as the Object Management System (OMS), can normally range from any ad-hoc and application specific storage system to modern DBMSs with flexible object-oriented modeling facilities [3]. The OMS is the core component of an SEE: it is used as the key platform to achieve tool integration and communication [1] while primarily contributing to the construction of an integrated CASE environment [4, 5].

This study emphasizes two important goals of modern software development environments, namely their *extensibility* and *interconnectivity.* Extensibility and interconnectivity are two of the most essential features of modern SEEs. There is clearly a need for systems to evolve over time: it is expected that new tools will be gradually added. Moreover, since many (if not most) software projects are developed on computer networks it is also reasonable to expect that the domain of the local data will exceed the boundaries of the local OMSs. To cope with this issue it is required to interconnect the individual SEEs (physically distributed over different workstations) by providing the

[a]The term object is used in a generic sense, it bears no direct connotation to the object-oriented programming style. What constitutes an object is relative: it largely depends on the object management system used and on how users utilize the typing system of this particular model to define software objects.

operating services of a distributed object manager capable of handling objects of diverse types.

Extensibility implies the ability of tools to be easily augmented in terms of the operations performed and the data they operate upon. An SEE is intended to be extensible in order to support experimental investigation of software process models and evaluation of novel tools in the context of a complete environment. Extensibility leads to the notion of system *openness* where integration of software development tools is supported in such a way as to facilitate the task of adding new tools to the environment. Interconnectivity, on the other hand, implies the ability to support the smooth integration and maintenance of multiple SEEs developed over a network of computing resources. Interconnectivity leads to the notion *tool interoperability* where tools are viewed as interoperable processes.

This paper outlines the technical problems associated with the topics of tool integration, extensibility and interconnectivity and proposes appropriate solutions. We start by briefly explaining how tools in an SEE can be integrated and how they can communicate via the use of an object management system. We then outline the various technical problems and conflicts associated with tool integration and propose solutions in terms of a common set of modeling requirements that should be offered by future OMSs to guarantee extensibility and interconnectivity. Finally, we explain how different SEEs can become interoperable and can exchange information and services under the use of a common integrating platform which exhibits "intelligence" behavior.

2. The Organizational Impact of Using Multiple Tools

An SEE consists of a set of CASE tools which assist users with various software development activities of the software development life-cycle. CASE tools support all the aspects of system design and construction. Depending on their functionality CASE tools may be divided into *upper* and *lower* CASE tools. Upper CASE tools include tools that support techniques like structured analysis [6] conceptual data modeling (e.g., ER-modeling, entity life-cycle history), and techniques such as pseudo-code specification, action diagrams or minispecs. Lower CASE tools comprise traditional fourth generation systems (i.e., application generators with tools for dialogue design, screen painting, automatic generation of database schemas, code generation, etc.). Both upper and lower CASE tools must have connections to *implementation tools* which facilitate code production (e.g., program-development tools such as editors and command interpreters) and manipulation activities (e.g., language-specific tools such as compilers, linkers and loaders, symbolic debbugers, test tools, etc.). A tool[b] can be viewed as comprising a set of functions which accept as operands (and manipulate) the various objects created by other tools or users [7, 8]. Commands, i.e., invocable tool services, are essentially interpreted as the application of tools on objects and the production of new objects as a result of applying tool operators on input objects.

2.1. *Types of tool integration*

Conventional CASE tools specialize in automating diverse very specific software tasks offering, thus, only a very limited support for the various phases of the software development life-cycle. In some cases tools offer a functionality which is complementary to that of some other existing tools. The objective is to combine, or *integrate*, these tools into a coherent, comprehensive, automated software development environment which supports users in activities related to software development tasks. In fact, there exists a necessity to integrate upper CASE with lower CASE tools, and both these types of tools with implementation tools. It is also important that the integration is achieved in such a manner that changes in the upper and lower CASE tools are automatically reflected in the implementation level. Tool integration must accomplish the following two interrelated purposes:

1. Software developers should have at their disposal a uniform working environment where distinction between different tools is completely transparent.
2. Tools must support the diverse tasks that a software developers may choose to perform during the systems development life-cycle.

The foundation that allows integration of tools is the object repository: tool combination and inter-tool communication is achieved at the data, viz. the OMS, level. The true value of tool integration may be defined as the ability of tools to create and manipulate objects (according to agreed-upon definitions from the part of tools) which are freely shared and have common applicability across all the integrated tools. As a general rule, all tools must have complete access to the OMS so that they can define the various types of objects required for their tasks, and obtain access to the objects produced and shared by other

[b]Henceforth signifying an upper, lower CASE or implementation tool; unless otherwise stated.

tools participating in the same or related development activities. The results of operations performed by tools can be seen by all other tools, which in turn can contribute to that operation. This form of integration may be described as a *tight integration* of tools, as they are required to communicate only via shared access to a common object repository and object management system.

In tightly integrated tool environments the communication traffic and data interchange between tools is delegated to the OMS which provides the standard tool interface through which tools can create, access and modify objects associated with the software development life-cycle. This shared repository maintains information about the semantic content of objects in a common semantic dictionary, together with tool-specific views that specify modes of tool interaction. Typical examples of this approach include structure editor-based environment [9, 10] and some modern knowledge-aided systems like Marvel [11] and Worlds [12].

The tight form of tool integration offers numerous advantages such as fine-grain tool cooperation, data sharing at an abstraction level, with a common homogeneous kernel—viz. the OMS, providing a common interface to all tools and guaranteeing tool evolution, reusability and extensibility. To achieve tool integration the OMS must provide upgraded data modeling facilities suited to SEE infrastructure and should also cater for both data exchange and integration services [13].

2.2. *Tool composition and data interchange*

Tool integration may be thought of as the complex task of allowing the diverse tools used in different life-cycle phases to operate together to produce the total software product [14]. Regardless of whether objects of an SEE are local or distributed (they span local or remote workstations), several generic mechanisms must be provided in order for an OMS to be in the position to keep track of consistent creation, deletion, re-definition and transformation of objects. For practical purposes we may differentiate between two kinds of activities which underly the OMS framework: *conceptual modeling* and *object implementation* activities.

Conceptual modeling activities capitalize on the standard repertoire of modeling primitives, provided by the OMS, and are used to prescribe the appropriate solution in the context of the desired application domain. Here, the abstract components, i.e., tools, making up the system are identified and their respective data structures, structural relationships, and the pattern of tool communication are specified. Object implementation activities, on the other hand, employ those data management techniques that are required to implement and coordinate the objects that result from conceptual modeling. In the following we will outline these two kinds of activities and examine the implications they bear on the task of multiple tool integration.

1. **Conceptual modeling activities** employ two complementary methodologies to represent functional tool constituents and specify the type of data exchanged between tools. We refer to the former methodology as the functional composition of tools and to the latter as the data interchange methodology. In the following, we will examine how these two techniques provide the basis for composing tools and combining multiple tools for constructing integrated toolsets.

- *Functional composition of tools*: An SEE must be a vehicle for providing extensive and growing tool capabilities. These capabilities should be furnished primarily by collections of tool fragments, rather than by a few, large, monolithic tools. Under this perspective, a tool is seen to be composed of a series of functional fragments each one implementing specific portion of a tool operation, e.g., a symbolic debugging tool may be defined as an object providing a collection of methods for displaying the status of a program in execution, browsing through the call history, inspecting actual values of data structures, stepping through the program calling sequences, etc. Function composition aims at mapping identifiable physical fragments of tool functionality into a set of functions and to synthesize tools from related tool fragments. Tools should be viewed as aggregates to tool fragments whereby inter-fragment dependencies are explicitly specified. A further requirement is the ability to combine existing functions, distributed across multiple tools into a single functional unit. For example, the task of prettyprinting may be synthesized from a collection of tool fragments which include a lexical analyzer, a parser and a formatter. This results in promoting consistency of operations and avoiding the duplication of implementation efforts.

  One of the main advantages of composing larger tools out of smaller fragments, or tools for that matter, is that if the tool fragments are carefully chosen they will prove to be usable as components of a variety of larger tools, thereby enabling the creation of those tools at much reduced costs. It is, thus, obvious that this methodology serves as a basis for extensi-

bility and reusability. Here, a specific tool fragment may be replaced by another as long as this replacement produces and draws upon objects of the same type as the other tool fragments in the tool. This enables not only considerable flexibility by replacing tool fragments with equivalent ones, but also facilities the integration of new tool fragments.
The value of the functional composition methodology lies in finding autonomous operational tool fragments. Once these fragments are identified, one can identify their data interchange needs and satisfy them through the functionality provided by the OMS.

- *Data interchange methodology*: Functional behavior can be defined in terms of input and output objects involved in or produced by tool invocations. The type of these input and output objects as well as the possible ways of combining and/or structuring them to satisfy the data requirements of tool fragments is guided by the data exchange methodology. The tool data exchange methodology makes sure that tool fragments or individual tools are able to communicate by either producing compatible objects to be read by other tool fragments or tools, or by reading objects produced by other tools or tool fragments. Consider for example, a pretty-printing tool which must work in conjunction with a lexical analyzer and a parser. If the pretty-printer were to access the output of a proven lexical analyzer and parser and be conceptually based on such data constructs as lexical tokens, parse trees, and symbol tables, this tool is likely to be better for its reliance on a robust and proven code than had it been created from scratch.

  The most basic form of data interchange between tools is through a mutually-agreed-upon format of exchangeable data (objects) defined as the interface between the tools. Thus, tool fragments accesses a needed object only through an accessing primitive designed to accept as parameter the type of which this particular object is an instance. This enables tool fragments to share and manipulate objects created by other tool fragments while also incorporating those primitives that will eventually ensure the integrity and extensibility of an SEE. This methodology guarantees tool interoperability at the level of data interchange, viz. at the object-level. For our purposes two or more tools are interoperable if they are able to communicate or interact to perform software development tasks jointly or in a cooperative fashion.

The aim of the preceding methodologies is to facilitate the development of a versatile environment that supports the activities of software developers by coordinating their actions and operations. However, to meaningfully compose and integrate tools it is not necessary to employ the functional composition and data interchange techniques but also to resolve all kinds of incompatibilities which may arise during the tool composition and integration process. In general, the inherent inability to freely interchange data (objects) across a diversity of tools stems from at least three forms of incompatibilities which arise as a result of the attempt to achieve a meaningful integration of multiple tools:

(a) *Functional incompatibilities*: There are incompatibilities which arise from the diverse data requirements imposed by the fragmentation of the tool functionality and by distributing different tool functions across many tools. The data requirements of tool fragments which need to be combined into a single tool and tools which need to communicate may be based on different data structures and representations. Consequently, in order to integrate tools one needs to cater for the rectification of structural and semantic incompatibilities found among the exchangeable forms of data [15, 16].
(b) *Methodological incompatibilities*: Such types of incompatibilities arise from the use of differing *methodologies* promoted by different tools. A methodology may be defined as an ordered collection of *methods*, like structured analysis, ER-modeling, and project management methods, performed by tools in order to develop a software product. A method may be viewed as the specific approach taken to solve aspects of a software development related problem. For example, data flow diagrams represent a method for developing process decomposition during the requirements phase. As different tools promote different methodologies, any viable tool combination must resort to consistency checks carried out on different parts of the specification. If say, two CASE tools are used in conjunction, one promoting data flow diagrams (DFDs) for functional specification and the other one ER diagrams for data definitions, then it should be made sure that the data stores on the DFD hierarchy correspond to entities and/or relationships on the ER diagram and that their respective names match. As a result we must ensure that correspondences between equivalent structures of differing degree of granularity and detail are established. As already stated, it should also be perceivable to develop a certain software product by following different development strategies, e.g., by using different tools with overlapping functionality.
(c) *Distribution incompatibilities*: The tool data exchange methodology may

be viewed from the perspective of multiple cooperating developers who rely on communicating toolsets distributed among different workstations with each workstation possibly relying on its own private object-base for data management. This specific category of incompatibilities introduces not only incompatibilities between different OMS data definition constructs but also incompatibilities which arise from the use heterogeneous machine configurations, operating systems and so on.

One of the major purposes of the OMS is to resolve these forms of incompatibilities by making sure that the structure of the shared data is made conformant to all interacting tools in a toolset. The OMS handles the details of tool connectivity, including representations for data structures, organizing the structure of shared data and checking consistency between connections. Our view is that the desirable conceptual modeling primitives which assist the OMS in their effort to resolve all forms of incompatibilities can be provided by recent developments in information systems technology, i.e., object-oriented and knowledge-based data models.

2. Object implementation activities require a common data repository for coordinating access to and storage of the objects shared by tools. Thus, the object implementation activities instrument the conceptual modeling framework. This repository handles functions which span conventional data management activities such as storage management, concurrency control and recovery and extend them by providing persistence for typed objects. Such issues have been extensively researched and are addressed by the relevant literature [17] and, thus, will not be examined in this paper.

In the following section we will first elaborate on the desirable OMS modeling primitives and explain how these primitives can be used for managing the structure of the data exchanged between the tools, and consequently promote tool extensibility and interoperability, and then we will explain how these features can be used to resolve inter-tool conflicts and incompatibilities.

2.3. *Desirable OMS modeling primitives*

The objects which require management in an SEE range widely in size and character. Sophisticated object management support is required to faithfully represent objects of varying granularity such as parse trees, abstract syntax graphs, symbol tables, source codes, test plans, designs and so on. This suggests that the SEE's infrastructure must provide the basic facilities for explicitly modeling the intricate structure of software objects which represent information both at a coarse and at a fine grain level. Several systems have been, or are being, developed around semantic or object-oriented data modeling facilities [2, 3, 8, 18] to provide a rich repertoire of object management facilities regarding the definition, manipulation and storage of complex entities which may be used to model software objects.

The use of the OMS as an integration platform unfolds the possibility of building powerful information retrieval facilities which can collate and present component information generated at different stages in the software life-cycle. The OMS employs an *object-base schema* to publicly define the types of objects that are handled by tools and specify the data structures communicated among tools. Object definitions, thus, do not belong to the code of specific tools but are made publicly available by the OMS.

This section summarizes the most salient conceptual modeling features that contribute to the overall OMS functionality. The proposed conceptual modeling features combine object-oriented programming with rule-based modeling. Each feature is studied from the perspective of OMS extensibility and with a view to ultimately supporting OMS interoperability. The capabilities sought for each of these issues and some interesting problems are briefly discussed below.

- *Typing facilities*: The OMS can manage objects produced by tools used in all phases of the software development life-cycle. The key factor to the OMS's expressiveness is the notion of *typed* objects. The OMS enforces typing which includes definition of type properties (e.g., file objects and associated properties like the name of a file, content of a file and so on) and behavior (i.e., how an object acts in terms of its state changes and message passing) as a set of operations (typed methods) attached to a typed object (e.g., operations on file objects such as create, open, close, concatenate and so on). In an SEE where all objects are instances of abstract data types, it is easier to share objects or to modify their implementations. Thus, the OMS is able to hide the internal structure and implementation of objects behind well-defined interfaces and can accordingly control the operations performed on those objects.

  The type system needs to be flexible and powerful enough to capture information which relates to tools, processes, and even types themselves and treat it as objects. This implies that we may have objects which are types of types or *meta-types*. Recently, work on type systems, in the context of object-oriented OMS models, has dealt with these and related problems and has focused on forming a compatible set providing the rich typing capabilities required for SEEs [1, 3, 8, 9].

- *Support for composite and complex objects*: For the administration of objects, it is often desirable to use the notion of object composition as a way to collect together related objects into a single composite (or complex) object. Composite/complex objects can be treated as a single unit while their component objects can be treated as separately identifiable and accessible units.

  Complex objects possess the ability to establish simple inter-object references, whereas composite objects exploit this mechanism further by granting existence dependency properties to inter-object references. Consider for example the attribute *compiles-into* that relates a *source-code* object to its object code counterpart. If we choose to represent the *source-code* object as a composite object, then the *compiles-into* object becomes an integral "part-of" the *source-code* object. If the *source-code* object is deleted then its *compiles-into* counterpart object is also automatically deleted.
- *Varying object granularity*: Most conventional SEEs are able to store large objects, like programs or documents, as a single unit. However, it is desirable that such coarse objects are decomposed into smaller components. For example, it is desirable to store each of a programs procedure's as a separate object, rather than storing them in a single coarse object, as is the current practice with file systems.

  The granularity of objects in modern SEEs is normally chosen to be in a fine-grained form so that the administered objects are compatible with the data structuring mechanisms encountered in high-level programming languages. This choice of granularity at a coarse level poses a real threat: sub-granular references should be kept to maintain the consistency and validity of information. When objects get modified, existing sub-granular references to them may be invalidated. This is a typical case when dealing with program code modules (e.g., Ada packages) where we need to support libraries of compilation results.

  The issue of granularity is very much related to that of complex/ composite objects as they are used when dealing with larger software units, such as program systems, documents or even entire projects whose structure must be made available system-wide. Such objects cannot be stored in the OMS as a single unstructured object. They must be modeled as an abstraction of a set of related simple or complex/composite objects and their interrelationships. Therefore, it is evident that with the use of complex/composite objects the problem of sub-granular references to component objects (the integral parts of the composite object) can be eliminated by appropriately mapping it to that of representing simple or existence dependent references towards the component objects.

- *Inter-type relationships*: The ability to capture and maintain relationships between objects in an SEE is closely related to its ability to define and maintain typed objects. Through the typing system, relationships between types can be properly expressed and manipulated. An association between objects may itself be considered as a typed object and further relationships may be built upon this relationship type. For example, the fact that a particular *object_code* module is related to some *source_code* module by a relationship *compiled_from* is an important property as it indicates that the *link* operation may only be applied to instances of that type.

  Currently, there exist several tools which reason about or exploit relationships among objects. Typical examples include version control systems and automated system building tools. As a rule, defining the relationships among the environment's tools and information contents, viz. objects, facilitates the upgrading of the environment since the effect of upgrades (modifications) can be relatively easily determined by examining the inter-object relationships.

- *Constraints*: Depending on the domain and semantics of object properties, it may be necessary to constrain object creation in such a way as to ensure that their attributes assume only permissible values which belong to a specific range of the value domain. This feature guarantees consistent creation of type instances as opposed to unconstrained creation which involves the obligation to verify data consistency a posteriori (and thereby scales down the performance of the environment considerably). Constraints are incorporated into the type definitions of objects, a fact that gives the OMS additional versatility and expressive power.

  Existing constraint mechanisms can be characterized as value-based and, thus, do not support constraints that can explicitly specify and delimit permissible operations on objects. However, modern OMSs require

action-based constraints applied on types and their instances. Action-based constraints are provided by modern OMSs through the trigger concept (similar to exception handling mechanisms in programming languages, and to demons in AI systems) [8, 9]. Triggers enable a repair activity to perform certain corrective actions so that their associated constraints are always satisfied and object integrity is preserved. A typical example of the use of triggers is for automating, replanning and rescheduling tasks when software development activities have to be redefined and/or re-initiated [9]. For example, a change in a specification requires the design activity to be reinitiated. Such events are otherwise manually entered into the OMS which subsequently triggers compensating activities depending on the specified events.

- *Rules*: Rules can serve as the main agents which control active participation in the software development process in terms of activities (e.g., text editing, compilation or debugging) carried out using tools such as editors, compilers, debuggers, etc. Rules define the conditions that must be satisfied for a particular tool to perform an activity which must be carried out on a set of objects; and also specify the effects of the tool invocation. Rules normally implement a chaining model to impose their effects and maintain consistency. In fact, rules are used to implement action-based constraints, just like triggers, and control corrective actions.

  Rules may also by used to automate activity initiation by automatically performing activities which otherwise would have to be carried out manually. For example, in response to the completion of implementing a program module, the rule-system may initiate the testing activity for this particular module. Another important use of rules is that they may be used to apply a backward chaining policy, similar to that of Marvel [11], for invoking mechanisms to rectify attribute mismatches (see Subsec. 2.4). In general, rules are attached to types as *multi-methods*, which are sent to a collection of objects of different types, making thus use of inheritance of structure and operators.

To summarize, we may state that the four basic approaches, based on the above OMS modeling primitives, which seek to rectify inter-tool conflicts and improve efficiency via the use of objects are: ***abstraction and information hiding, functional decomposition/composition, parameterization*** and ***rule-based processing***. With the use of abstraction we produce intermediate abstractions for tools whereby tools pay no attention as to how their counterparts came into effect; with functional decomposition/composition we partition the tools into, or synthesize tools from, disjoint fragments which materialize complementary functionality; with parameterization we identify which system parameters affect which tool fragments; and finally with rule-based processing we guarantee automation, consistency and integrity of inter-tool invocations.

2.4. *Resolution of inter-tool incompatibilities*

The focal point of our discussion in this section concentrates on how the OMS modeling primitives like typing, behavioral modeling, inter-type relationships, constraints and the rule system can be used for the resolution of functional and methodological incompatibilities. Physical distribution incompatibilities are the subject of the next section which elaborates on the concept of corporate software development environments.

It is important to point out that tool management capabilities complement object management capabilities: tools are viewed as functional agents defined and acting upon objects, where objects are the instances of types tailored in such way as to satisfy the data requirements of the functional tool fragments. Object-orientation provides the natural framework and set of modeling primitives for supporting effective tool management, resolution of inter-tool conflicts and subsequent tool integration. The usefulness of the object-oriented paradigm as basis for the resolution of functional and methodological conflicts does not only stem from its superior expressive power (the object model lends itself to the construction of software environments that embody the properties of well-structured and complex systems) but also from the fact that it provides natural support for the data-driven analysis and top-down decomposition methodologies [16, 20]. In the following we will examine how the OMS modeling primitives (based on the object-oriented and knowledge-based paradigms) aid in resolving inter-tool incompatibilities.

The process of resolving functional inter-tool conflicts is a three step activity. First we assert the existence of the relevant tool fragments involved in a certain development sequence; then, we evolve their interfaces in terms of conformant data interchange patterns; and, finally we embed them into a single organizational unit, the object tool type. A tool fragment architecture is always materialized in terms of its functional components and the data structures upon which these functional fragments operate. It is important to point out that the data requirements of the functional tool fragments are of paramount importance: the functional fragments of a tool are completely described in terms of the input and output objects that this specific fragment accepts as parameters or produces as results. Once the data requirements of the functional fragments have been specified, as a result of performing some form of data driven analysis, the input and output objects of the tool fragments that are to be combined are compared to ascertain their commonalities and degree of compatibility. The objective of this step is: (i) to guarantee that functional fragments which are placed in the same tool use compatible data structures (and if not to devise some mapping mechanism); (ii) to additionally develop uniform interfaces in order to facilitate tool fragment interaction with their intra- and inter-tool counterparts. The final step in this process requires that all identified data structures and functional components are incorporated as structural and behavioral properties in their encompassing object type which materializes a concise tool in the SEE.

We exemplify the three steps of the resolution of functional incompatibilities by means of the debbuging tool depicted in Figs. 1, 2 and 3. This debugging tool is seen to comprise the three identifiable tool fragments (or methods in the object-oriented sense): *ReadObjectCode, SetUpStructures* and *Interaction* (see Fig. 1). This figure also depicts the data requirements of those fragments specified in terms of input and output (IN, OUT) in object type parameters. These tool fragments represent the three major functional fragments of a rudimentary debugger and perform quite independent tasks. The tool fragment referred to as *ReadObjectCode* accepts a core file object as input and produces an object of type hash table (of the compiled program) as output. The fragment *SetUpStructures* is responsible for setting up the appropriate structures required for debugging. It accepts as input the hash table object produced by the previous functional module, and produces a set of internal table objects. Finally, the fragment *Interaction* is responsible for providing user access: it accepts as input the set of internal table objects produced by the previous fragment and produces I/O structures for interaction with users.

The specific approach taken to resolve functional and methodological incompatibilities by bestowing an object-oriented flavor on the debugger's (and for that matter any other tool's) functionality is succinctly examined below.

1. *The use of composite objects and inheritance to resolve functional incompatibilities:*

When analyzing the functionality of a tool in terms of the behavior of its particular constituents, we obtain several self-contained functional fragments.

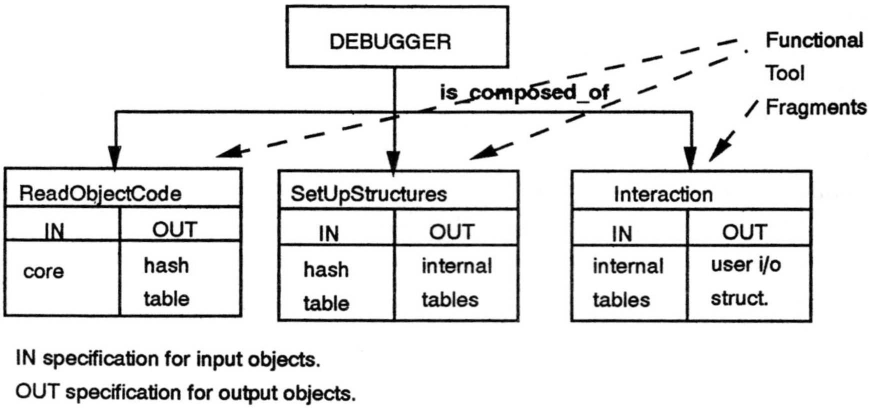

Fig. 1. Functional composition of a debugger tool.

These fragments accomplish a narrow and specific portion of the overall tool functionality. As shown in Fig. 1, these tool fragments may be represented by the nodes of an is_composed_of, or *functional composition hierarchy*, with each leaf node contributing towards a portion of the functionality of its root node. Nodes signify tool fragments, while the root of the hierarchy signifies their common defining object type, i.e., the debugger in Fig. 1. The tool solution space is seen as being composed of a set of functional units and the process of tool synthesis defines the overall behavior of the tool as a concise object which inherits and is fully characterized by the individual behaviors of diverse tool fragments.

The resolution of functional incompatibilities is accomplished from the fact that any defined component objects directly reflect the functionality of the fragments of a tool, and describe how they are interfaced with the remaining intra-tool fragments. At the same time the functional fragments define an outwardly (inter-tool) visible behavior in that they may be potentially accessible from every object in the environment. It is worth mentioning, that other objects in the SEE will be in the position to access functional tool fragments as long as they "know" how to tailor their message interfaces to the data structures required to achieve inter-object tool fragment invocations.

This particular methodology employs the concept of composite objects to provide the means for referential sharing of object types, allowing, thus, individual tools to be combined (or grouped together) into a higher-level abstracter tool. A composite object may be profitably viewed as a tree defining an is_part_of hierarchy, represented by the dashed lines in the figure. The composite object itself is the root of the tree and the objects which it aggregates are its component objects. Consider for example the case of the composite tool type called *Program_Development_Toolkit* and shown in Fig. 2. This tool type contains the tools *Compiler, Linker, Loader* and *Debugger* as its component object types to produce higher level functionality.

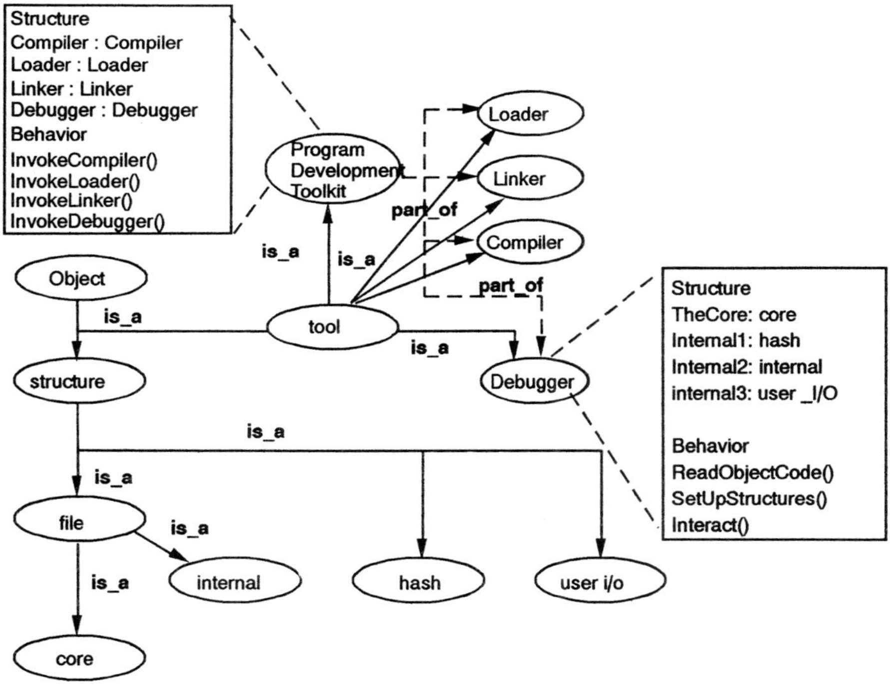

Fig. 2. The tool object type hierarchy.

The functional tool composition and the is_part_of hierarchies can be easily combined with the *schema object type*, or is_a, hierarchy, represented by the solid lines in Fig. 1, through which tools in an SEE are classified. In this way tools and tool fragments define their attribute domains in terms of object types organized in the object hierarchy. The organizational criteria for the formation of the object type hierarchy are not the same as those of the functional tool composition and is_part_of hierarchies: with these hierarchies no sub-typing relationships (signifying property inheritance) are possible. One can only ascertain which functional tool fragments or tools are constituent parts of other tools, but not whether a functionality or a tool is more generic than another—which is the criterion for classifying tools.

Reverting to the debugging example; the specification of input and output data types used as parameters for the tool fragments of the debugger can be organized in a generalization hierarchy as shown in Fig. 2. In addition to this hierarchy, Fig. 2 also shows the individual structural and behavioral properties of the debugger. For example, *The_Core* property specifies the memory map (or core) file object needed for initializing the debugger, while the rest of the debugger's structural properties correspond to the input and output type parameters utilized by its functional fragments like *Set_UpStructures* and *Interaction*. Notice that all the debugger structural properties draw their values from the object types defined in the is_a hierarchy. This principle is also employed in the case of the type *Program_Development_Toolkit* depicted in Fig. 2. In the is_a hierarchy object types like *Structure*, *File* and so on define a generic structure and behavior exhibited by many object types serving as parameters for either tools or tool fragments.

The preceding discussion has illustrated how the problem of tool composition and construction relates to the general bottom-up strategy of software development which library-based object-oriented design naturally implies.

2. *The use of relations and rules to resolve methodological incompatibilities:*

As already stated, methodological incompatibilities are inherent to the utilization of particular tool fragments during the completion of a specific software related task. To be completed successfully such tasks require a synergy of different tools and tool fragments.

The main problem in defining a methodology for a software development related task lies in providing appropriate input and output data structures that suit the data specifications of the tools or tool fragments used to perform this task. The key issue here is to be able to transform the output data of tools to a format which is compatible to the input format of the next tool or tool fragment in the sequence of the methods required to satisfy a chosen methodology. During this sequence of events all parameter mismatches must be rectified.

Another important problem in the definition of methodologies is whether a specific order of tool fragment invocations will lead to an effective completion of the requested task. Consider for example the methods of the *debugger* type in Figs. 1 and 2. Although a separate invocation of any method associated with a particular tool fragment in the body of the type *debugger* makes sense, the invocation sequence *ReadObjectCode(core):Interaction(internal)* will lead to inconsistencies. The reason is that these two functional fragments are not called in the right order: the functional fragment *Interaction()* expects to receive as input an object of type *internal* which is unavailable. This object will be properly set up after a call to the functional fragment *SetUpStructures()* which accepts as parameter an object of type *hash* (produced by a previous call to the functional fragment *ReadObjectCode()*) and returns as result an object of type *internal*. In order to prevent this situation from happening, the OMS should be in a position to detect the "functional" gap and data inconsistencies resulting from the ill-chosen method invocation sequence and invoke the appropriate functional tool fragments in the right chronological order.

Both of the aforementioned problems can be solved by using inter-object relationships and rules. Relationships help to rectify methodological incompatibilities and the problem of ill-chosen tool invocations by stating additional dependencies between object types used either as input or output tool fragment parameters. Such dependencies are concerned with providing information regarding the compatibility of input and output functional fragment type parameters during a sequence of tool fragment invocations. For example, in Fig. 3 the ternary relationship *inter_structure_transformation(structure_1, method_name, structure_2* provides information about the equivalence between its input and output tool fragment parameters *structure_1*, and *structure_2* by returning the name of the method which allows to transform the structures of one type into those of the other type. The figure shows three instances of this relationship with the first instance signifying the fact the objects of type *internal* can be transformed into equivalent objects of type *hash* if the method *int_hash()* is invoked.

To utilize this information, one can think of an additional auxiliary tool, represented as a type called *method_check()*, whose purpose is to check the validity of a given methodology and rectify attribute mismatches. This type is shown in Fig. 3 to implement the functionality of a checker module responsible for establishing the compatibility between input and output tool frag-

inter_structure_transformation

structure	method	structure
internal	int_hash()	hash
core	core_int	internal
hash	hash_user()	userI/O

method_check

transformed_into: Structure
equivalent: Structure

Rule
IF transformed_into ≠ equivalent
THEN look_up_structure_to_structure_production(transformed_into, equivalent)
invoke(method(transformed_into))

Fig. 3. Relationships and rules for methodological conflicts and irregularities.

ment parameters used during a sequence of debugging activities. To achieve this effect the checker module uses a rule which ascertains and invokes the method needed to transform an object of one type into its equivalent counterpart of a different type. Consider the call sequence with the steps *ReadObjectCode(core):interact (internal)* again; the checker type is in the position to find out whether the attribute *core* conforms to the type *internal* and if not, to find out which sequence of methods is needed to establish this equivalence. The method *look_up_structure_to_structure_production(transformed_into, equivalent)*, called from within the rule where the formal parameters *transformed_into* and *equivalent* correspond to the actual parameters *core* and *internal*, utilizes the relationship *structure_to_structure_production* to find out that the method *core_int()* will eventually have to be called. This method is subsequently automatically invoked by the rule in the checker module, see Fig. 3. It must be pointed out that since the method *look_up_structure_to_structure_production()* accepts arguments of type *structure* it establishes polymorphic references to objects defined in the is_a hierarchy.

The use of rules to rectify methodological inconsistencies is in accordance with the concept of *opportunistic processing* whereby simple development activities can be performed automatically by the model so that software developers need not be bothered with them [11].

3. Toward a Corporate Software Engineering Environment

It is anticipated that large software development projects will gradually evolve toward a growing set of tools that can be used from a variety of workstations with each workstation managing its own object-base. In this environment different members of a development project may invoke the same or different tools to operate on one or more of the same objects stored either on a local or a remote data repository. When multiple developers cooperate on a corporate software development project, they share a single conceptual (virtual) object-base physically dispersed between multiple client and server processes and workstations with each workstation possibly supporting its own OMS and object-base. Currently, interrelated projects have no means to remotely invoke tools or exchange objects stored in (heterogeneous) data repositories. However, with true integration of multiple SEEs this is very desirable feature: products generated by projects relying on different types of OMSs can be reused within a common network.

The inherent inability to access and integrate objects across a variety of SEEs, henceforth referred to as *distributed objects*, and tools stems from differences in structural and semantic content of similar, or almost similar, objects created by different tools in different OMSs. When integrating multiple SEEs it is reasonable to expect that models of different kinds are used by their associated OMSs to represent the data relevant to the software development process. Obviously, the elementary manageable resources in the corporate SEE are the objects produced and managed by the individual OMSs. For reasons of simplicity we assume here that the individual OMSs in the corporate SEE support some variant of the object-oriented data model. In reality some of the OMSs may support filing systems, may be based on the relational or a navigational data model or variants thereof. The coexistence of two (or more) heterogeneous data models in an integrated environment preassumes that these models are in a position to acquire data from one another and subsequently convert these data to their internal representation format. This requires the ability to establish a common means of expressing software development activities within the corporate environment; to keep track of these activities; and finally, to provide support for distributed object management in order to allow multiple users and tools to work conveniently on the corporate object-space. Distributed tool sharing poses the problems of introducing various layers of distribution incompatibilities such as those hinted at in Subsec 2.2 and unfolded in the following:

- Incompatibilities due to the use of heterogeneous data models: differences in the representation of objects utilized by projects which rely on diverse data models. To bridge these differences a meta-model, or *canonical representation*, which comprises a super-set of the underlying data models, must be utilized. The purpose of the meta-model is to facilitate inter-OMS conversion: OMSs of one kind must be in a position to understand the type model of a different kind of OMS.
- Incompatibilities in object-base schema definitions: an additional problem is the inter-OMS differences encountered at the object-base schema level. Presenting the same kind of objects (local or remote) through different perspectives, requires a mechanism for keeping views and actions upon them consistent with respect to the base objects from which these views have been derived. This may be alleviated by adopting corresponding techniques from the database research field, namely distributed database and view integration methodologies [21, 22].

The problem of distributed object management and the resolution of its associated conflicts represents an active area of distributed systems [23] and distributed database systems research literature [24] and poses a series of technical issues and problems such as dynamic migration of objects, dynamic connections and disconnections of workstations, effective communication protocols, concurrency and distributed transaction management and so on. Although the above issues represent challenging problems, attention will be focussed on the problems identified so far which in fact are the immediate derivatives of distributed object sharing in a corporate SEE. Additional information about the previous problems can be found in the information systems literature [21, 22, 25].

3.1 *Inter-OMS communication*

In the corporate SEE environment, tools are considered to be processes connected to and communicating via a common network. Communication can be performed by issuing remote procedure calls. For example, this kind of inter-tool communication can be achieved through a broadcast message server [26] where communication between tools that reside in remote workstations can be implemented by using TCP/IP-domain sockets.

Remote tools that work together share the behavior and the view of the object-base schema defined by their respective OMSs. We assume that each tool that can be remotely called is supplied with a strict interface which spec-

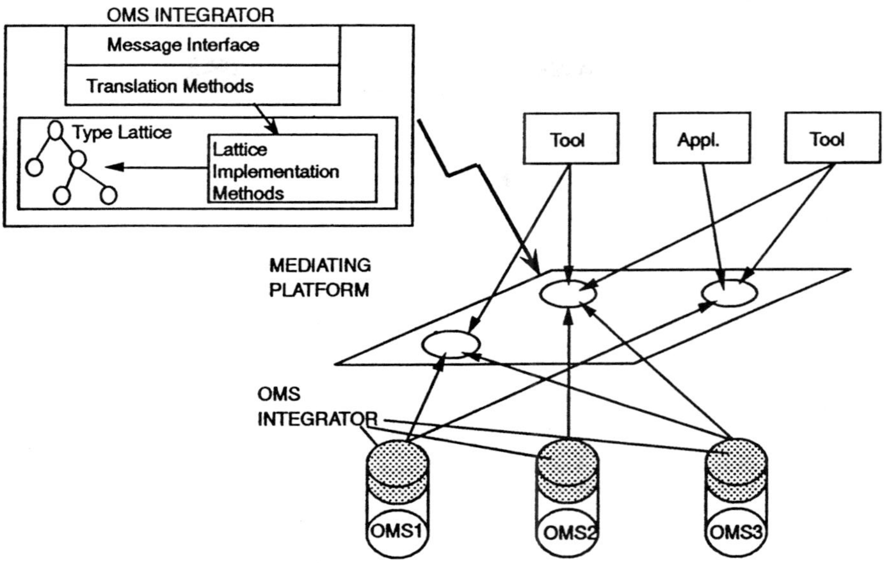

Fig. 4. Use of a set of uniformizing integrators between OMSs and tools.

ifies the constructs that the tool imports or exports. Such constructs may include tools, types, relationships and rules. A tool may have its import ports connected to several export ports of remote tools and vice-versa. With this scheme name clashes between imported and local facilities are treated as different views of the same construct. The general objective here is to establish interconnection between tools and tool fragments in terms of services required and services rendered.

3.2. *Inter-OMS Cooperation*

Even when inter-OMS communication is existent, it is extremely difficult to guarantee that meaningful network-wide references can be established from local tools and users to remote heterogeneous objects and services. Distributed tool sharing in a corporate SEE concerns itself with the sharing of a set of distributed objects which draw their data from diverse object-bases—physically situated at different workstations. To resolve the severe technical problems and diverse forms of incompatibilities exhibited by the OMSs a novel architectural framework must be introduced. With this architectural framework, distributed object management can be achieved whereby each local OMS will still be in charge of the objects and pre-existing applications developed on its workstation, and would cooperate with remote OMSs to achieve sharing of remote tools and objects.

The proposed approach attempts to address these issues by using a blend of object-oriented and knowledge-based techniques. It entails transforming the rather "passive" local OMS components into *active agents* by attaching to them active front-end extensions which embody sufficient contextual knowledge. Each local OMS will entail an *OMS (logical) integrator* and will accordingly be transformed into an agent which is able to reason about a corporate project domain, perform transformations which need to be applied to local OMS components, and automate many corporate software development activities. These advanced abilities grant the OMS the attribute of being *active*.

3.3. *Functional view of the corporate environment*

The functional view of the corporate SEE architecture entails a federation of cooperating agents implementing an additional layer on top of the already existing local OMSs, i.e., OMS 1 to 3 in Fig. 4. This figure shows how the OMS integrator is interfaced with its underlying local OMS. It is assumed that an OMS integrator (the shaded areas in the figure) will be attached as a front-end extension to each local OMS in the network and act as a mediator in order to provide information processing and requests addressing remote applications. Project management and administration of inter-project objects will not be performed on the premises of a single centralized OMS in the network. Rather, existing OMSs will cooperate, through their integrating component, and transparently access distributed heterogeneous objects residing at differently structured OMSs. The logical integrators are the only means by which local OMSs can communicate. The entire OMS integrator community may be perceived as forming a distinct mediating layer interposed between the diverse tools and object-bases (see Fig. 4). The mediating layer, or platform, makes the software developers' applications independent of the local or remote data resources and data management intricacies and is used as a vehicle for the unification of local and remote data and services.

Many of the near insurmountable problems which characterize corporate SEE object management would be solved if the tools in the different workstations were to share a single object representation employed by each OMS integrator. The idea of having all remote tools operating on the same data structure is very attractive as it guarantees full integration: with only a single representation of inter-OMS data, tools can communicate directly. The integration mechanism on the OMS integrating component performs several services such as keeping compatibility maps which describe how operations on data in one workstation OMS translate into equivalent operations on the same or equivalent data objects originating from remote workstations, i.e., the translation methods in Fig. 4. Moreover, the logical integrator uniformizes data, views and services provided by the diverse OMSs and makes them available to applications and tools operating on network-wide available objects.

The corporate object space entails virtual objects (depicted as circles in the mediating platform) which draw their data from either remote or local address spaces. Such objects are described in the canonical representation scheme used by the logical integrators which employ a common object type lattice to define the overall corporate schema (see Fig. 4). Existing OMSs retain their autonomy in that local OMSs will not be tampered with. However, software developers who require remote object support will have to utilize the canonical data model to achieve this purpose. In all other circumstances users can still rely on their original data model for software development purposes.

As the logical integrator basically provides the same functionality that a distributed database management system provides in the traditional database world [21, 27] detailed description of these and related technical issues is beyond the scope of this paper. In the following section we will confine ourselves to the issue of choosing the appropriate modeling capabilities to support inter-OMS integration and remote tool access and cooperation.

3.4. *The corporate SEE modeling requirements*

To choose the most suitable OMS approach for supporting corporate software development, the OMS conceptual data requirements must be identified first, exactly as it was done back in Subsec. 2.3. The present section investigates these issues and then based on the desired capabilities, concludes that an enhanced object-oriented data model in the form of a tight coupling of data and knowledge based formalisms, as already implied in Subsec. 2.3, is most appropriate for supporting corporate SEEs.

The overriding consideration behind the corporate SEE is the provision of a complete development system for practical complex design environments based on object-oriented technology. The logical integrator's extended functionality is driven by a supply of extensive domain and operational knowledge organized as a form of tight coupling between the AI-based knowledge oriented mechanisms and conventional database technology [28]. Such advanced capabilities include the advanced modeling primitives which facilitate the development of well formed interfaces to a collection of heterogeneous information sources, and knowledge representation facilities (mainly through the use of the rule-based system) used to resolve the acute problem of data incompatibilities in the integrated application environment.

The usefulness of the typing and abstraction mechanisms (described in Subsec. 2.3) are well recognized also for the case of distributed tool invocation and object management. For example, inter-type relationships offer very attractive features for OMS integration: capabilities that rely on relationships, such as reference and derivation [3], will ultimately facilitate inter-OMS integration by allowing users to interact with the environment at a high level, while leaving the intermediate mapping steps to be automatically determined. Through the establishment of inter-object relationships software objects in some space can refer to software objects in another: two source-code objects represent programs $P1$ and $P2$ can have references to objects in a common subroutine library which is represented by a separate object space. However, in our view the issues which are of paramount importance for materializing distributed tool invocation are the use of knowledge and meta-knowledge for OMS integration purposes.

Knowledge in the canonical model can be represented by means of rules which are used to represent inter-object dependencies. For example, one rule may state that a user object at a workstation-A can modify the remote parse tree represented by a program object at workstation-B. Another rule may state that a precondition for a user at workstation-A to resume execution of a program at workstation-B is that no changes have been made to any procedure already on the run-time stack. Rules will also be used externally and will not be embedded in the general tool functionality as suggested in [7, 11]. Adding this kind of knowledge to the logical integrator level would make its functionality relatively intelligent.

The logical integrator is designed not only to store the initial low level information, i.e., the objects, but also information used to facilitate corporate SEE tool invocation. This type of knowledge pertains to the structure and functionality of both local and remote objects and software development activities. The central repository of the logical integrator is a knowledge-base which contains information about inter-OMS structural and operational dependencies, application knowledge, software tool knowledge, and can also be used as a vehicle for communication between the individual OMS components in the corporate environment. Software tool knowledge is expressed as a form of understanding of how local and remote software methods and tools tie together and is used as guidance to produce correct and effective products. In particular knowledge of this type entails information on how to construct and maintain the corporate object space and how to conduct controlled automation by forward and backward chaining among the rules defined by local or remote strategies. We collectively refer to this kind of knowledge, which for operational purposes needs to be shared by the entire OMS integrator community, as the *meta-knowledge* portion of the corporate SEE.

In sum, combining object-oriented data modeling primitives as described in this section and Subsec. 2.3 provides a firm foundation for addressing the complex distribution problems. Both paradigms increase software development productivity and reduce inter-object integration and maintenance costs. Object-orientation provides support for data abstraction, knowledge encapsulation, reusability, and extensibility while rule-based processing provides support for representing expertise and inferencing.

4. Conclusion

Until very recently software has been developed predominantly on large centralized computer configurations using a collection of tools bearing little or no relationship to one another. There has consequently been marginal support given to the software developers during the software life-cycle. It is against this background that the concept of SEEs has evolved. An SEE is a development environment into which tools supporting all of the various phases of software life-cycle are integrated.

The important issues which we addressed in this paper were tool integration, SEE extensibility and interoperability. It was explained how the OMS supports internal tool integration and extensibility by providing advanced modeling primitives and by managing the properties of objects as part of the product management policies and the software development process rather than embedding them in the tools themselves. In this way a given tool may be used in different contexts with different policies and methods and this will ultimately facilitate software tools to be usable on a distributed network of

SEEs. Given the trends toward greater portability and distribution, the value of tool integration will be the ability to create and manipulate objects according to common definitions and have distribution applicability across all tools no matter if they are local of remotely accessed in the network. Throughout this paper, we have concentrated on the extensibility and interoperability issues and identified several problems associated with these issues, raised some important open questions and suggested some promising research directions and methodologies.

Acknowledgments

We deeply appreciate the numerous excellent comments and suggestions made by Dan Cooke and Bernd Krämer. Their enthusiasm, help and interest is gratefully acknowledged.

References

1. M. H. Penedo, E. Ploedereder and I. Thomas, "Object management issues for software engineering environments," *SIGSOFT* **13**, 5 (1988) 226.
2. A. van Lamsweerde *et al.*, "Generic lifecycle support in the ALMA environments," *IEEE Trans. Softw. Eng.* **14**, 6 (1988) 720.
3. S. Hudson and R. King, "The CACTIS project: database support for software environments," *IEEE Trans. Softw. Eng.* **14**, 6 (1988) 709.
4. A. Wasserman, "The architecture of CASE environments," Technical Report, Interactive Development Environments (1989).
5. V. Stenning, "On the role of environment," *9th Int. Conf. on Software Engineering*, Monterey Ca. (March 1987) p. 30.
6. E. Yourdon, *Modern Structured Analysis* (Prentice-Hall, 1989).
7. M. Larcroix and M. Vanhoedenaghe, "Tool integration in an open environment," *European Software Eng. Conf: ESEC'89*, Coventry, England, p. 311.
8. R. Taylor *et al.*, "Foundations for the Arcadia environment architecture," *SIGSOFT* **13**, 5 (1988) 1.
9. S. Horowitz and T. Teitelbaum, "Relations and attributes: a symbiotic basis for editing environments," *SIGPLAN Notices* (1985) 93.
10. B. Krämer and H. W. Schmidt, "Developing integrated environments with ASDL," *IEEE Softw.* (January 1989) 98.
11. G. Kaiser, P. Feiler and S. Popovich, "Intelligent assistance for software development and maintenance," *IEEE Softw.* (May 1988) 40.
12. D. S. Wile and G. D. Allard, "Worlds: an organizing structure for object-bases," *SIGPLAN Notices* (January 1987) 16.
13. E. Adams, M. Honda and T. Miller, "Object management in a CASE environment," *Procs. Software Engineering Conf.* (1989) p. 154.

14. D. Smith and P. Oman, "Software tools in context," *IEEE Softw.* (May 1990) 15.
15. B. Mayer, "Reusability: the case for object-oriented design," *IEEE Softw.* (March 1987) 50.
16. G. Booch, *Object-Oriented Design with Applications* (Benjamin/Cummings, 1991).
17. W. Kim and F. Lochovsky, ed., *Object-Oriented Concepts, Databases, and Applications* (ACM Press Books, 1989).
18. S. Reiss, "Working in the garden environment for conceptual programming," *IEEE Softw.* (November 1987) 16.
19. D. Bobrow *et al.*, "Common loops: merging lisp and object-oriented programming," *OOPSLA '86 Procs.* (October 1986) p. 17.
20. Special issue on Object-Oriented Design, *Commun. ACM* **33**, 9 (September 1990).
21. S. Ceri and G. Pelagatti, *Distributed Databases, Principles and Systems* (McGraw-Hill, 1984).
22. S. Navathe, R. ElMasri and J. Larson, "Integrating user views in database design," *IEEE Computer* (January 1986) 50.
23. D. Decouchrant, "A distributed object-manager for the Smalltalk-80 system," in *Object-Oriented Concepts, Databases, and Applications*, ed. W. Kim and F. Lochovsky (ACM Press Books, 1989).
24. P. Bernus and M. P. Papazoglou, "Knowledge based architectures to integrate heterogeneous distributed information systems," *2nd Conf. on Tools for Artificial Intelligence* (November 1990) 682.
25. M. Manino and C. Karle, "An extension of the general entity manipulation language for global view definition," *Data Knowledge Engineering*, **1** (1986) 305.
26. M. Cagan, "HP softbench: an architecture for new generation of software tools," *SoftBench Technical Note Series*, SESD-89-24, Hewlett-Packard, Software Eng. Systems Division (November 1989).
27. M. P. Papazoglou, "Knowledge-driven distributed information systems," *14th Computer Software & Applications Conference: COMPSAC-90* (October 1990) p. 671.
28. L. Kerschberg, "Expert database systems: knowledge/data management environments for intelligent information systems," *Inf. Syst.* **15**, 1 (1989) 151.

Management Benefits of CASE

ESTABLISHING THE CONTEXT OF CONTINUOUS IMPROVEMENT FOR TECHNOLOGY TRANSFER

GREG BOONE

President, Systems Research, Inc., 211 South Garden Street, Bellingham, WA, 98225, USA

ABSTRACT

Although the majority of professional trade press and academic attention regarding CASE (Computer Aided Software or Systems Engineering) has focused on technology, software developers have not been deluded by overinflated promises regarding productivity gains attributed to those and similar technologies. Truly profound technologies require a concomitant change in methods, practices, and techniques. Unfortunately, the majority of the software industry has had the expectation that CASE and other technologies could automate the development of information systems without a significant rethinking of work practices. Changing work practices particularly among highly independent-minded software developers, who prize independent creativity more than team engineering of systems, may be one of the most difficult challenges facing the advance of the information technology management profession. This paper is a revision of a paper which examined the rate of CASE adoption and the necessity of a continuous improvement infrastructure which the author felt was necessary to accelerate its successful adoption. In the last three years, much evidence has accumulated which verifies the practical value of continuous improvement systems in organizations for the facilitation of technology transfer.

1. Introduction

The gold rush is on. However, today's gold rush is the mining of wealth in the form of information. Instead of heavy mining machinery, we have mainframe computers. Instead of steel pans, we have PC's. As the entry cost to mining diminished and was put into the hands of many, whole new towns were built, expectations rose, commerce flourished, the entire Western United States was transformed. With the advent of computer technology, so too have new organizations arisen within businesses, business organizations themselves are changing, and expectations are high. But with the gold rush, the basic commodity of wealth was limited. With the modern gold rush, the basic commodity of wealth is information, whose limits we have yet to find, and maybe never will. The changes to organizations and how those organizations respond to change as a result of information technology, continues to be profound.

This paper is a revision of an article conceived in 1987, presented at various conferences, written in 1989 [1] and then published in 1991 [2]. The fundamental ideas, organization, and commentary has been kept as much the same as possible. The most notable addition concerns the Business Improvement Maturity Model, which describes the most elementary dimensions of improvement in the business environment, and is an outgrowth of the work done in the earlier versions of this paper.

Since then, many events have taken place which corroborate the suggested approaches which were stated in those early presentations and papers. For example, the Software Engineering Institute of Carnegie Mellon University has validated and popularized the notion of process improvement [3]. Their "Process Maturity Model" has become well-known throughout the data processing industry. The Hewlett-Packard Company has been one of the leading pioneers of the application of a process improvement approach, especially the move from a software testing emphasis to a defect-prevention emphasis through the use of process instrumentation and metrics [4]. Their work was inspired by their investigation of Japanese manufacturing techniques as early as 1978, and is a valuable contribution to software engineering as well as a significant departure from the generally accepted thinking about metrics at that time [5].

Other specific industry experiments conducted since then directly support these notions. Even before the Hewlett-Packard experiences, and as early as the late 1960's, Japanese companies such as Hitachi, Toshiba, NEC, and Fujitsu had instituted a completely different approach to software development than US firms; instead of a hand-crafting approach, they desired a more organized, disciplined approach. They emphasized process improvement first rather than product invention [6]. They conceived of "software factories," a metaphor for the application of a manufacturing paradigm to software development capitalizing primarily on a "provide from stock" or "assemble to order" model instead of the "make to order" model [7]. They followed engineering principles for process analysis and control, skills standardization, systematic reusability, computer-aided tools and integration, and incremental product/variety improvement. Their experiment is still unfolding, has its challenges, but seems to be quite successful, and they have been doing so with very little fanfare to international academic or industrial audiences.

The subject of this paper is change and continuous improvement as a driver for action rather than technology transfer as a driver. Too often, technology becomes an end in itself, and means are diligently sought to make its use successful. The approach presented in this paper is not intended to be narrowly used as a tool for technology transfer. Instead, continuous improvement is a broader achievement whose objectives are logically prior to technology transfer. Along with continuous improvement systems is the need for management of organizational change. Inspired from the work done by organizational development specialists, there are models and methods which can be built into continuous improvement systems which expand their application and greatly improves the probability of success. Once the objectives of continuous improvement are established, then experiences with technology transfer will go more smoothly, predictably, and successfully.

But what about the claim regarding the management of change? Is there really anything practical that can be done about it? Are not some changes too broad and intractable? Without experiencing managed change, how easily do we give up on an improvement opportunity before we have even begun? Instead of threatening unmanageable, and unpredictable, change can be constructive and manageable. When change is initiated at increasingly lower levels in an organization with the appropriate infrastructure for control, change tends to be less threatening and destructive. Yet of these three aspects, predictability can be the most troublesome to overcome. Although prediction has been considered an art since ancient times, our ability to predict the shape of things to come can improve if we "cast our net" over a broader domain of knowledge and expand into other subject disciplines. Only as we see the wholeness of systems will we begin to apprehend their consequential progression.

So it is with information technology management, specifically software development. Conventionally, computer professionals tend to devote their time and attention nearly exclusively to technology and technology related subjects. But the limiting factor for the effective adoption of technology has much less to do with individuals' intellectual and technical abilities as it does with engineering work processes for a team environment, improving management practices, and human factors. Then, predictability becomes less important when an organization gains confidence in its ability to continuously improve.

Continuous improvement is the ability for organizations, particularly teams, to learn from their experiences and apply that learning to the transformation of their work environment. Unless the infrastructure for continuous improvement exists within an organization, unless roles, responsibilities, attitudes, and the work culture is amenable to incorporating every worker's constructive suggestions for improvement, then it does not matter how potent, powerful, or promising a new technological innovation may be. Putting such technology into an environment devoid of the ability to accomplish team learning will only produce limited results. This aspect of organizational behavior is just beginning to receive popular attention [8, 9].

This paper uses the example of the enormous changes beginning to take place as a result of the introduction of CASE, or Computer Aided Software Engineering, in order to understand the importance of continuous improvement principles. Even by its own definition, CASE is much more than just a technology for productivity improvement [10]. It represents a whole new approach which in time, will move data processing from a software crafting approach to more of a true software engineering discipline. What this statement truly means will become an important agenda for interpretation for the 1990's and beyond.

Unfortunately, the "CA" of CASE, computer aided, has become much more important than the "SE", or software engineering aspect of CASE to most of the industry. CASE is perceived almost exclusively as a technology, not as a disciplined paradigm for organizing and conducting the management of information technology. Take for example, the commonly held view that object-oriented approaches are an alternative to CASE, a disturbing confusion to say the least. The two are not inimical, they are related. CASE has slipped into more of a vendor driven technology phenomenon than a work practice redesign phenomenon. Just the reverse exists in most of Europe, where more formal, disciplined approaches are de rigueur.

The rate of CASE adoption and the current means of CASE adoption are limiting factors against forward progress in information management. Certainly, the need to speed up system deployment, deliver correct, useful solutions, and improve system reliability is a problem for which CASE can provide unique solutions.

However, there are important lessons from other industries and disciplines that can accelerate CASE adoption. Major advances have been made in manufacturing and some service sectors through the application of industrial engineering techniques, particularly statistical process control. These engineering techniques have evolved to the level of management practices which embrace the philosophy of total quality management; and through the techniques of organizational development, which have made such headway in understanding how to facilitate organizational change. As widely known as these subject areas are, they are still quite new to most of the data processing profession. What is most troubling, is that these concepts are the most vital, yet missing in most CASE implementation efforts or other technology transfer opportunities.

The current attempts at CASE implementation have been primarily and exclusively at the tactical level, dealing with such issues as tool evaluation and selection, or choosing pilot projects for application of those tools. These tactical approaches have met with extremely limited success, and a growing number of experienced users are sharing the opinion that this situation will continue unless CASE is approached strategically, using the principles of continuous improvement and management of organizational change.

2. What the CASE Experience Has Been

Information management professionals are constantly working to automate the flow of information within businesses, and to some extent, actually automate some jobs. Now we have CASE, which has been acclaimed as yet another technology which can dramatically improve the productivity of information management professionals—indeed "automate" the software development process. So to many, it is a rather novel idea to try to automate the automators!

For veteran data processing professionals, this is not the first time efforts have been made to automate data processing. Relational databases, fourth generation languages, and programmer workbenches, are all examples of some of the technologies which have been hyped with great promise. Even COBOL and FORTRAN programming languages were once considered to be major technological advances with the purpose of improving productivity. Yet, according to *The Annual CASE Survey 1988* [11], early CASE usage did not point to improved productivity as a tangible benefit, but rather it pointed to improved quality. To the early pioneers of CASE, improved quality as the primary benefit came as a surprise. This finding from the survey along with many others, directly conflicted with the prevalent corporate culture which put productivity before quality in importance.

That CASE is greeted by data processing professionals with some skepticism should not be surprising. Nor should it be surprising that this group has endured very little change in terms of self-examination of work practices, organization structure, or development methods. Consequently they are even more resistant to change than those they have been "automating" for many years. Like the rugged individualist prospector from the gold rush days, resourceful and independent, the software developer of today is finding himself forced into situations which demand greater interdependency and a greater spirit of cooperation—both with their clients and their fellow developers.

2.1. *CASE means cooperation*

Quite simply, it might be inconceivable for a group of several artists to get together to jointly conceive and execute an artistic endeavor. Yet we have scores of engineers who work collectively on projects and express great creativity and imagination. Why is this? What makes engineers different from artists?

Engineers have been enlisted to work on efforts of a much larger scale, or on parts which are intended to fit into a larger whole. They have dedicated themselves to serving the wishes of their customers as closely as possible, and manifesting their customers wishes. They have not merely sought an outlet for their own individual expression or "self-actualization." Engineers have a common language, a common means of expression, a common set of methods, and established standards. They have the means to effectively communicate with one another and their customers. Yet software development today is still more of an artistic, crafting activity. The saying that a team of one to two programmers is more effective than a team of ten is more an indictment of the lack of maturity of the software development discipline than it is about the nature of software development itself.

One of the important myths that underlies software developers in the corporate environment is that a loose organization of programmers, arranged in a confederacy, can somehow, through cumulative individual efforts, achieve a satisfactory, collective information management capability for an enterprise. As an analogy, after every possible creek had a prospectors claim on it, and the simple, individually oriented methods had been exhausted, gold miners eventually resorted to more cooperative efforts through the use of heavy machinery for hydraulic erosion, pit mining and other methods.

Likewise, when the visible pieces on the surface which were easy to pick up were gathered, or by analogy to data processing, when the easy systems had been built, data processing professionals are now faced with problems of much larger scale, higher complexity, higher interdependency, more demanding user interfaces, and systems with quicker responsiveness. Due to these problems, we must achieve new levels of cooperation. These new levels of cooperation are needed not only among the disparate technologies that have been amassed today, but also among individuals and groups, among both developers and customers.

Nowhere has the spirit of cooperation met with so much resistance in the data processing community than with the introduction of CASE. Always anxious to find tools to make what is already being done easier, programmers are astonished to find that instead, the new tools demand a change in what is being done. When they are not as successful at using the new technology as they expected, they find themselves needing to perform their work in new ways; ways that change their perception of their work and their individual roles; ways that are sometimes threatening. Ways that force individual developers out of rather isolated roles and into tighter relationships with an increased demand for team communication.

Although many programmers are having a difficult time making the transition to a CASE environment, it is the management and the customers that often have more difficulty. For example, the amount of effort expended in the early stages of a project when using CASE may be as much as twice the effort compared to a conventional project. During this period a much better job of communication of requirements or specifications is generally being made with the customer and between project team members, possibly through the use of joint application design techniques (JAD), and/or more complete and rigorous examination of the functional design. All of this is taking place before any code is written. Yet managers unacquainted with CASE get very uneasy and react unfavorably. They sense that the project may be going out of control, so they relinquish the use of CASE and revert to traditional methods, pushing the team to rush on to the production of the more tangible result: code.

Not only are software developers impacted by CASE but also their customers. In many organizations, customers are learning elementary structured analysis techniques and are active participants with software developers in actually drawing and diagramming their proposed systems. For some developers, this can be threatening. For some users, who expect to simply tell the software developers what they want and do not want to talk to them until the system is finished, such participation is very different from that to which they are accustomed. For most, it is a very constructive, beneficial experience.

Even the so-called, "safe" pilot project can become a source of resistance. When CASE tools are introduced on a pilot project, usually the best developers are chosen and it is the pilot project team that gets the glory. What can remain for most others, if the pilot was successful, is a dull obligation to adopt the new technology and/or methods pioneered by the pilot team; methods and technology which probably are not well understood by anyone other than the pilot team. Therefore, resistance in many forms arises, maybe in the guise of "show me the numbers," or "the pilot project was unfair, it received unusually favorable treatment," or the "the pilot was different from the kind of applications we usually build," "why should we follow the lead of that other project, we can choose our own CASE tool," or many other forms of passive hostility and skepticism.

Overall, these are just a few examples that point out some of the numerous sources of resistance to CASE. However these sources of resistance can actually pose an opportunity for developers and their customers to challenge their ideas about themselves, their roles, their work methods, and their purpose.

More recent evidence is dispelling the myth about teamwork in software development. According to Randall Jensen, Chief Scientist of the Software Engineering Technical Laboratory of Hughes Aircraft Ground Systems Group, "... we have run experiments that more than double productivity. These experiments show that just changing management styles, a no-cost proposition, can often double productivity." [12] In one of these experiments, they had programmers working in pairs, sharing a workstation, and writing code together. "The result was over 100% improvement in productivity, and a decrease in errors by three orders of magnitude."

This and other findings from the Hughes teams, should be alarming to those who have believed that more innovative, powerful technology is the answer. In fact, not only do nontechnological solutions hold the most promise today, but should serve as a powerful warning that if new technology is introduced, even more attention needs to be placed on management, processes, methods, and techniques.

2.2. *The impact on software development*

The introduction of CASE, as mentioned earlier, is not the first time that the identity and role of the programmer has been challenged. Several years ago, James Martin predicted the demise of the programmer in *Application Development Without Programmers* [13]. We now know that has hardly been the case.

Instead of programmers disappearing, the more technically oriented programmer has gravitated towards developing more general purpose software, such as database management systems, file management systems, repository managers, configuration management software, local area network communications software, spreadsheets, word processing applications, fourth generation languages, reusable software environments, and various object-oriented environments. The less technically oriented programmer has vastly increased his or her understanding of the business environment in order to build applications more relevant to the business user, "standing on the shoulders," so to speak, of the work done by the more technically oriented programmers.

So there is this stratification that is becoming even more pronounced through the use of CASE approaches and technology. Technically oriented programmers are developing more generalized tools for other software developers who wish to spend more of their energies solving business problems rather than just technical problems. Overall, this stratification is broadening to include an increasingly greater percentage of people in any organization. More and more people are taking advantage of the use of computers, and not in just the strictly polarized "developer-user" role that has stereotyped our thinking in the past. With more and more user developed systems, or joint user-developer systems, organizations have been forced to take a fresh view of how systems should be developed, or find themselves adrift on a sea of technology that has become more heterogeneous and confusing, and even more so with the addition of CASE.

Instead, new roles are evolving, including not only systems programmers, application programmers, data base administrators, data administrators, information center personnel, development center personnel, network administrators, PC support specialists, and so forth, but also user-directed and user-managed application development, development of specifications by "users," prototyping of applications by users in PC-based products like PARADOX or ACCESS, or mainframe based fourth-generation languages. In the future, we will see new roles emerge for software developers who are skilled at integrating tools into an environment and customizing them for group or team-oriented development approaches. Users want more direct control over the business process redesign catalyzed by computer automation.

Also, the nature of demand for information management services is beginning to undergo a fundamental transformation. It is not just that we need to develop systems faster, it is that the systems we have to build are now an order of magnitude more complex which requires higher levels of discipline, and rigor.

Enforcing rigor and discipline among groups of people can be highly challenging, especially among software developers. But the new systems we now have to build cannot be crafted, they must be engineered. We have a vast inventory of aging systems of enormous complexity that need to be integrated with one another. Hardware capabilities and user insistence are pressing for the splitting of system functionality among multiple hardware platforms, in the form of cooperative and distributed processing. We have distributed databases that users are starting to want to merge with one another. We have enormous problems of data correctness, integrity, consistency, and reliability. These issues span traditional departmental boundaries, and therefore are strategic issues.

Creativity transcends the technical problem (programming) for the business or problem-oriented developer and the real creativity lies in the ability to effectively match information management technology to the real business need. Those business needs are stratified: they are at all levels, from the operational levels to business strategy formulation levels.

Effectively matching information management technology to business needs is what a lot of front-end CASE tools are really all about: doing a better job of understanding user information management needs, helping users better understand their information management needs, and doing a better job of communication, both developer to user, and user to developer. If CASE is the new idiom for expression, then a great deal of its power lies in its ability to create a common means for communication. Consequently, creativity is no longer held hostage by the technology or the technologist, but broadens to include a wider spectrum of people in the organization.

But like the nature of the challenge of CASE itself, the pending identity crisis of software developers is not to be solved solely on the individual level. It is not a simple matter for a person to decide one day to be different. There is a complex set of existing work relationships, organizational structures, reward and compensation systems, company values, existing expectations that all present competing forces which shape behavior. The challenge of CASE is very much a matter of culture change. But what aspects of the culture needs to change, and how does one go about facilitating such a change?

2.3. *The receptivity to change*

Once a CASE tool has been brought in and some preliminary experience has been accumulated, a number of questions invariably arise among users. "How do I get my organization to effectively use CASE?" "Why am I not getting the productivity increases that I was promised?" "What is it that prevents software developers from more fully embracing CASE?" "Where do I start in order to begin changing this situation?" Although existing CASE users are just beginning to recognize these as real challenges, this is not the situation for prospective CASE users. Unfortunately, the grim reality of prospective CASE users remains obsessed with primarily one question, "What is the best CASE tool to buy?" To many vendors, this is obviously an important question, and indeed it is an important question. What is discouraging is that industry as a whole including potential CASE users feels it is the most important question. Vast amounts of energy are put into product selection, and very little into training and implementation. It should be no surprise then, to either vendor or user of CASE, that success with the product might be less than expected. The receptivity to change is diminished if CASE users do not raise the right questions and reformulate what does need changing.

Even more discouraging is not the fact that users feel product selection is the most important question, but the fact that software developers only seem to be able to learn in an incremental, experimental fashion. They have to touch, see, do, in order to embrace something new. They have to do this for themselves, and have little trust in others' experience. Advances are made individually and inductively, reasoning from small, particular experiences before changes are made to values and beliefs about software development.

The problem is that this rate of adoption by software developers is abysmally slow compared to the responsiveness needed to meet changing business information management requirements with rapidly changing technology. It takes a lot of small, particular experiences with lots of organizational communication and synthesis before more general policies become established or institutionalized into the company culture. For example, how long has it taken software developers to use relational database technology? How many understand that a significant part of the productivity improvement possible with the relational model has to do with DBMS enforced referential integrity rather than programmer enforced referential integrity?

One of the underlying problems behind slow CASE adoption is that CASE requires a quantum leap in conceptual understanding as well as a corresponding quantum leap in implementation effort compared to previous automation attempts. It presents an entirely new paradigm for software development. It would be nice if industry could make this paradigm their own, and deductively apply the general vision to their own particular experiences.

But as things are right now, industry does not appear to be able to do this. Not until there is a much wider wealth of experience from other companies setting examples, will prospective CASE users be able to thoughtfully assess the risk and benefits of the implied changes. But there may be a more effective way to accelerate the successful implementation of CASE. In order to accelerate the rate of change and to insure the right kinds of change, the very means of change must be expanded beyond good intentions and wishful thinking. The good news is that change can be better managed—good diagnostic and analytical techniques are now available. When change is unmanaged, or when the rate of change happens faster than we can make the necessary accommodations in order to feel comfortable and secure, then we experience what Toffler calls "future shock"—the state of becoming either individually or collectively dysfunctional [14].

In the face of incredible technological change, it is no wonder that software developers have not had the chance to make all the necessary changes to their work practices to optimize the use of the new technologies. Mastery of materials is a stepping stone to mastery of methods. But just when an adequate mastery of the materials (hardware platforms, operating systems, languages, data base management system, etc.) is attained, those materials change and the fundamental steps of learning the characteristics of the technology start all over again. Little time remains then, to figure out how work methods might be improved. Nevertheless, the heavy preoccupation with technology must shift in favor of improving the methods and the process.

The real goal should not be successful CASE implementation but the improvement of the software development process. Too often, CASE is approached as an end in itself. Unless we realign our goals commensurate with business requirements, success with CASE will probably continue to be disappointing. Therefore, we should be more concerned about the slow adoption of CASE, not for the sake of CASE itself, but for the sake of reversing many of the management principles which hinder quality and productivity. Typically, we have placed productivity before quality, creativity before discipline, individualism before team approaches, autocratic decision-making before participative management, product before process in order of importance. All of these beliefs need to change. All of these attitudes limit the continued progress of improved software development capabilities. The resistance to CASE is really a reluctance for software developers to adopt new principles and methods.

This is a work culture challenge and therefore, more difficult to attain. In the Japanese work culture there is an fundamental ethic to improve—Kaizen. Unfortunately, the U.S. culture is dominated by the ethic of maintaining the status quo, or sidestep improvement and embrace innovation. It is as if there is some static ideal that if once attained, is all that is necessary. Then, all efforts for improvement can cease, and the primary job is to maintain the standard, prevent deviation, and seek control. Although the latter tasks are necessary and valid, they become misapplied if improvement is not viewed as a dynamic, continuous goal. Unfortunately, this ethic has been reinforced over hundreds of years in Western Culture through institutions of religion, government, and academia.

An excellent example of this contrast in cultures is provided through the experience of Japanese automobile manufactures. Subsequent to establishing U.S. factories, the Japanese obtained auto parts from U.S. firms. In Japan, as time moves on, a supplier improves its ability to manufacture parts or components and consequently, the price of parts is expected to decrease. This is in sharp contrast to the U.S. practice where increases in overheads are not absorbed by improvements in manufacturing, but rather the increases are passed along to the customer. The Japanese, expecting a decrease in costs, have been surprised and intolerant of annual increases demanded by U.S. manufacturers.

For the U.S. to turn to a true commitment to quality, it must put aside the desire to maintain the status quo and replace it with a desire to continuously improve, not just stop because some temporary level of excellence has been achieved. In order to emphasize quality, organizations need to adopt a process orientation which stresses prevention of defects over detection of defects [15]. The industrial engineer Edwards Deming [16] admonishes businesses to adopt the following practices:

1. Build quality into the process; do not rely on inspection.
2. Foster teamwork and dismantle the barriers that divide disparate departments.
3. Provide managers and workers the training they need to fully participate in the improvement process.
4. Have top management chart a company-wide strategy for continuous improvement of products and services.

In a study conducted at the end of 1989, CASE Research Corporation surveyed the use of CASE methods and tools [17]. The results were startling.

Adoption rates followed nearly exactly the well-known "S" shaped curve model, (or sigmoid curve) originally inspired by cell growth models from biological sciences. This model has also been applied in sociology to the diffusion of technology in society [18]. Structured methods have been about 18 months ahead of life-cycle methods since 1986. Back-end CASE is three or four years older than front-end CASE. Adoption of both back-end and front-end CASE took off in 1987 when the use of front-end CASE passed back-end. This data seems to support the notion that CASE technology transfer is accompanied by changes in methods and practices, which slows its adoption. Management must recognize this in order to improve the effective infusion of CASE technology.

3. What the CASE Experience Could Be

3.1. *Change the playing field*

Although there can be significant benefits when the goal of CASE implementation is on a tactical, project-by-project basis, enough is known about the nature of CASE to suggest that the real payoff will come when it is approached strategically. The real challenge is to get the entire organization to use CASE—not just a few pilot projects. As discussed earlier in this paper, a whole new level of cooperation among software developers, a strategic cooperation, will be required. To get the real payoff from CASE, incremental step-at-a-time change will be inadequate. Like a chemical reaction, a combination of elements need to be brought together under the right conditions for the reaction to happen.

Changing several things simultaneously is a strategic change, because it involves planning and coordination of multiple organizational units towards a common vision and goal. Strategic change requires knowing where you are and where you want to go. It requires identifying the resources critical to the change and describing their mobilization in a coordinated, well-timed fashion to meet objectives. It means the adoption of common principles and guidelines. But few organizations have the vision or see the importance of taking the time to establish this kind of groundwork. But look what happens when this groundwork is ignored.

Let us start by analyzing how change happens. Change comes about because of externally driven factors, (i.e., competition, change in technology or technical environment, mergers, acquisitions, downsizing, reorganizations, etc.) or because of internally driven factors (e.g., a seemingly compelling desire for something better). Generally, CASE is brought into software development organizations on a voluntary, internally motivated basis. Ever on the search for a more technologically advanced means of accomplishing the information management function, developers have begun experimentation with CASE. Expecting minor change, if any, they have been caught by surprise with major change. Unfortunately, when internally motivated change, e.g., change that seems relatively benign and merely a "good idea," unexpectedly produces a deeper and broader impact, it can often be abandoned. In other words, if the true cost of the change was known up front, it could well be that the proposed technology transfer opportunity would not have been undertaken to begin with. Or, preparation could be more intelligently made to meet the capital, organizational, and procedural requirements of the new opportunity.

There are two alternative solutions to the CASE implementation challenge or other technology transfer opportunities. First, make the benefits of the technology imperative to the very existence of the organization by showing it as a solution to a critical problem. If the pain of not changing (failure to adopt the new technology) is sufficiently great, then the change will at least receive the attention it deserves. (This is not to be confused as the sole requirement for successful change). But, it is rare for many organizations to be able to contrive such a situation if no critical problem really exists. The net effort of such political maneuvering might not be desirable.

If the technology transfer opportunity really is critically tied to the solution of a major organizational problem, then it ceases to belong to a choice of alternatives. There simply is no alternative but to adopt the technology; but the question remains, how to accomplish the adoption successfully. However, both situations still lead to the second alternative.

Regardless of the extent of the technology transfer imperative, this leaves only the second alternative: create an infrastructure for continuous improvement that allows CASE or any other technological, methodological, or improved technique to be adopted on a continuous and economical basis. Such an infrastructure would not only provide the means for introducing such a change, but once introduced, make the appropriate micro-changes to accompany it in order to make it actually work! This is the new context for CASE, or any other technology transfer opportunity [19].

When this context is established, it changes the rules and the playing field for technology transfer. An entirely different work culture is established. Receptivity to change is much higher. Change is viewed as a fact of life, rather than something to be resisted or fought. Change is more desirable and to be expected. Organizational systems exist under broader employee participation and control which gives everyone greater confidence that change will be positive rather than negative. Improved communication from these systems makes the change more understandable and meaningful, to everyone. Greater levels of cooperation are created so that separate operating units cease working at cross-purposes or in a destructively competitive manner. A common vision that binds all efforts together in a more meaningful way increases individuals sense of contribution, self-worth, and value. Overall, motivation is much higher for successful technology transfer.

3.2. *Getting started with the new context*

One of the most important aspects of establishing an infrastructure for continuous improvement is to create a vision for change. Not just one individual or small constituency, but a *shared* vision among the majority of an organization. This vision should be compelling, substantive enough to have meaning, and clearly articulated throughout the organization. And it should be backed up with endorsement by the leadership of the organization through active participation. Sound simple? Common wisdom? It is. But how many organizations are following this common wisdom?

To progress from the vision to action requires knowing where you are presently. Knowing where you are requires an assessment of current applications (the application portfolio, information architecture, repository, etc.), current software development tools and methods, organizational culture, cost of poor quality, and the nature of customer demand. Knowing where you want to go requires coupling the improvement vision with the enterprise's objectives. Knowing how to get there requires a strategy for the creation of the continuous improvement infrastructure.

Where does one start, and how, to create a continuous improvement infrastructure? Are there changes in the organization that are necessary? How much does it cost? How long does it take before results can be seen? Will it really work? Will it be worth it? These and many other questions beg the need for a rational, organized approach.

However, this opens up the enormous subject of Total Quality Management or TQM. There are no simple answers to those fundamental questions of cost, benefit and feasibility. Some of the answers can be found by delving deeper into the definition of TQM. Inherent in the word "total" of TQM is the unique systems viewpoint, viewing the whole, seeing the "whole cloth" of continuous improvement and not just a part. To truly appreciate TQM, it must be seen in all its dimensionality, not just in terms of a few techniques.

But who wants to wrestle with TQM when implementing CASE or some other new technology transfer activity on a project or organization-wide basis? That may already seem a sufficiently daunting task on its own. Indeed, individuals who initiate or become involved with such broad organizational programs like TQM that do not have specific product or service oriented deliverables are rarely rewarded if not punished unless management has first made a firm commitment to such a program. But if one appreciates the degree of peril associated with CASE implementation when the proper context is missing, the so-called burden of additional work may appear more attractive than wasting effort on a failed CASE implementation project.

How one goes about building a continuous improvement infrastructure goes beyond the scope of this paper. However, a brief introduction to what that infrastructure looks like will help provide initial direction to at least establish awareness of the necessity to do so. TQM, or specifically continuous improvement, along with the management of organizational change, has become such an enormous subject that it is easy to get lost and confused. Both to alleviate confusion as well as provide a practical tool for developing continuous improvement strategies, a model has been developed to describe organizational improvement methods. As mentioned earlier, seeing the whole of TQM is necessary to appreciate its essence.

Change is like a chemical reaction that takes a combination of elements and environmental factors before the reaction will succeed. It is important to examine each of the various elements of the "chemical" reaction needed to adopt TQM. The fundamental elements and how they work together are described in what is called the "Business Improvement Maturity Model" [20, 21].

3.3. *The business improvement maturity model*

Trying to categorize, eliminate, generalize, analyze, and synthesize the most critical aspects of something as complex as business improvement methods is certainly not easy, and possibly an overly ambitious task. Creating a model which depicts the most important nature of TQM may be an impossibility. Nevertheless, the model presented in this paper is certainly a simplification but hopefully a simplification that will aid in differentiating between various business improvements approaches, especially various types of TQM approaches.

It is also an important diagnostic tool that can identify those aspects most lacking in an organization and most in need of attention. This model can serve as a compass to those business managers who are trying to diagnose the deficiencies in their own improvement efforts. This provides the vital information necessary to truly construct a relevant and practical improvement strategy. It helps narrow the choices from a broad set of quality improvement choices so that resources are used wisely. This model was developed by the author after several years of analysis of improvement methods used since the time of Fredrick Taylor in the 1920's. It has been used successfully in many practical applications for the implementation of continuous improvement programs.

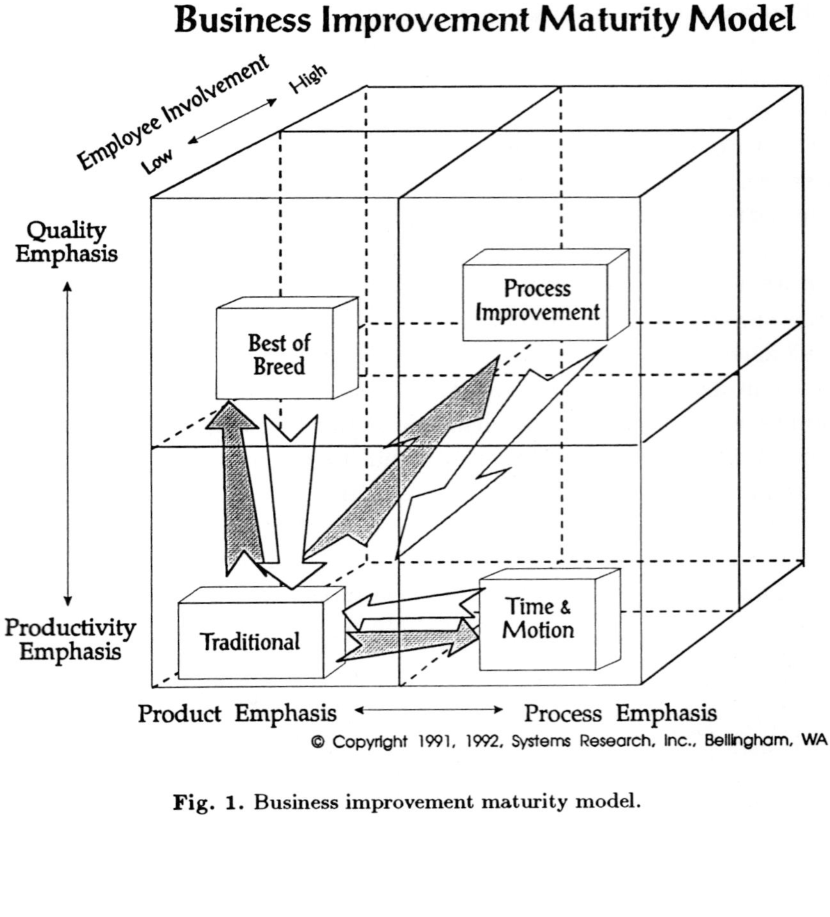

Fig. 1. Business improvement maturity model.

The Business Improvement Maturity Model (Fig. 1) depends on the use of three fundamental continuums which form the three basic dimensions of the model. These dimensions are described below and then followed by a discussion of the "chemistry" of sustainable change.

3.3.1. *The product versus process dimension*

Upon examination of all the best known management practices, certain continuums of values can be found to be common to all the various approaches. For example, it is interesting that although the early time-and-motion studies of Taylor focused on the efficiency of the manufacturing process, most American managers were obsessed with efforts to generate product. The only real process innovation was Henry Ford's invention of the assembly line. After that, the assembly line became the dominant production model and managerial practices focused on work fragmentation, which resulted in today's hierarchical organizational structures. In reality, a manager needs to balance his efforts and the efforts of his workforce between producing product or service and investing in improving the means of delivering that product or service. Therefore, the first dimension of the model shows the continuum between a focus on product versus a focus on process. The major improvement approach is broadly called "Time and Motion."

Each of these dimensions connect to the other. The product/process dimension cannot be divorced from the quality dimension. Once the US industry better understands that the quality of a product is dependent on the quality of the process that produces it, the question for software developers may be, "just how much dependency?" Problems of poor cost and schedule estimation, unresponsive computer departments, high maintenance costs for existing systems are just some examples that should be thought of as quality problems. Even time-to-market, or speed of application development can be thought of as a quality problem, since a higher quality software development process would eliminate redundant effort, and minimize rework due to errors. These are all problems that might be solved by improving the process of software development.

To show how product oriented most of the software industry seems to be, it is estimated [22], that only about 10 per cent of the software development community is using any form of disciplined, structured methods for software development, and about the same percentage is using some form of CASE. More recent estimates may be closer to 15 to 20 per cent. Proponents of

CASE are now recognizing that not only the tools of software development need improvement, but also the practices surrounding their use. They say CASE can serve as an influential catalyst for change, as long as the larger cultural and methodological implications of the change are acknowledged. Slowly, the process improvement focus is growing through heightened attention to forms of structured analysis and design methodologies, life-cycle support methodologies, and object-oriented techniques.

3.3.2. *The productivity versus quality dimension*

Quality versus productivity is another continuum in the model. Companies which offered the highest quality products were equated with high production costs, long delivery times, extravagant product cost to the customer, and market appeal only to the most wealthy elite. Being "Best of Breed" was commendable, but often subject to the instability of shifting customer desires. And, by definition, very few companies could occupy such a niche. So, companies had to choose between a focus on productivity versus a focus on quality. Of course, the traditional approach has been to lean more heavily in favor of productivity, at least until more recently.

As businesses become increasingly aware that the application of information management technology can make a crucial difference in satisfying consumer/market needs, and therefore competitive position, so too does the demand to productively apply that technology. There has been a long history of attempts to get software developers and workers in general, to do more in less time. Productivity rather than quality has been emphasized. Only recently have businesses begun to yield to the understanding that the quality of goods and services produced is more important than productivity, because this increases market share, and therefore survivability and profitability. Quality is now rising in importance over productivity as a new management ethnic.

So much attention has been directed to the information management resource in the name of improved productivity. When the very nature and character of that resource remains a mystery to most managers, it is difficult to associate the ideas of improved quality with software. Why worry about the quality of software when it does not seem to be produced or maintained fast enough?

To properly answer this question requires more discussion than can be offered here. But one of the first clues comes from looking at the definitions of productivity and quality. If productivity is an efficiency measure, (quantity of output divided by the amount of resources used), then quality is an effectiveness measure, which by its very nature has a subjective, customer orientation.

The concern with an effectiveness measure is to make sure the right thing is being done, rather than only being concerned with doing it right. Although data processing organizations are working harder to find out how they can become more customer oriented, they have been hampered by both a lack of business knowledge as well as an overwhelming need to master an extremely complex technology.

Although both productivity and quality are difficult to measure, quality poses the larger challenge to the data processing professional. Efficiency measures do not count for very much if what is being delivered is the wrong solution.

For example, many studies indicate that a significant number of software development projects are abandoned midstream; the completed applications never get used, or are used for a less than expected short duration and then abandoned. Most data processing organizations today do not even know how many of the application systems they have built are really being used. This kind of wasted effort far outweighs the so-called productivity improvements currently sought from CASE or other technology-based automation efforts. So, the new quality improvement initiatives can significantly decrease waste, which in turn improves productivity. Productivity is a by-product of quality improvement, and can only be attained through quality improvement.

But what is quality? Does it just refer to product "goodness?" Quality is a characteristic of customer needs and desires. That is not to say quality can only be defined by the customer, for if that were true, where would fresh innovations come from that pose new possibilities? Quality is defined by the joint, reciprocal transaction between supplier and customer. Each must equitably listen to the other.

However, quality as an abstract ideal does not exist alone. It is connected to the other dimensions of the Business Improvement Maturity Model (see Fig. 2). One of the lessons learned from the Japanese is that product quality is not as dependent on the ability of the individual worker, as it is on the quality of the environment that worker is in, the quality of the raw materials he is given, the quality of the tools and machinery he is given, the knowledge he possesses about the materials, methods, and tools, and the work methods which he uses.

Collectively these things comprise what is termed the process of production. The definition of a process is the combination of resources and resource trans-

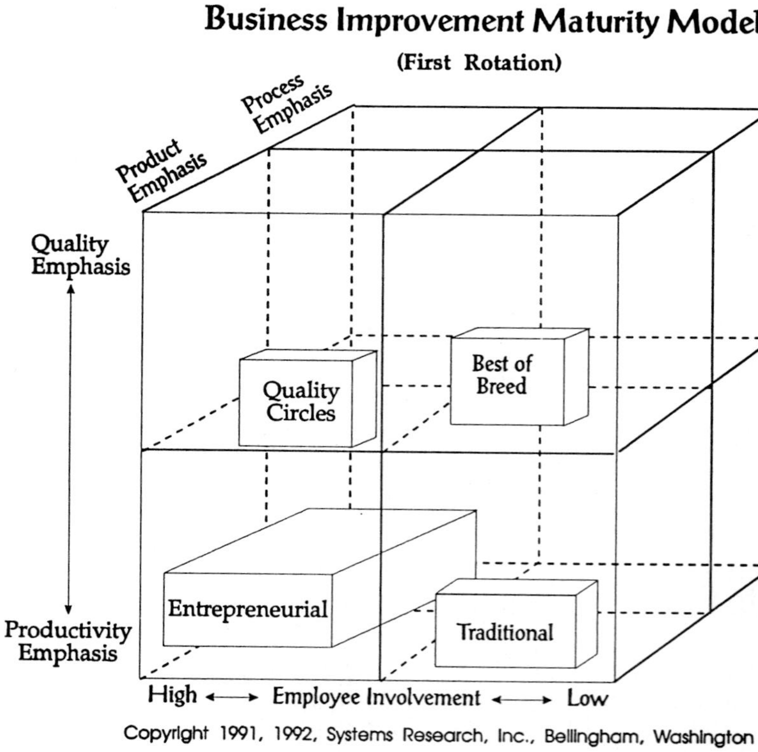

Fig. 2. BIMM, first rotation.

formation that are repeatable. Processes are hierarchical; there are smaller processes contained within larger processes. So it is possible to look at processes in organizations at many levels. The trouble is, due to the high "intellectual content" of the system development process, most software developers believe the process is "invisible," "creative," and impossible to make explicit to others.

The new quality improvement ethic is only beginning to be passed along to the data processing organization from the operating business units. Unnoticed by most individuals in the data processing profession, new principles of management are being adopted at a very rapid rate by higher levels of corporate management. In time, these business units will come knocking at the door of data processing management, asking that these values receive attention. Already, we are seeing the beginnings of this trend [23].

3.3.3. *The employee empowerment dimension*

Then, another family of approaches acknowledging the restrictiveness of the authoritarian, hierarchical, bureaucratic organizational structure, came into being, all which can be roughly labeled as "entrepreneurial." Theory X versus Theory Y management, getting decentralized business units to act as profit and loss centers, flattening the management hierarchy, engendering a more participative work culture, fostering innovation—all of these are examples of how companies tried to improve through higher employee involvement. Therefore, another continuum or dimension of the model involves the extent of focus on employee involvement as an improvement strategy.

Employee empowerment is a current, popular, management term which is terribly misunderstood, but essential to tapping the improvement potential of an entire workforce. Basically, employee empowerment is the exercise of authority and the ability to make decisions, take initiative, or take "routine" action as low in the organization or as close to the customer as possible. This does not mean "power to the people" in an unmanaged fashion in which all control is delegated to lower ranks. First, it means allowing employees at all levels to take the initiative for those matters of a more detailed nature that does not require management attention. Second, it means allowing employees to act responsibly in a program framework of continuous improvement which establishes ground rules and mechanisms for communication, team problem solving, measurement, and team recognition. Third, it means providing the education and training necessary for personal mastery of the knowledge and skills to achieve superior job performance. Fourth, it means instilling a set of values towards quality improvement that is more than an afterthought or mere contractual requirement, but is internalized into the work culture and becomes natural behavior.

According to Willem Roelandts, V. P. and General Manager of Network Systems at the Hewlett-Packard Company, "Empowerment of employees is a cultural question ... It cannot be buzzword or an idea that a few progressive people have; it has to be part of the company's vision of who they are, in everyone's mind ... You can't have empowerment unless people know there is not a penalty for trying and failing. The penalty should come for failing and not abandoning what made you fail." [24]

Already, major changes in attitudes towards workers are taking place. Where once workers rights were represented by unions, now workers are represented by attorneys. Where management conduct was once a prerogative, now much of it is considered intolerably abusive [25].

Knowing when and what kind of change is necessary or tolerable may require a new set of guiding principles. Perhaps through a greater understanding of the process of change itself, individuals and organizations may be able to better judge which changes are tolerable and necessary, as well as to increase their capacity for change. In improving the receptivity to change, the good news is that there is a way to avoid the dysfunctionality which ensues from "future shock." As intractable as the issues surrounding change seem to be, we believe there are exciting prospects for a solution. A number of interesting patterns among CASE users have emerged; we have studied what other industries have been doing and we feel there is real promise. Bringing together principles and techniques from industrial engineering and a branch of behavioral science called organizational development, a whole new perspective for managing change has emerged, a new context for technology transfer.

For example, studies conducted by ODR, Inc. [26], an organizational development research and consulting firm, has shown that change initiatives fail for many reasons, including:

1. Management was only concerned with the change when negative reactions were obvious or inevitable.
2. Management could not decide when special implementation planning was required.
3. Management approached change as an event rather than a process and had a low tolerance for ambiguity.
4. Management's orchestration of key roles of change assumed that issuing directives were synonymous with successful implementation.
5. Management failed to demonstrate strong commitment by playing an active, visible part in sponsoring the change.
6. Management approached resistance as an unexplainable force that mysteriously affects people, rather than understanding it to be a natural human reaction to disruption.
7. Management assumed "change agents" could deal with any implementation problem that would arise without special training.

3.3.4. *One-dimensional moves*

For each of the major improvement approaches mentioned above, "Best of Breed," "Time and Motion," and "Entrepreneurial," movement away from the traditional model is one-dimensional; it exercises the application of only one aspect of improvement, whether it be higher quality awareness, more engineering-like attention to process, or a human factors approach either intentionally or unintentionally encouraging a more participative and motivated work force.

Unfortunately, most of the one-dimensional approaches had limited success. The early time-and-motion studies by Taylor did nothing but infuriate and alienate workers. Operations research two decades later introduced formal reasoning and quantitative tools, but met with similar results only on a larger scale; both management and workers were infuriated, and even more alienated by the sterility of the so-called scientific approaches. Operations Research as the "new savior" discipline pretty much fell out of vogue in the latter part of the 60's. Companies following these highly process oriented approaches generally reverted back to a focus on product and productivity under the traditional, authoritative, hierarchical organizational structure. So there is generally a persistent reversion back to the traditional model (see Fig. 1).

So too with companies who pursued entrepreneurial approaches. Entrepreneurial approaches contained the seeds of failure from the beginning; as the entrepreneurial organization grew, its old lines of communication informal relationships began to increasingly fade in favor of more formal, bureaucratic structures it originally abhorred. The entrepreneurial model is more feasible for smaller scale companies, but as they grow, the communication required for high employee involvement causes time delays which are often impractical to remain efficient and competitive. Securely in the hands of a few owners, relatively high self-determination and autonomy goes out the window in favor of greater revenues and profitability. Along with power, employee involvement also goes out the window of decision-making, which then puts such organizations squarely back into the traditional model. Again, there is a reversion back to the traditional model.

So-called "Best of Breed" organizations can only move up or down on the continuum of quality versus productivity. Either they are or they are not best of breed, either by management intent or by market acceptance. By definition, only one company can occupy that tenuous position. In either case, Best of Breed types of organizations hardly represent a business improvement strategy at all. But indeed it became so de facto for many companies, because occupying the number one position in any given industry generally causes them to fail to see the importance of implementing any improvement strategy. The Best of Breed approach can blind companies to having any strategy for improvement. So the Best of Breed group really pursues a strategy of no strategy. They

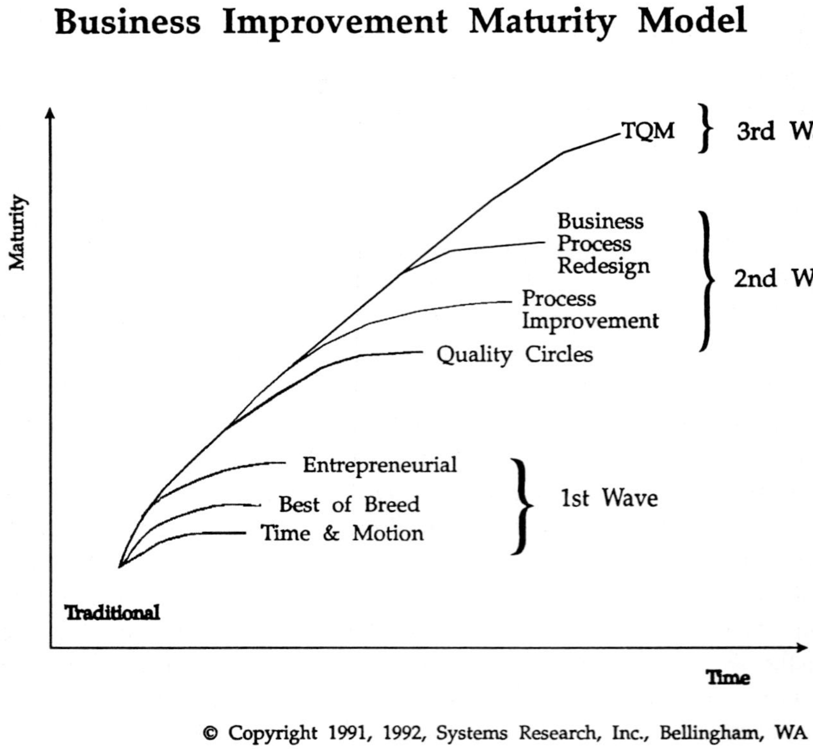

Fig. 3. Business improvement wave model.

rely on improvement by accident or high ego, either from their management or engineering or sales. And once again, like the previous one-dimensional moves, there is generally a reversion back to the traditional model.

Another one-dimensional improvement strategy, cost reduction methods, almost always have a predominantly process focus, productivity emphasis, and very low employee involvement. A favorite venue for management consultants, very often cost reduction methods are couched in quality improvement language, and as such, they are used to help reduce waste. The important difference in cost reduction methods between a single dimensional move and a two-dimensional move is whether the cost reductions are aimed at eliminating cost on a one-time basis or the systematic removal of chronic waste. If it is the latter, then the cost reduction method is more of a two-dimensional move.

Why are these efforts generally so unsuccessful? Why are they popular for such relatively short durations of time? In light of the Business Improvement Maturity Model, it is easier to arrive at some interpretations. Notice that each of these approaches moves in a one-dimensional fashion. Time-and-Motion approaches move only on the product-process continuum. Best of Breed only moves along the productivity-quality continuum. Entrepreneurial only moves along the employee involvement continuum. These are all one-dimensional moves and constitute "First Wave" business improvement (see Fig. 3), an improvement strategy that does not abide by the principle of multi-dimensional change and, therefore, is not a sustainable improvement approach.

3.3.5. *Two-dimensional moves*

More recently, we have seen the adoption of the new quality ethic coupled with employee involvement, called quantity circles (see Fig. 2). This was a radical step forward because it moved the traditional organization in two of the fundamental dimensions simultaneously: both the productivity-quality dimension and the employee involvement dimension. This appeared to be proven in practice in Japan, but like Just in Time Manufacturing (JIT), the full context and meaning did not reach U.S. shores. So the deficiencies were numerous.

Quality circles were generally assigned to trivial problems. Quality circles picked problems independently of one another. Participation was voluntary, so the perception of those who got involved in quality circles was "those are the discontents,"—a stigma of a short career life in most conformance and control oriented organizations. Employees were not really trained properly to describe improvements in management language, but worst of all, management would decide whether the improvement should be implemented or not. This occurred for many reasons, but mainly because management was looking for low cost product improvement suggestions, not process improvement suggestions. Although the Quality Circle was supposed to move organizations further in the employee empowerment dimension, it met with a new kind of failure (see Fig. 4.). Not only did quality circles fail, but it taught employees to be highly cautious about management overtures to encourage their participation.

It is too early to declare success or failure regarding the more recent approaches which bring high innovation to fundamental business processes, sometimes called business process redesign. Usually these approaches are administered by outside consultants, advisors, or a special group of insiders charged with making radical changes. There is little to no intent for bottom-up, employee-inspired involvement. Those who are involved consider themselves highly elite subject-matter experts who are the most capable and in the best position to make sweeping recommendations. Because their Hamiltonian overtones are incongruent with more common Jeffersonian political values, it may suffer the same kind of short-term success seen with other improvement approaches. But then, it may be a short-term necessity in order to put out raging fires which threaten to consume an organization. Still, those improvement approaches that make some positive movement on the employee involvement dimension will probably enjoy longer term success.

These two improvement approaches, Quality Circles and Process Improvement, move in two-dimensions simultaneously, and constitute "Second Wave" business improvement (see Fig. 4).

Challenges with Quality Circles

- Inadequate employee empowerment
  - Autocratic rather than participative environment
  - Employee involvement as a motivational tool
  - Lack of employee training
- Assignment to trivial problems
- Teams pick problems independently
- Participation is voluntary
- Quality Circles do not do causal analysis of specific defects but pursue problems perceived by the circle to be important
- Limited to changing what its members are able to change
- Implementation is usually done on a members own time
- Management "funding" for QC activities is usually inconsistent and may evaporate over time

Fig. 4. Challenges with quality circles.

3.3.6. *Three-dimensional moves*

The most recent and also misunderstood improvement approach is generally termed Total Quality Management or TQM. Going by several other names, such as Continuous Process Improvement, Continuous Quality Improvement, or most recently, Total Quality Improvement, this approach radically redefines management thinking on a number of fronts. As shown in the Business Improvement Maturity Model, TQM can be characterized by a simultaneous focus on the process, on quality, and high employee involvement. With such a focus, organizations move in three dimensions simultaneously from the traditional model, which constitute "Third Wave" business improvement.

Although the operating premise of this model is that failure results from one and two dimensional moves, and success only comes from three dimensional moves, there are some caveats that interprets the potential for improvement success in degrees of advocacy of the new dimensions.

For example, many organizations are simply not ready to buy-in to the new "religion" of quality. It is not all that clear that productivity is a by-product of improved quality, and that costs of production decrease. It still seems that higher quality product has higher costs of production. It still seems that tremendous inefficiencies accrue from high employee involvement and all the communication that it requires. It still seems that the product is what counts and all you have to do is hire the best workers to produce it; what is the process anyway and what can be done about it? The objections are too numerous to all list here.

Nevertheless, TQM represents an ideal state that can eventually be attained. Walking before running has always been sage advice, and there are a number of steps which must be taken, even before the staunchest quality advocates say it is possible to apply *all* their methods and techniques. Even when the goal of a full TQM implementation is presented to an organization by its management, the reality of implementation occurs in steps and stages.

For software developers, getting started depends on a number of factors relating to the maturity of their organization and the type of software development activity. For an internal MIS (management information systems) organization providing computer services to the rest of the corporation or agency, a customer satisfaction survey leading to the formation of quality improvement teams may be the best approach. For a third-party, independent software developer where time to market is of paramount importance, establishing process improvement teams with the goal of improving product launch coordination between engineering, marketing, and production as well as reducing cycle time may be the best strategy.

In almost all instances, few companies are stepping up to the plate with the goal of hitting a home run for TQM implementation: TQM is first viewed as a means towards some specific, tactical end, such as doing a better job of adopting advanced CASE technologies. In these cases, the Business Improvement Model can be used to diagnose which dimension is the most limiting for the successful adoption of improvement initiatives, and direct resources to remedy that deficiency.

3.3.7. *Business improvement maturity model as a diagnostic tool*

Every organization's work culture varies to the extent they hold quality in high esteem, actively practice process improvement, and do both or either of these in the context of high employee involvement/empowerment. Increasing the degree to which each of these dimensions is followed suggests an organization specific strategy.

For example, if an organization has worked conscientiously on process and procedural improvements with involvement from all employees, then what may be relatively deficient is a focus on quality. It may be very difficult to conceive of an organization who has made the prior accomplishments without at least an implicit appreciation for quality. Indeed, by the definition of the Business Improvement Maturity Model, higher one-dimensional accomplishments are highly unlikely. There are strong forces to revert back to the traditional model. Therefore, higher levels of process focus accomplishments are probably unlikely without attention to quality. So consider in this example how this organization has made its operations quite efficient, but has lost its customer focus, or needs to increase its customer focus. Through the use of diagnostic instruments which measure the relative strengths of organizations according to each of the three dimensions of the Business Improvement Maturity Model, the weakest dimension would be identified and questions which can point to specific, critical deficiencies.

Or as another example, consider an organization which has enthusiastically embraced the quality ethic. Maybe their management has read a book which presents the pursuit of quality both as laudable and at no cost. Maybe their management has gone to a seminar which has galvanized them into action regarding quality because of the shocking losses due to waste and reuse their accountants never told them about. Their workforce has heard and seen the speeches, exhortations, and memos. By now, you might have a management "all pumped up with nothing to lift." Their muscle of enthusiasm has increased but cannot be practically applied to do anything useful. Why? Because the tools for process improvement and/or employee involvement are lacking. Far too many companies fall into this category, and it is little wonder why their efforts to build improvement infrastructures quickly run out of steam. The Business Improvement Maturity Model show this relative imbalance and suggests questions which can lead to a more balanced improvement strategy; such as training teams in the use of process mapping, process stabilization, and process engineering, as well as being encouraged by management to use these tools. With these tools, employees could actually do something rather than merely feel embittered at their helplessness and the poor quality made all the more manifest because of the heightened attention given to it by management.

These are just a few examples of how the Business Improvement Maturity Model can be used as a diagnostic tool for creating an implementation strategy for continuous improvement in an organization. In the next section, suggestions are made for how to begin the broader task of implementing a continuous improvement system.

4. Establishing the New Context

4.1. *The broader relevance of continuous improvement*

Certainly, it is hard not to generally adopt some of the new quality ethic. Catchy platitudes such as "doing it right the first time" or "zero defects" have become well-known slogans of the quality improvement movement. However, not only can these slogans become tiring, but software developers already feel buried under the demands of rapidly changing technology and new business requirements. Information management and software development seems more like a "hit-and-miss" research and development activity characterized by constant exploration of the unknown and unfamiliar, than repetitive, manageable activity where TQM has been traditionally applied.

Also, there are strong pressures for outside package solutions, outsourcing downsizing, rightsizing, and an ever-increasing share of computing performed on an individual or group level on personal computers. In the face of these pressures TQM may look like another diversion which could dilute an already scarce resource, diminish the Information Systems function, or even depersonalize software production.

But TQM is not a mere diversion. Although TQM applied to information technology management and software development is still very much in its infant stages, the mandate of the business climate clearly says TQM is becoming mainstream. There are many forms of TQM being applied in U.S. corporations today, but few have specially applied them to information technology management.

According to the Business Improvement Maturity Model, TQM means working in three fundamental dimensions simultaneously: quality improvement, process improvement, and employee involvement. Working in these three dimensions simultaneously is critical for improvement to be sustainable. The process of improvement is like a chemical reaction: unless all the necessary conditions are present in terms of pressure, temperature, etc., and the right chemical ingredients are together in the right proportions, the reaction will not take place. A lot of business improvement approaches in the past have been heavy on the "temperature and pressure" but have failed to bring all the necessary ingredients together in the right proportions. Technology transfer would be more successful if accomplished in this context of continuous improvement and management of change principles.

4.2. *Preparing for the new context*

Practically speaking, few organizations are really prepared to make the investment in a continuous improvement infrastructure, although it could also be said that few can afford not to. To get started, there are a number of steps that can be taken without having to adopt a formal program and gain widespread commitment. It is always best to work with what you have, rather than always looking for what is missing (resources, management commitment, etc.) as an excuse for inactivity. Obviously there may be major obstacles to attain the ideals for improvement that are being sought. But it is also surprising to take inventory of what does exist and find how unexploited and unleveraged those items have been. These steps are outlined in the following subsections and shown in Fig. 5: Preparing for the new context for technology transfer.

Few, if any organizations, even have the vision to approach the implementation of continuous improvement as an infrastructural device. Instead, they are viewed as a "program," possibly independent and competitive with other programs. With all the attention being placed on quality, Total Quality Management, and other organizational improvement approaches, few of their practitioners have really thought out or had experience with service oriented organizations, particularly managers of information technology. The rush to apply the nouveau techniques like the Shewhart Cycle, House of Quality, statistical control charts, Ishikawa Fishbone Diagrams, and so forth has obscured the need to first apply some simple industrial engineering. It is highly important for any organization interested in applying the new quality principles to not get overly impressed in these techniques without adequately preparing themselves. Here is the fundamental industrial engineering that needs to be applied: few information technology management organizations have been able to sufficiently stabilize their processes, understand at the simplest level possible how they work, or achieve reasonable levels of repeatability and predictability. Applying statistical process control techniques to unstable processes is sheer disaster, but the current generation of software metricists are rushing headlong to do so. Process stabilization is a prerequisite to the establishment of a continuous improvement environment. There are no shortcuts. This is the bitter pill that may significantly slow down technology adoption in favor of a process stabilization emphasis. This is a bitter pill few organizations are prepared to swallow, unless they better appreciate the nature of organizational change.

Preparing for the New Context for Technology Transfer for Information Technology Managers

- Exploit Known Process Conformance Mechanisms
- Exploit Known Feedback Mechanisms
- Undo Damaging Practices
- Define Your Software Development Process
- Obtain Executive Sponsorship for the New Context

Fig. 5. Preparing for the new context.

4.2.1. *Exploit known process conformance mechanisms*

Process conformance mechanisms are those which insure that the process, to the extent it is understood, is actually followed in practice. Project management skills and tools are almost always underdeveloped and underutilized. Project managers still find themselves making unrealistic estimates, caught beetween the politics of managers or customers who do not want to hear the bad news, and self-preservation. This self-preservation ethic becomes an even larger demon as the project goes on, and news regarding missed deadlines, unmet milestones, and budget overruns are creatively redefined or delayed.

Then, too, the deployment of information technology systems to customers has generally been a "black box" to the customer. They generally have no idea of what the process is for how systems are developed. They just expect to see a finished product. But if the development team can communicate their process to the customer, then communication improves, expectations are more realistic, challenges are faced more rationally, and conformance to proven methods generally improves.

4.2.2. *Exploit known feedback mechanisms*

If a system has no feedback, it has a high chance of going out of control. There are many well-known feedback mechanisms in software development, few of which are put into practice by today's software engineers. Post implementation reviews, phase reviews, structured walkthroughs, are some, just to name a few. Knowledge transfer through a Development Center is a way to observe, record, and distribute information about software development.

4.2.3. *Undo damaging practices*

There are many practices which seriously undermine any attempt at sustained improvement. The remedies are: (1) Provide training to employees when they need it, (2) discontinue the mere use of slogans, exhortations, etc., (3) discontinue the use of software metrics to measure merely the people, their performance, or the product, (4) change the employee annual review process, merit system, etc., to recognize contributions to the improvement of process capability and capacity, (5) get management to "walk the talk" of quality, (6) improve the work culture through participative management, increase trust, and decrease fear.

Although some of these points may seem enormous in magnitude and scope, they will only have to be addressed during the course of a formal continuous improvement program if not before. Again, exerting some activity in this direction can do much to properly assess the feasibility of establishing a continuous improvement infrastructure.

4.2.4. *Define your software development process*

Without a doubt, this is a highly difficult, complex activity that seems to have little intrinsic benefit. But those organizations which have taken the time to do so, at least at a high level, have discovered incongruities, inconsistencies, nonvalue-added activities, and so forth that required very minor changes which resulted in large paybacks. It is always a source of astonishment for a group of software developers to see, graphically laid out in a concrete form for all to see, how their group performs their function. Just the clarification from doing so begins to ease numerous communication difficulties, hand-off problems, interface problems, and integration challenges. This is the most fundamental step for process stabilization.

4.2.5. *Obtain executive sponsorship for the new context*

Sponsorship needs to exist for whatever scale or scope of implementation. There are some who advocate that only an enterprise-wide improvement program can be effective, sometimes called the "top-down" approach. There are those who are not necessarily against a "top-down" approach, but who claim that efforts inspired from lower ranks in small groups can also be effective. These "bottom-up" efforts are often necessary to "prove the principles" and their small but marked successes can inspire the rest of an organization to do likewise. Sometimes, one group's success within a larger organization can invoke jealousy, and the "not-invented-here" syndrome, thereby resisting the application of the other group's approach. On balance, the quality movement has attained sufficient stature and momentum that this latter situation is less likely to occur. When an opportunity arises to secure sponsorship, at whatever level or scope, take it. Do the best with what you have.

4.3. *Establishing the TQM context*

It is not enough to cheerlead the workforce in understanding the new quality philosophy, explaining what TQM is. How TQM is to be implemented must also be thoughtfully planned. Particularly with the enthusiasm of senior management for the new quality thinking, it can be all to easy for them to escape the operational realities of what it will really take to make TQM work successfully. They tend to make a tacit delegation of such responsibilities to the workforce, who generally react with bewilderment and frustration. By properly planning the "how" of TQM—the methodology used in making TQM happen—the risk of a failed implementation is considerably lessened.

Too many organizations take an “ala carte” approach to TQM. They pick one or two TQM techniques and introduce them to the workforce. Although some short-term successes can be achieved, which do serve to offer proof of the principles of improvement, such attempts can also build barriers which make subsequent improvement efforts more difficult.

For example, without a methodology:

- The techniques picked are often the easiest but does not produce the highest impact. Quality improvement becomes perceived as interesting but trivial, anecdotal rather than relevant.
- The techniques picked are incomplete unto themselves. Merely instructing a workforce in the use of various statistical control techniques, for example, without a team structure which permits them to improve processes, can lead to significant frustration.
- Without a context for the techniques, including a clear vision for the quality improvement effort, which directly relates to the business plan and/or organizational mission, as well as specific quality improvement goals, the quality improvement program can be misinterpreted as a scheme for work-speedup, a political ploy, or irritating pressuring by a zealous few. Even if these misinterpretations do not occur, the quality improvement effort in time will lose direction and focus, thereby putting the program up for grabs by special interest groups or individuals, who may or may not be popular with the organization at large.
- Some TQM techniques depend upon prior mastery of other TQM techniques. For example, over a decade ago, JIT (Just-in-time) manufacturing techniques from Japan were advocated in the U.S., but largely failed. Although the idea of zero inventories and the benefit of nonproductive capital being tied up unnecessarily was appealing, JIT was unsuccessful because companies had not mastered the principles of continuous process improvement which created better synchronization of material flows. In other words, US managers wanted to go straight to the benefits without understanding the hard work which had to preceed the attainment of those benefits.
- Likewise, many companies try to jump to advanced TQM techniques such as Quality Function Deployment, Hoshin Planning, or Business Process Innovation without having mastered the fundamentals of team approaches, making decisions based on data, or having even stabilized their existing processes. The consequence is a failed or seriously flawed implementation whose fault is directed at the techniques, rather than the implementation strategy.

- Quality improvement is a long-term process. Without a suitable architecture for implementation, the improvement effort can appear to the workforce as inconsistent, incoherent, disruptive, and confusing. It is important to do as thorough a job of planning as possible, so that roles and responsibilities are made clear.

So, the benefits of a methodology for implementation of quality improvement are numerous, rather than attempting a relatively unplanned application of a set of techniques. Therefore, a methodology:

- Establishes clear purpose, direction, and expectations.
- Increases cooperation and team involvement when everyone knows the rules.
- Lessens the risk of workforce resistance to the improvement effort.
- Builds upon previous efforts so that skills acquired are cumulative.
- Provides a standard of comparison which helps keep the improvement effort on track and not diluted by diversions.
- Provides a means of evaluating progress directly attributed to the quality improvement effort, rather than relying only on anecdotal and subjective evaluations.

5. Conclusion

Just as getting information management technology more directly into the hands of business users increases the effectiveness of that technology, so too will getting the knowledge of organizational development and change management techniques into the hands of data processing professionals. The rapid rate of the introduction of new technology creates increasing demands for groups to reorganize in different ways. But as information technology management is becoming the responsibility of all business users, not just a few data processing professionals, the principles of continuous improvement become even more significant.

Efficiency measures are now seen to be very short-sighted in comparison with effectiveness measures. Effectiveness demands an increased customer orientation. Profitability is tied more to market share, rather than efficiency of production, and attainment of market share is accomplished through improved quality. Total quality commitment is almost becoming synonymous with teamwork and training.

Despite the "new wave" of enthusiasm for improved quality, even the most critical skeptic in data processing needs to come to terms with this changing attitude and take a position. It is easy to be adverse to trendy movements, but is there a real message, a real lesson that can be learned? If nothing else, we must agree that competitive survival will depend on the ability for human groups to manage very rapid change.

Companies should approach CASE implementation from a holistic viewpoint. CASE magnifies shortcomings in the existing software development process and poses unique characteristics which require additional transformation of the software development process. Without the capability for continuous improvement, CASE technology can actually be detrimental rather than beneficial. Companies which pay attention to this new context for CASE have been more successful. Without such a context, bringing in CASE is like "putting old wine into new bottles," it just does not work. Instituting teamwork and an organization-wide program for continuous improvement will provide the right context. In turn, the software development process cannot undergo significant transformation without paying attention to the human response and managing organizational change.

References

1. G. Boone, "CASE and its challenge for change," Publication No. CB-070889, CASE Research Corporation, Bellevue, Washington, August 28, 1989 (now available from Ernst & Young, Center for Information Technology and Strategy, Boston, Massachussetts).
2. G. Boone, "CASE and its challenge for change," *Int. J. Softw. Eng. Knowl. Eng.* **1**, 2 (1991) 151–163.
3. W. Humphrey, *Managing the Software Process* (Addison-Wesley, 1989).
4. R. Grady and D. Caswell, *Software Metrics: Establishing A Company-Wide Program* (Prentice Hall, 1987).
5. Some of the more notable experts in software metrics, such as Capers Jones, Howard Rubin, or Thomas McCabe, had more specialized intent with metrics, than to measure the process from a process improvement viewpoint. See, for example, Jones, Capers, *Programming Productivity* (McGraw Hill, 1986).
6. M. A. Cusumano, *Japan's Software Factories* (Oxford University Press, 1991).
7. Terms adopted from John Zachman, by personal conversation with John Zachman, Zachman International, Glendale, California.
8. "Management's New Guru's," *Business Week* (August 31, 1992) p. 44.
9. P. Senge, *The Fifth Discipline* (Doubleday, 1990).
10. G. H. Boone and V. Merlyn, "CASE classification model," CASE Bulletin No. CB-050389, May 27, 1989, CASE Research Corporation, Bellevue, Washington (now available from Ernst & Young, Center for Information Technology and Strategy, Boston, Massachussetts).

11. G. Boone and V. Merlyn, *The CASE Experience: Annual CASE Survey 1988*, CASE Research Corporation, Bellevue, WA, 1988 (now available from Ernst & Young, Center for Information Technology and Strategy, Boston, Massachussetts).
12. "Making teamwork work in system development: an interview with Randall Jensen, Chief Scientist, Hughes Aircraft Ground Systems Group," *System Development*, Applied Computer Research, Phoenix, Arizona (August 1992).
13. J. Martin, *Application Development Without Programmers* (Prentice Hall, 1982).
14. A. Toffler, *The Third Wave* (Bantam Books, 1980).
15. R. G. Mays *et al.*, "Experiences with defect prevention," *IBM Syst. J.* **29**, 1 (1990).
16. W. E. Deming, *Out of the Crisis*, Massachussetts Institute of Technology, Cambridge, MA (1982).
17. G. H. Boone, V. Merlyn and R. E. Dobratz, *The Second Annual Report on CASE*, CASE Research Corporation, Bellevue, WA, 1990 (now available from Ernst & Young, Center for Information Technology and Strategy, Boston, Massachussetts).
18. E. M. Rogers, *Diffusion of Innovations*, 3rd ed. (The Free Press, 1983).
19. G. Boone and V. Merlyn, "Getting the process right," *Computerworld* (June 10, 1991).
20. G. Boone, "Continuous process improvement: the new context for progress," *People & Systems Conference*, September 11–13, (1991), Boston, MA.
21. G. Boone, "The applicability of TQM to software development," *Proc. 1st Int. Conf. on Software Quality*, October 7, 1991, American Society for Quality Control, Milwaukee, Wisconsin.
22. See Ref. 11.
23. Personal discussion with V. Merlyn, Director for the TQM Multi-Client Study, Ernst & Young, Center for Information Technology and Strategy, Boston, MA.
24. *Computerworld* (July 1, 1991) p. 8.
25. "Good Bye Mr. Dithers," *Business Week* (September 21, 1991) p. 52.
26. V. Merlyn, D. Conner and G. Boone, "Winners and losers: management's role in orchestrating the change that comes with CASE," Working Paper No. 7, February 1992, Center for Information Technology Strategy, Ernst & Young, Boston, MA.

PROJECT MANAGEMENT UTILIZING AN ADVANCED CASE ENVIRONMENT

JOHN M. BAKER

Software Engineering Strategies, 327 Lochside Dr.,
Cary, North Carolina, 27511, USA

ABSTRACT

An advanced CASE environment would dramatically improve the analytic activities of a project manager. Management by exception will become more effective as the CASE environment generates warnings of abnormal situations. Participatory management will become more effective because, while team members will be able to create their own work tasks, the manager will be able to more accurately review the activities against plan.

1. Introduction

Managing a project involves several activities including:

- Estimation
- Determining resources
- Tasking the resources
- Controlling tasks
- Managing trade-offs of schedule, resource, and quality over the development process.

The management must perform these activities with incomplete information, and continuously adjust the project due to unforeseen events that may impact the object. Software projects are particularly difficult to manage because the inherent capability of software to be modified encourages change during the development process.

Several models for the management of software projects have been developed (e.g., Waterfall [1] and Spiral [2] models). These models attempt to break the activities of the development team down into manageable units that are linked to each other by sequential dependencies. Tools such as the PERT and

Grant charts help managers define and visualize these dependencies and determine the resultant completion date based on critical path analysis. However, experience managers recognize that these models do not accurately reflect the natural tendency of developers to iterate rapidly between many small jobs during the development process [3]. Many managers are faced with the dilemma of keeping two sets of project books, the official PERT chart and what is really happening on a daily basis between team members. One significant reason for this discrepancy is that we do not have an effective means of capturing what each member of a project team is actually doing. Weekly time sheets or even daily diaries cannot accurately reflect reality.

This paper looks at how project management might change if:

- Every member of the project utilized a CASE-like environment to accomplish the majority of daily project activities.
- The CASE-like environment automatically captured a profile of the activities of each user.

2. Estimation

Estimation models such as COCOMO [1] or BANG [4] are used on raw units of work modified significantly by different coefficients. Unfortunately, the manager must estimate many of the coefficients. This can result in random and bias errors.

An estimation module to a CASE product could improve estimates due to the following factors:

Units of work could be based on integral products of the CASE environment. This would allow early life cycle units to be measured as compared to later life cycle units such as KLOC's. The early life cycle units would depend on the method hosted by the CASE environment. For example, in an information modeling method, entities, relationships, and attributes would be components declared during a requirements definition phase. These units would correlate to overall system effort.

The CASE product would also tend to normalize the units of work due to the consistent environment in which the work is done. This would allow more accurate comparisons of effort between projects and companies that used the same CASE environment to capture the data. The predictive models would be refined by analysis of the large set of normalized raw metrics from the group of users of this CASE environment, resulting in more accuracy.

The CASE environment would transparently capture the audit trail of individual productivity. Since the individual contribution is the most significant factor in project success or failure [5] it is imperative that the project manager is able to quantify this and track it against expectations. In order for a productivity profile to be meaningful it is necessary to capture more than keystrokes per hour. The basic unit of work would be the volume of repository units delivered. A verification and validation step must be part of the development cycle so that there is feedback on whether or not the unit of work being measured over time is acceptable. It is the volume of acceptable work per unit time that the CASE environment archives. Once a profile had been recorded it should give a manager the ability to build hypothetical teams during the planning process.

A significant cultural problem that must be overcome is the "big brother is watching you" syndrome. Can the developer profile accurately reflect the competencies of the developer? Will employees submit to a computer analyzing every keystroke? Would such a system be secure from unauthorized access and sabotage? The profiles must be reviewed periodically by the developer's manager to ensure that they agree with the manager's assessment of productivity. The employees must be involved in the decision to have their work automatically measured. In addition, the information must be protected with the same level of security as other confidential personnel records.

As DeMarco [3] points out, as soon as an employee figures out that some metric will influence their salaries then that employee will work to optimize the metric and not do what they think is necessary to build a good system. A colleague of mine was once called into his boss's office and asked why he was not working. When he replied that he thought he was working hard, the manager pulled out a computer printout that showed the activity rate on the department's mini-computer. Compared to his peers he was using the least number of CPU minutes per day. My colleague then went back to his office and wrote a small task that would activate at random intervals and do nothing.

3. Determining Resources

Resources (people, computers, facilities, etc.) would be defined in an enterprise level repository. Project managers would be able to quickly match needs to available resources and generate draft project resource plans. Trade-offs between using more people of less capability or fewer people of greater capability could be studied. Team members that have capabilities that are complementary could be matched. The profile of an individual changes based on:

- The changing experience of the individual
- The other team members whom the developer worked with
- The development and target technologies
- The business and political issues surrounding the project.

The more the new project differs from the projects upon which the productivity profile was captured the less certain that profile will be. The large number of factors that contribute to the productivity profile, the relatively small sample size (how many projects does a developer work on in his/her career?), and the non-repeating nature of many of the factors will introduce error to the productivity profile. Does this make the profile useless? No. The ability to bring together individuals with capabilities and personalities that combine into an effective team goes beyond the capability of the CASE environment. However, the data captured and the analysis provided to the project manager should significantly assist the manager in performing this job.

4. Tasking the Resources

A comparison of the traditional project management module and one that is part of an advanced CASE environment is given in Table 1.

The ability of team members to modify tasking on the official project management model is a fundamental change from the hierarchical management

Table 1.

Traditional PM tool	Advanced CASE PM
Number of tasks at start of project = n	Number of tasks as start of project = 10n
Number of tasks at end of project = 1.5n	Number of tasks at end of project = 100n
Tasks are defined by project manager	Most tasks are defined by team members
Mean task duration = m	Mean task duration = .05m
Mean number of concurrent tasks = .1n	Mean number of concurrent tasks = 30n
Effort against task is estimated by developer and then manually entered into PM tool.	Effort against task is measured by CASE PM tool and is part of repository.

philosophy used in many companies [6]. A manager's role under a participatory management style as supported by a CASE environment would be to review the tasking as it occurs and correct the conflicting activities. The ability of the CASE environment to document the existence of small units of work will more accurately reflect the project. A suggested level of granularity that would be maintained by the project management module would be as small as a half day total duration contained within a two year development project. In addition, the CASE environment would capture the activities assigned to a given task within a resolution of one minute. Thus, during a typical work day, a developer might shift between a dozen different work tasks and spend a few minutes focusing on one, jumping to another for an hour, returning to the first, etc.

5. Controlling the Tasks

When is a specific task in problem? Often on a project this is hidden from view, with slippages only announced to successive management layers when the major milestones on the official Gant chart are passed. If the tasks are broken to a fine enough level of granularity and forced through objective gating criteria such as quality peer reviews, then the manager will be able to closely monitor potential trouble spots. The manager would still have to determine what went wrong and how to correct the problem.

The CASE environment would also assist in the process of identifying abnormal situations. For example, a classic problem that occurs during a project is the issue of completeness. A manger will try to assess the completeness of various components of a project, usually by asking the responsible engineer. The inevitable response is "90 per cent complete" or some variation on that theme. Other ways in which project managers fool themselves about the completeness is the delivery of major documents signifying the completion of a project phase. If the project is scheduled to be thirty per cent done when the functional requirements document is delivered, and if the that document is actually published near the scheduled date, then obviously, the project is thirty per cent complete (*ipso facto* ...).

An alternative to completeness is stability. If one accepts the concept that a system component is never really "done", but continuous to evolve over its entire life then the stability of a component is a more useful measure of its utility to other components of the system. Stability is the trend in the changes to a component as measured over the cumulative development effort (see Fig. 1).

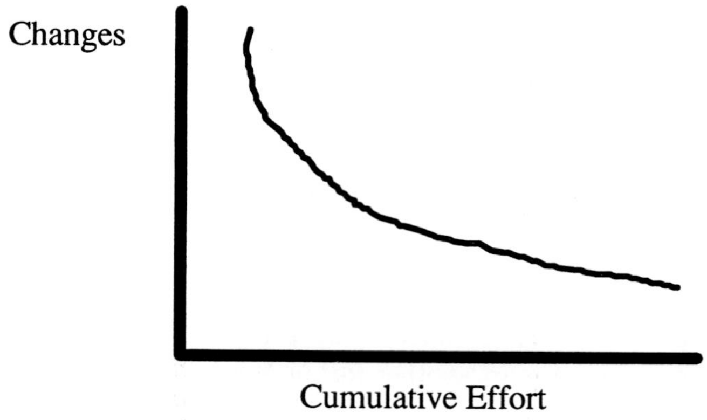

Fig. 1.

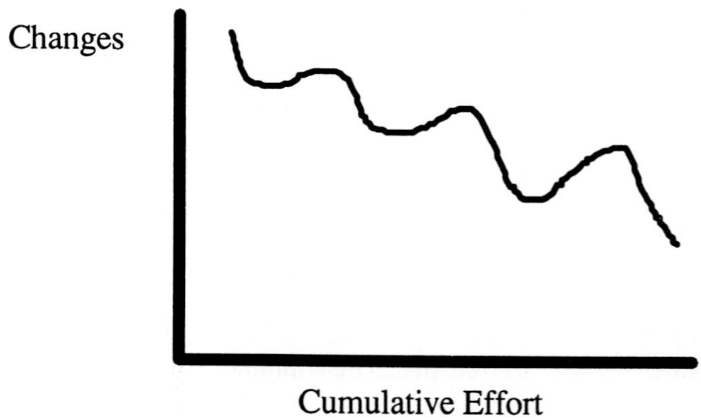

Fig. 2.

The stability shown in Fig. 1 is an idealized situation where the changes are monotonically decreasing towards zero as the component matures.

It is expected that as the project team documents more detailed information about the system, changes will be recorded based on errors detected and new features desired. This is shown in Fig. 2.

However, if the CASE environment gives a warning based on the stability given in Fig. 3 then the manager should find out why it is unstable, what is the necessary correction, and how it will impact the schedule/resources/quality.

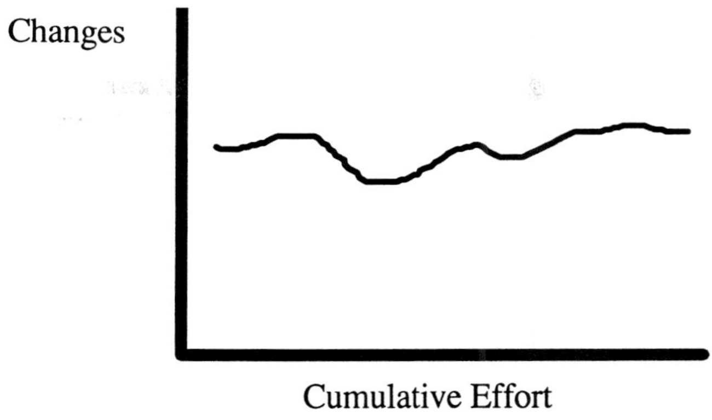

Fig. 3.

Table 2.

Type of Change	Weight
Delete due to verification error	1.0
Add due to verification error	1.2
Delete due to validation change	1.8
Modify due to verification change	2.0
Add due to validation change	2.8
Modify due to validation change	3.0

The change value for a component would be weighted by the type of change as given in Table 2.

A verification error is an inconsistency of the component based on the rules of the method. This type of error should become less likely as the CASE environment becomes more sophisticated. A validation change may come from new information, resource constraints, or a simple change of mind. The values of weight are the author's opinion and are not based on quantitative research. However, the complexity of change caused by deletion of a defect is much less than that of modifying the system due to new customer requirements. If a structured method is used that supports abstraction through encapsulation (leveling), then each primitive component would have a weighted change value equal to the sum of the components.

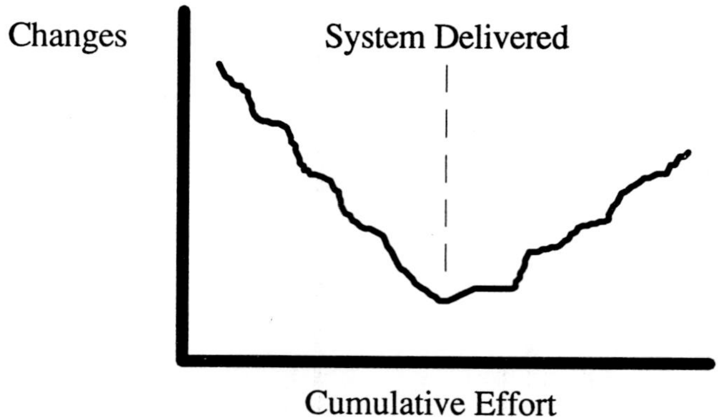

Fig. 4.

$$C_j = \sum_{i=1}^{n} C_i \qquad (1)$$

Where c_j is the change value of the jth level of abstraction and i is the number of child components at the $j+1$ level. The cumulative effort is the sum of creative and review effort spent by all people on a given component.

The smaller the component, the more likely it will be to see wider fluctuations in stability. However, the larger components (e.g., a requirements model) will tend to reflect a mean of the overall stability. A requirements model that has not reached a threshold of stability is not "complete". It is unwise to force stability by not allowing the component to be changed based on the verification and validation effort. Projects that constrain change during development to meet schedule will have a stability curve as shown in Fig. 4.

6. Managing Tradeoffs

The CASE environment would maintain the raw metrics for schedule, resource, and quality. A set of predictive models would continuously update the target estimates of schedule, resource utilization, and quality. Figure 5 shows a traditional approach to estimation of the completion date.

This stereotyped project has the following characteristics:

1. The estimates occur infrequently.
2. The estimates occur near a milestone that has slipped.

3. The estimates occur more frequently as the project nears completion.
4. All estimates are optimistic.
5. The closer to completion the more accurate the estimate.

Compare this with the predictive model that a CASE environment should provide as shown in Fig. 6. The characteristics of this project are:

1. The estimates are available in real time.

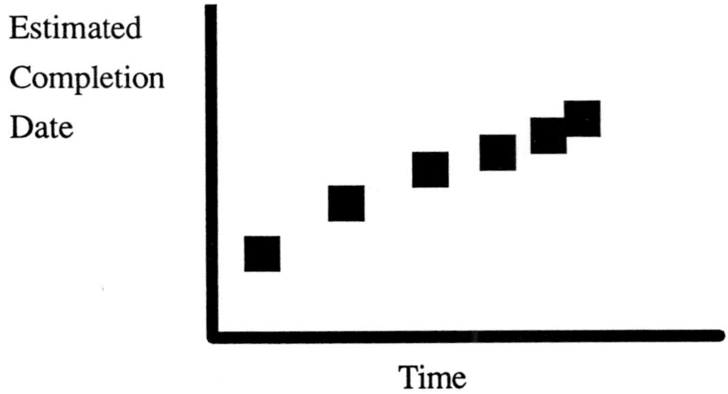

Fig. 5.

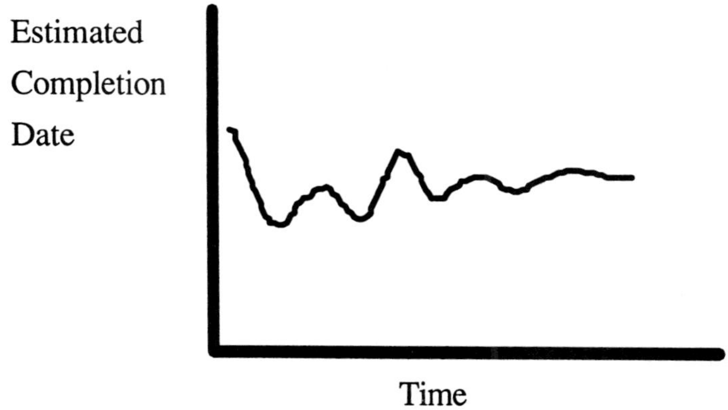

Fig. 6.

2. The estimates show both pessimistic and optimistic error compared to the actual delivered date.
3. The closer to completion the more accurate the estimate.

The correctness of the models would have to be constantly evaluated by a metrics group at the enterprise level so that more accurate estimates would be possible based on the recorded experience within the enterprise.

7. New Models of the System Development Life Cycle

If the system life cycle is patterned after the way individual developers actually succeed in delivering a product then it might be best described as opportunistic chaos. Opportunistic because developers work with the information at hand. This information may be based on preceding work or on new information coming at unanticipated times. Chaos because the number of unknowns is large. Chaos theory [7] indicates that for many systems predictive modeling is impossible due to the sensitivity of the system to the smallest initial perturbation. The systems development process may be a chaotic system.

The nature of opportunistic chaos is that individuals and teams iterate rapidly between exploration, declaration, validation, and pruning, and back to exploration across a broad front of issues. The size of the component to which this process may be applied may vary from an entire system down to primitive components of function, data, or dynamics.

The four steps are described below as applied to an arbitrarily sized component.

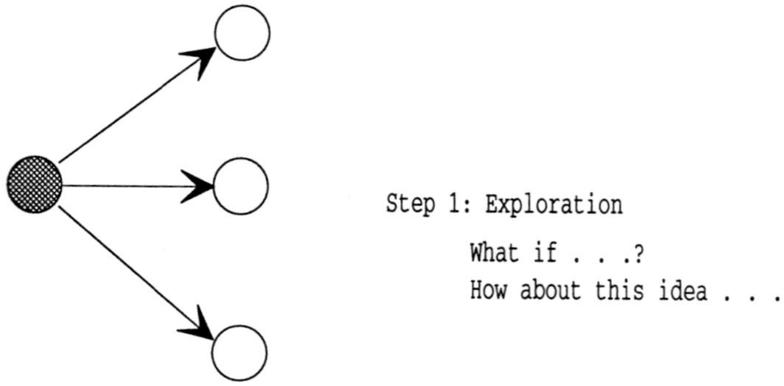

Fig. 7. Exploration.

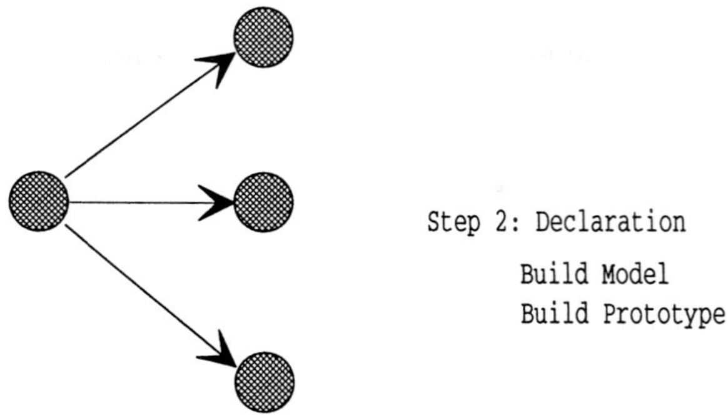

Fig. 8. Declaration.

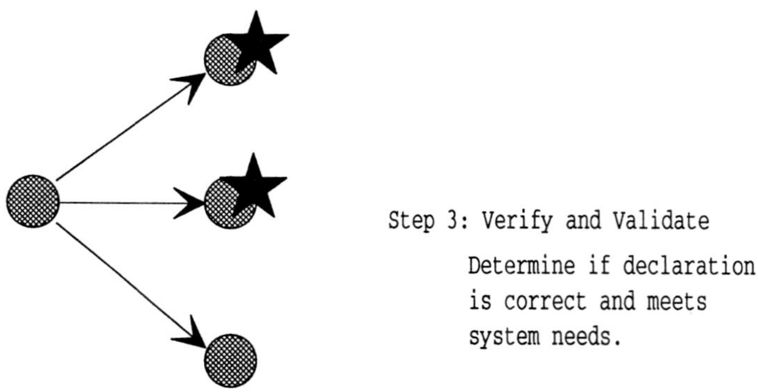

Fig. 9. Validation.

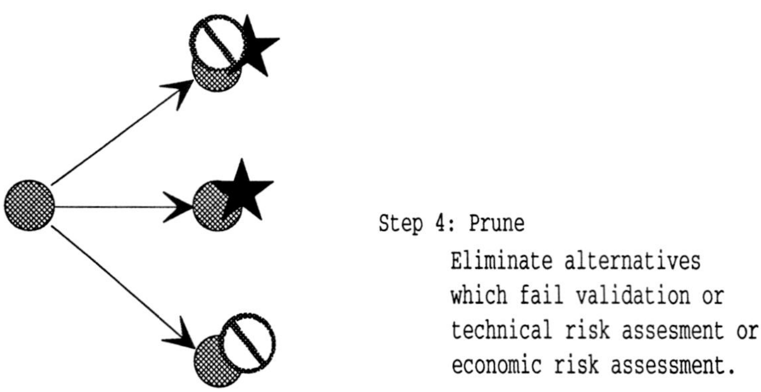

Fig. 10. Pruning.

During an exploration step the developer attempts to discover alternative representations of the system. Some of the alternatives are different ways of representing the same systems, others might involve systems consisting of different features. The more alternatives explored the higher the probability of building an optimum system. However, the more alternatives explored the higher the cost of development.

The declaration steps adds sufficient detail to the component to allow adequate validation. If there is not enough information available to complete declaration then this branch may be left hanging as an immature branch. However, another possibility is that by gaining further insight to the component during declaration more alternatives will be discovered.

Validation is a review of the component to determine if it will meet the needs of the system. Depending on how the component is defined validation may involve review of static representations (such as data flow diagrams), simulation of the component by the CASE environment, or examination of the delivered system on its target platform. Validation is another activity that will be a source of new alternatives to explore.

Pruning is the mechanism by which alternative branches are eliminated because they are not valid, there is a stronger alternative, or the project cannot afford to examine all the outstanding alternative branches.

The CASE environment must be able to store all the alternative branches, provide an intuitive navigation mechanism through alternatives, and assist the manager in determining if the team is applying the method effectively. The method may be applied recursively to several different components simultaneously.

This approach is fundamentally different from the traditional system development strategy that quickly converges to a unique baseline representation. While this baseline may go through changes the number of changes and the number of alternatives explored is much less then that proposed for an advanced CASE environment. The approach taken by object-orient programmers in browsing, inheriting, and prototyping is similar to that proposed for the CASE environment and the reason why they are similar is that in both cases the computer off loads a significant fraction of the cost of looking at alternatives.

Successful management involves balancing the cost of this cycle as applied to some number of alternatives with the benefit of finding the optimum path to a successful delivery that meets the project constraints on schedule, cost, quality, and usability.

The introduction of an advanced CASE environment that significantly lowers the cost of each cycle allows for more alternatives to be rigorously examined, that will increase the probability of achieving success.

8. Conclusion

As the powers of development platforms increase to allow sophisticated CASE environments to capture accurate information about fine grained activities, the role of the project manager will change. Management by exception will become more effective as the CASE environment generates warnings of abnormal situations. Participatory management will become more effective because, while team members will be able to create their own work tasks, the manger will be able to more accurately review the activities against plan.

However, due to the chaotic nature of systems development the process may never be deterministic. The predictive aspect of the CASE environment will always carry some error.

References

1. B. W. Boehm, *Software Engineering Economics* (Prentice Hall, 1981).
2. B. W. Boehm, "A spiral model of software development and maintenance," *IEEE Computer* **21**, 5 (1988) 61–72.
3. R. Guindon and B. Curtis, "Control of cognitive processes during design: What tools would support software designers?" *Proc. CHI' 88. ACM* (1988) pp. 263–268.
4. T. DeMarco, *Controlling Software Projects* (Yourdon Press, 1982).
5. J. D. Valett and F. E. McGarry, "A summary of software measurement experiences in the Software Engineering Laboratory," *J. Syst. Softw.* **9**, 2 (1989) 137–148.
6. J. Scully, *Odyssey* (Harper & Row, 1987).
7. J. Gleick, *Chaos* (Viking, 1987).

Software Process Modeling

A PROCESS MODELING APPROACH AND NOTATION

ROBERT CHI TAU LAI
International Software Process Constellation, 2255 Wheelwright Court, Reston, Virginia 22091, USA
E-mail: 7146.1442@compuserve.com (703)620-0584

ABSTRACT
This article forms the foundation of the bridge between guidance and automation on software development process. It offers a process notation PASTA (Process and Artifact State Machine Transition Abstraction) that will enable a process engineer to model any process to any level of detail. It is this flexibility that makes this process notation so powerful and the precision that is conducive to process automation.

1. Introduction

The Software Productivity Consortium is working in the area of process improvement to help software industry better manage large, complex software development projects. Some of the other Consortium's activities are:

- The Consortium conducts the Software Engineering Institute (SEI) Software Process Assessment.
- The Consortium offers a variety of guidebooks that help guide the practicing engineer to perform his task more efficiently. Examples include the Software Measurement Guidebook, which focuses on metrics collection and analysis, and the Evolutionary Spiral Process Guidebook, which specifies a

This material is based in part upon work sponsored by the Defense Advanced Research Projects Agency under Grant #MDA972-92-J-018. The content does not necessarily reflect the position or the policy of the U.S. Government, and no official endorsement should be inferred. Produced by the SOFTWARE PRODUCTIVITY CONSORTIUM under contract to the VIRGINIA CENTER OF EXCELLENCE FOR SOFTWARE REUSE AND TECHNOLOGY TRANSFER SPC Building, 2214 Rock Hill Road, Herndon, Virginia 22070.

process incorporating risk management and iterative development and specifies methods to implement the process.

- The Consortium prototypes a software engineering environment that will provide process management tools for supporting automated software development.

By building on the simple paradigm that people (roles) and resources perform activities that lead to products (artifacts), and by providing a rich set of relationships among those basic ingredients of a process, it is possible to model virtually any process and to maintain state tables that maintain information about the completeness of the product. Therefore, it is possible to know, at any given time, exactly what the state of completeness of all artifacts is, and hence the state of completeness of the activities and project. This provides the project manager with great insight and control over the events in the project.

Furthermore, by offering a notation that is flexible enough to allow state transitions based on the partial completion of activities, it is possible to model both deterministic and nondeterministic events. Hence, by allowing a partial ordering of events, it is possible to take advantage of opportunities or address risks as they present themselves.

The process modeling notation described provides benefits because it:

- Provides a precise, unambiguous description of the process.
- Provides a basis for building and integrating process tools, thereby recording process measurements, enforcing standard representation, and automating parts of the process.
- Allows all parties concerned (technologies, developers, managers) to agree (standardize) on the process.
- Provides a basis for process improvement/process evolution.
- Provides information for process and project management to reason about the status of a project, thereby providing insight as to how the process may be made more efficient.

Process modelers use the techniques of generalization, metaprocess, macro, parameterization, object-oriented, procedure calls, abstraction, and instantiation to describe a software process. Just as software is a description based on an abstracted model of a real-world problem, software process description is based on an abstract model of a software development process. From machine code to fourth generation language, several layers of languages represent different layers of abstraction. Compilers are developed to convey the real-world problem to lower level and machine-oriented abstractions. The trend is to use higher level abstractions which are close to the application for the process modelers' convenience. The more high-level software process abstraction a process notation offers, the easier a software process modeler's job will be.

A process description may offer a certain degree of support for how general a process can be described. There can be more different levels of abstraction between mathematics and the real software process, but only four levels are of interest in this paper.

- Process: Represents a real software process for a project, e.g., implementing module 23 or performing a code inspection on module 23.
- Process model: Represents a set of processes where the process model catches the variation of the set of processes, e.g., spiral process model, waterfall process model.
- Generic process model: Represents a set of process models where each generic process model can be used to represent a process model, e.g., PASTA, Entry-Task-Validation-Exit (ETVX) diagram, Petri, state machine, and Structured Analysis and Design Technique (SADT).
- Mathematics: Represents all of the possible generic process models, e.g., set, bag, group theory, graph, logic.

This paper describes a generic process model and a process notation, PASTA, and its application to process definition and modeling.

2. Process Definition

2.1. *Generic process model*

Figure 1 shows all of the key terms with directed arrow connecting them. In the following list, each term represents one relation between two elements.

- ***Refer-to.*** Analysis on the software process always refers to an artifact, A-state and P-state.
- ***Composed of.*** A P-state is composed of the operations that a software processional can currently perform and a role is composed of the activities that the role is able to perform.
- ***Change.*** An operation changes (promotes or demotes) an A-state.
- ***Manipulate.*** Operations manipulate artifacts.

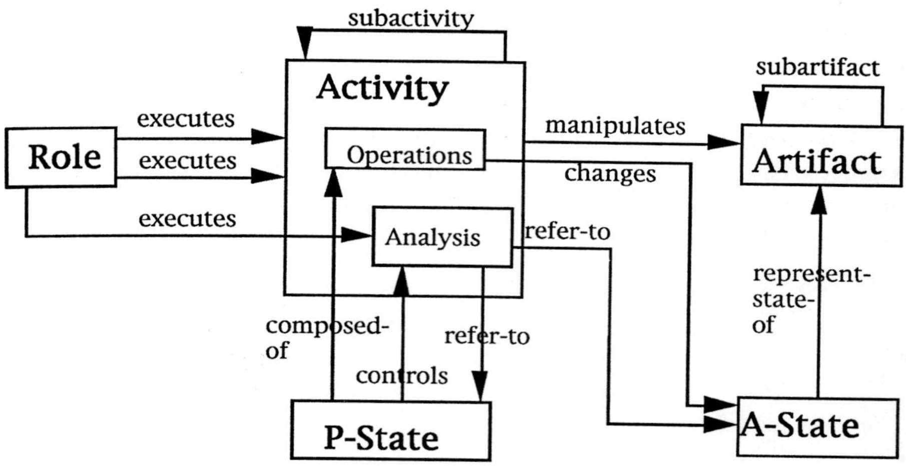

Fig. 1. Relationships defining the design model.

2.2. *Primary elements of a generic model*

A software development process is a sequence of decision-making activities. Software development is a process of making decisions about what programs should implement the software requirements and what the required properties of those programs are, including properties such as their structure and interfaces.

Artifacts capture the decisions made during the software development process. Examples of artifacts are a description of the decomposition of a design into a set of components (such as modules, objects, packages, or subroutines) and a specification of the interface of one of the components. To characterize the state of a software development process, the engineer must characterize the state of the artifacts produced during the software process, e.g., whether or not the software decomposition is complete. However, merely characterizing the state of the artifacts is insufficient to describe a complete software process. The process modeler must also describe the activities that may be performed on artifacts, the conditions under which those activities are performed, and the roles of the people who may perform them. For example, activities that the engineer might perform on an interface specification of a software module are creating the specification, checking it for completeness and consistency, and conducting a formal review of it. He performs the review after he has created and analyzed the specification for completeness and consistency. The reviewers may include designs other than the creator, implementors, and quality assurance personnel.

Software processes vary in many ways, including the way the software is organized into parts and the relations used to define dependencies among the parts. A particular software process may be defined as a sequence of decisions made in different states. The process modeler may model a methodology by a set of predefined states, i.e., it is a prescription for the artifacts to be used, the activities to be performed and their sequencing, and the roles that people play. The definitions of a set of states are the interpretation of the methodology. An engineer using the methodology proceeds by following the activities prescribed by the states to produce the prescribed artifacts in the prescribed order. Figure 1 illustrates the elements from which a generic software process model is composed; it is derived from Potts [14].

Artifacts are the work products of any software process and are typically documents. Most artifacts are composites or aggregates, i.e., they are composed of a number of parts, each of which is also an artifact. At some level of organization, the parts may be considered elementary, i.e., for the purposes of software development, they are not further decomposable or the decomposition is not of any interest to the process modelers.

The goal in identifying artifacts as part of a method is to find artifacts whose states the engineers can easily assess. The engineer needs to associate a rationale with an artifact. Whereas the artifact represents decisions that he has made, the *rationale* for the decision—what issues led to making the decision, what alternatives were considered, and what the justification was for the alternative chosen—is a separate concern from the decision recorded by the artifact.

The PASTA model has two levels. The lower level is based on the state of the artifacts produced during the software process; such states are called artifact states (A-states). Because A-states alone are insufficient to describe the software process completely, descriptions of activities, operations on artifacts, analyses that the engineer can perform on artifacts within the state, and the roles of the people involved augment them. The augmented states in the upper level state model are called process states (P-states).

The two-level model allows the separation of the process description from the representation used for the artifacts. For example, the upper level model may specify operations to be performed on interfaces to information hiding modules [11] without specifying the representation of such interfaces. The specification of the representation may be confined to the lower level model, where the state of the artifact that represents such a module is defined.

Different software projects may choose to use different methods for any step or sub-process for their software processes. For different methods, the artifacts used are different. An activity is the work that goes into producing or manipulating an artifact, i.e., each activity is associated with a particular artifact. Activities whose artifacts are composite have sub-activities, each associated with a component artifact.

Whether an activity is performable or not depends on the state of the artifacts. At any point in time, the set of performable activities represent the choice of artifacts on which the engineer may work. Those that are not performable represent the artifacts on which he may not work. The model prescribes a permissive ordering of activities (and on the work of the developer) by specifying which activities are performable and which are not at any point. Permissive means that the engineer is free to choose, from among the set of performable activities, those to pursue. The process modeler specifies a permissive ordering to support a realistic process. The model captures the information needed to produce a rational description of the work products of an opportunistic process [5].

In addition to specifying artifacts and activities, the process modeler also specifies the roles played by people involved in software development. As with artifacts and activities, different processes will specify different roles, such as designer, reviewer, implementor, and manager. The logical grouping of activities in which people may participate define the roles.

By augmenting state descriptions with activities and other process-related information, the process modeler can analyze the needs of the engineer at any point in the process. The goal of the analysis is to present to the engineer the information that he needs at the time he needs it. It also helps to focus on the concerns of what guidance to give to the engineer and what analyses the process modeler can perform on the software at any time. Finally, it helps to separate the concern of what information the process modeler should present to the engineer from how the process modeler should present information to him.

2.3. *The artifact state model*

2.3.1. *The relation and structure among artifacts*

Artifacts are the components that result from the decomposition of any software-development-related object. Relations among a group of artifacts create the structure of artifacts. Two predefined relations among artifacts are depends-on and is-composed-of. The relations described here are not necessarily a physical relationship among different artifacts. The relations are treated as an extra marking for process modelers to create relationships whenever necessary. The implementation of a process modeling language base on PASTA may implement the predefined relation is-composed-of as a physical object decomposition relation. The two predefined relations create two different kinds of structures among artifacts. The depends-on relation records the dependency structure which describes decisions about what artifacts are affected by changes to other artifacts. If, for artifacts X and Y, the convention (X, Y) is used to say that X depends on Y, X can be present and correct if and only if Y is also present and correct. X, then, is affected by changes to Y.

The other possible structure is an aggregation of modules and the is-composed-of relation. This is-composed-of relation, a relation among the artifacts, defines a tree. An artifact in the tree is composed of its children. The artifacts at the leaves of the tree are work assignments for individual software professionals or for a team of software professionals. Besides work assignments, the process modeler can define artifacts from different kinds of needs of software processes. The artifacts can be abstract artifacts or physical artifacts. The physical artifact is the artifact which really contains data objects related to software products. The abstract artifact is the artifact that the process modeler creates for the process model's sake.

2.3.2. *The rationale for an artifact*

By default, each artifact has a rationale associated with it. Since this is by default and is general for every single artifact, both predefined and user-defined, it is not part of the process notation. One of the attributes of a rationale is open issue. Because a software process is a sequence of decision-making activities and the artifacts are the work products of any software process, the process model must be able to capture the rationale for the entire software process. The predefined open_issues predicate will return a boolean value to reflect if there are open issues associated with the particular artifact.

2.3.3. *The artifact states*

English definition list and informally define the A-states. The A-state of an artifact describes the completeness of the artifact. The process modeler defines a partial ordering relation on the A-states which reflects the permissive ordering of activities. The A-states can be thought of as defining a state machine for each artifact. Activities performed by software professionals and other participants in the software process cause the state machines for the artifacts to transition from one A-state to another. The engineer uses the A-states, a formalization of the completeness of the artifacts, as a guide in completing the software artifacts.

Because the process modeler has defined a partial ordering on the A-states, the engineer can use the relational operators equal, greater than, less than, greater than or equal, and less than or equal on A-states. For example, for A-states M and N:

$$\mathrm{N} > \mathrm{M}$$

means that an artifact in A-state N is more complete than an artifact in A-state M. The three suggested default A-states which come with all of the artifacts are:

- ***Empty.*** There is no work associated with the artifact. It is empty. By default, it is the very first A-state at which an artifact will be.
- ***Named.*** The artifact is given a name. Giving an artifact a name is also a decision. It is the state that this artifact start to be able to be referenced. Therefore, there is one A-state to document the activity of naming an artifact. Implementation requires a system identification for all existing artifacts.
- ***Completed.*** No more work needs to be done for this artifacts. By default, it is the very last A-state at which an artifact will be.

2.3.4. *Elementary artifacts, composite artifacts, and predicates*

The engineer determines the state of an elementary artifact, one that is not an aggregation, by examining the artifact itself, whether there are any open issues that annotate it, and the state of artifacts on which the artifact depends. The engineer determines the A-state of an aggregate artifact by the state of its components and the A-states of artifacts upon which the aggregate artifact and its components depend.

Table 1. Definitions of predicates.

Predicate	Definition
Empty(x)	There is no work associated with the artifact instance x. The artifact is empty.
Name(x)	There is a name associated with artifact x.
State_of(x)	The A-state of x, where x is an artifact.
Open_Issues(x)	There are open issues associated with object x.
Completed(x)	Artifact x is totally completed.

Table 1 lists a set of predicates that are suggested to be available for a user-defined relation, user-defined artifacts and a user_defined object class. They are the only predicates which the engineer can use to define the A-state of an artifact. Since he defines all of the definitions of an A-state on top of this set of predefined predicates, the completeness of implementation for this process notation is possible. The Empty, Named and Completed A-states are from the suggested default A-state. The State_of is a predicate for retrieving the A-state by name of the artifact, "x".

2.4. *The process state model*

Table 2 shows the components of a P-state. The A-states of the artifacts associated with the P-state characterize a P-state. Consequently, the specification of a P-state includes a list of the artifacts associated with it.
In addition to artifacts associated with the P-state, a P-state specification also describes the entrance condition for a state entry and the activities that the engineer may perform in the state. The entrance condition is the condition that must be true to enter the state. The activities that the engineer may perform in the state are of two types:

- Operations, which the engineer may use to change the state of artifact.
- Analyses, which return information about the software development in general, including guidance on development methods, and artifacts in particular.

2.4.1. *Operations*

A pre-condition, the artifacts to which the operation may be applied, actions, roles, and a post-condition, may specify an operation as shown in Table 3. Pre-conditions are represented as predicates on A-states that determine when

Table 2. Components of a process state.

Components	Definitions
Name	The name of the state.
Entrance Condition	Condition required for entry of an activity and represented as predicates on A-states. The engineer uses this to determine when a process can enter a particular P-state.
Artifacts	A list of artifacts upon which work may proceed in the P-state.
Information Artifacts	The artifact which holds information required to support operations and analyses in this state. They are either artifacts which are returned by the analysis function or artifacts analyzed by the analysis function. These artifacts may include raw data and statistical data calculated by the analysis function.
Activities	A list of operations and analyses that the engineer may perform in the P-state. See Tables 3 and 4 for detailed descriptions of operations and analyses.
Post-Action	Action and predicates on A-states that determine when the process executes the action.
Exit Condition	Predicates on A-states that determine when the process exist the P-state.

Table 3. Components of an operation.

Components	Definitions
Pre-condition	Predicates on A-states that determine when the engineer can perform the operation.
Artifacts	The artifact manipulated by the operation.
Action	The function to be performed by the operation.
Roles	A list of roles of people who are allowed to perform this operation.
Post-Condition	Predicates on A-states that represent the condition when the operation is done.

the engineer can perform the operation. Post-conditions are represented as predicates on A-states that represent the condition when the operation is done. The engineer may perform an action when the pre-condition for the operation is true. The action embodies the effect of the operation. Accordingly, the description of an action is a formal specification of the effects of the operation.

As in other examples, the actions are assumed to be primitive functions and thus have not been defined in the process model in detail. They can be a tool, a micro-step in the process, or whatever size of step in the process at which the process modeler does not want to or does not need to model it in detail. Since not all operations are permissible to all people who participate in the process, an operation also has a list of roles of people allowed to perform the operation.

Table 4. Components of analysis.

Components	Definitions
Artifact	A list of artifacts related to this analysis.
Analysis	Specification of the analysis to be performed.
Roles	List of roles of people who may perform the analysis.
Trigger	How the engineer can invoke the analysis.
Result	The handling of the analysis results.
Action	Actions to be performed depending on the results of the analysis.

2.4.2. *Analyses*

In a P-state, an engineer can get information about the current status of the software project by invoking analysis. The information offered by the analysis helps engineers make decisions. Table 4 summarizes the components of analysis and their definitions. An analysis is defined by the artifacts to which it applies, the functions it performs, its types, and the roles of the people who may invoke it. The following attributes determine the type of each analysis:

- ***Trigger.*** The engineer can obtain an analysis in a predefined temporal situation, e.g., when entering a P-state, exiting a P state, whenever decided by the user, periodically, or before or after a certain operation.
- ***Result.*** The engineer may capture the result of analysis in some persistent storage, external file, or predefined data object class and shown the result in a predefined diagram type or predefined table type in a predefined text report type.
- ***Action.*** The engineer may specify response actions as part of the analysis definition for the cases when he finds certain condition to be true from the

analysis. Example actions include:

- prompt message (A-state, message). This action prompts the engineer(s) with the message when the analysis function returns A-state.
- save (A-state, file_name). This action saves the result of analysis in a file called file_name when the analysis returns A-state.
- mail reviewer (A-state, message, list of user_ID). This action mails the message to the engineers (list of user ID) when the analysis returns A-state.

2.4.3. *The process model as a state machine*

Because engineers are likely to be working on several aspects of a software project concurrently, the process modeler models the software process as a concurrent state machine, i.e., a state machine that can be in several states simultaneously. This permits an engineer to make progress in one state for awhile and then move to another without completing the first. It also permits several engineers to work on different parts of the software concurrently. By offering this capability, the process model allows the development team the freedom to act opportunistically yet still provide a means for guiding them in an orderly way. In addition, they can use it to record an opportunistic process so that they can plan the process and still hold the flexibility for the engineer to adjust to real situations when enacted.

Modeling the process as a concurrent state machine satisfies several concerns. First, it provides a precise definition of the methodology that the project needs. Designers, reviewers, and others involved in the process have a reference that specifies what they can do at any stage of the process. Second, it permits a parallel process since the model identifies opportunities for different engineers in a team to work concurrently and independently. Third, it provides a specification for a tool to support the process, i.e., a tool that can keep track of currently active P-states, record information about the software development, and provide the operations and analyses necessary for software professionals to make progress on the software project.

2.5. *Roles*

A role is a logical grouping of activities. A role defines the responsibilities of jobs associated with the software development task, such as designer, manager, or reviewer. A person who plays a designated role can determine what activities he may perform by looking at all the operations and analyses permitted for that role over all states. Roles are expected to vary according to the hosting organization as well as the method used, e.g., a reviewer's role in one method may be quite different than in another method.

3. The Process Notation

For a software process to be fully described under the PASTA generic process model, a notation is necessary for the process modeler to precisely define the process in his mind. The engineer can use this same notation to represent the necessary process-centered software environment for a project. Different projects may have different processes according to their needs, and the process-centered working environment should reflect that. The process modeler can do mapping by interpreting the software process description in a formal process notation and generating the activities coordination program to integrate tools. So far there are three forms of notation in PASTA:

- ***Form.*** The process is in terms of a set of forms, e.g., a form for describing an artifact, a form for describing a P-state. Each form represents a template which asks for some data to be provided to describe the process.
- ***Textual Language.*** It is the centerpiece of the PASTA's generic formal process notation. Together the form and graphical diagrams should contain a full set of information that the textual language will cover. Alex/yacc form of representation as well as Backus-Naur Form (BNF) representation of the language has been developed.
- ***Graphical Diagram.*** A graphical diagram notation is designed for the convenience of the process modeler. A process modeler should try to use the graphical diagram to model his process until he runs out of means.

3.1. *Form*

The following sections explain how to fill in each of the forms, with explanation of what kinds of data need to be provided, what fields are related among the different related forms, and how to interpret the information in the forms. They also explain the rationale for the default values which come with the implementation of the language. Some of the data for the form is formal. It is exactly the same as the data for the textual language. Some of the data is informal, i.e., an English description of an artifact.

3.1.1. *Artifact definition form template*

Table 5 shows the Artifact Definition Form used to record information about artifacts. The form has the following fields:

Table 5. Artifact definition form template.

Artifact Definition Form			
Name			
Synopsis	(English description here)		
Complexity Type	(Elementary or Composite)		
Data Type	(Name of object class, predefined or user-defined)		
A-State List			
A-State-Name	Put condition list over A-State of dependent artifacts here, if artifact is composite artifact.	(English explanation here)	
Sub-artifact List			
First Sub-artifact Name	(Name)	(English explanation here)	
Relations List			
Name of Relation	(English explanation here)		
	Type of relation (predefined or user-defined)	Direction (to or from)	Name of related artifacts

- ***Name.*** Each artifact needs to have a name assigned to it by a process modeler. If the process modeler is modeling a class of artifacts, he should suffix the name with a dot (.). If he is modeling an artifact from an existing, predefined class of artifacts, then artifact-class-name, name will be the name. If he is modeling just an artifact, what he needs to put in is a name. This naming convention is the same for all of the names in terms of modeling a process or a class of processes. In other words, this notation adopts the naming convention of using a dot to represent the relation between class and instance.
- ***Synopsis.*** This is the English explanation of the artifact being defined. Every form in PASTA process notation has a synopsis field to be filled in. An entry in this column is optional, but it is strongly suggested that they are filled to increase the understandability of the process model. This article will not explain how to fill in the synopsis for the rest of the forms in this process notation.

- ***Complexity Type.*** The process modeler can enter only one of the two reserved words, elementary or composite, in this column. A composite artifact is one that consists of sub-artifacts. An elementary artifact is indivisible.
- ***Data Type.*** If the complexity type of an artifact is composite, the artifact does not have a data type. In that case, it is optional for the process modeler to provide anything in the Data Type field. The process modeler does not and will not define the implementation of composition relationships among super-artifact and sub-artifact. It is the implementation of the process-centered software environment that makes the selections. It can be under the real object class hierarchy in the repository of a software project or just implemented as referencing mechanisms which reflect the sub-artifact relationships. Only the name of the object class can be put here. In other words, all of the names here need to end with a dot. When the process modeler or engineer enacts the process model, the implementation generates the name of the object's instance and maintains the name for them. They can provide two kinds of names here:

  Predefined Object Class Name. So far, the language only supports two data types, integer and string or text, and three basic types of object classes:

  1. Generic formatted text, e.g., the catalog name of desk-top publishing's text-formatting template set.
  2. Generic table, e.g., the number of the row and column and the data type of cells.
  3. Generic stick-ball diagram, e.g., the data types associated with each kind of stick and ball, the possible connections from kinds of sticks to kinds of balls and vice versa, and the name of the predefined graphic symbols and line font for the diagrams.

  The process modeler needs to provide the name of the class with a list of (parameter name, value) pairs which denote the instantiation of the generic object class for this artifact.

  User-Defined Object Class Name. The process modeler needs to provide the name of the object class and the instantiation parameters/instantiation value pair list.

- ***A-state List.*** The process modeler uses the condition lists to present the conditions when the artifact will be in this particular A-state. The condition representation described here is the same as in all the other places in the process notation. The condition may be composed of the following kinds of predicates:

1. State_of(x): An A-state retrieval predicate that comes with all predefined and user-defined artifacts by default.
2. Empty(x): A default predicate that returns a boolean to indicate whether an operation has been applied to an artifact after it was created. This default predicate comes with any predefined and user-defined artifact.
3. Open-issues(x): A default predicate that comes with all of the artifacts. By default, the process modeler can associate all artifacts with an issue database. Open-issue returns a boolean, indicating whether the artifact has an open issue in the issue database.
4. User_defined_relation(): A default predicate that comes with any predefined and user-defined relations.
5. There_is_one: There exists one or more artifacts.
6. For_all: Refers to all of the artifacts.

Only the following connectors for the predicates are allowed:

$>$ or GT: Greater than.
$> =$ or GE: Greater than or equal to.
$<$ or LT: Less than.
$< =$ LE: Less than or equal to.
$=$ or EQ: Equal.

The process modeler can use parentheses to clarify the meaning of the conditions. He can use only there_is_one and for_all, and he is only allowed to apply them over sub-artifact( ) and user_defined_relation(), two kinds of predicates. If an artifact is an elementary artifact, the process modeler is not required to put in the condition expression for each A-state. If the artifact is a composite, the condition list is required.

- ***Sub-artifact List.*** The process modeler needs to list only the sub-artifact names in the sub-artifact List field. An English explanation is optional.
- ***Relation List.*** The information captured in the Relation list reflects the necessary relations for the particular artifact that the process modeler wants to have. The process modeler needs to fill in a name of relation type (predefined or user-defined), the direction of relation, and the name of the class of artifact to which this artifact will be related. Again, the process modeler can provide an optional English explanation.

3.1.2. *Relation definition form template*

Table 6 shows the template for the Relation Definition Form. This form represents the user-defined relations. For each relation, the process modeler needs to fill the following fields:

Table 6. Relation definition form template.

Relation Definition Form			
Name			
Synopsis	(English description here)		
Possible Artifact Pair List			
From		To	
From		To	

- ***Possible Artifact Pair List.*** Each pair represents a directed relation from one class of artifact to the other.

3.1.3. *Process state definition form template*

Table 7 shows the template for the Process State Definition Form. This is the form to use to define a P-state. The form has the following fields:

- ***Main Role.*** This field optionally defines what role is responsible for completing the activities associated with the P-state. The main role has the ability to reassign role play for the P-state and to invoke the default operation version, baseline, commit, version query, and roll back to some earlier version of the artifact. The process modeler needs only to fill in the role name for the main role column. The main role also has the right to assign agents to roles.
- ***Entrance Condition.*** This field defines the condition required for entry into this P-state.
- ***Artifacts List.*** This is the list of artifacts operated on for this P-state. The components of this list may be in terms of artifacts or classes of artifacts:
  - A list of artifacts when modeling a process.
  - An artifact class list when modeling a class of processes.

Table 7. Process state definition form template.

Process State Definition Form		
Name		
Synopsis	(English description here)	
Main Role		
Entrance Condition		
Artifacts List		
Information Artifacts		
Operation List		
	Name	
	Description	
Analysis List		
	Name	
	Description	
Post-action List		
	Description	
	Condition	
	Action Function	
Exit Condition		

- ***Information Artifact.*** This is a list of artifacts which represents all the artifacts that the activities, operations, and analyses reference. They can be in terms of artifacts or classes of artifacts:
  - A list of artifacts when modeling a process.
  - An artifact class list when modeling a class of processes.
- ***Operation List.*** The name of an operation may be the name of a class of operations if the operation is listed as an instantiation parameter of this P-state. The name of an operation is the name of an operation instance; this means that the operation is an invariant of this P-state. To model a P-state, the name of operation may be an instance of a class of operations or it may be the name of an operation only defined for the use within this P-state.
- ***Analysis List.*** A list of analysis names. This is the same as the name of the operation listed in the Operation List field where they can be name of class of analysis or instance of analysis class.

- ***Post-Action List.*** Each post-action contains three parts:
  - Description: An English description of the post-action.
  - Condition: When the condition is true the engineer must invoke the action before exiting a P-state.
  - Action: The action to take place.
- ***Exit Condition.*** This field defines the condition required for exiting this P-state.

3.1.4. *Operation definition form template*

Just as an artifact is defined on top of object classes, operations are defined on top of methods/services of object classes. Table 8 shows the template for the Operation Definition Form, which is used for this purpose. The definition of an operation (class) should cover:

Table 8. Operation definition form template.

Operation Definition Form	
Name	
Synopsis	(English description here)
Pre-Condition	
Operation Type	(Manual, tool, function library, or state_control)
Artifact List	
Action	
Role List	
Post-Condition	

- ***Pre-condition List.*** This is a list of conditions. It is represented in the same way as the conditions for entrance and exit conditions of a P-state.
- ***Operation Type.*** There are several operation types that the process modeler can supply in this field:

  Manual. The operation is not automated or not modeled inside the process model being created: i.e., it is a black box to the process model. The person performing the role types in the password to signal that the task is done.
  Existing Tool. The action for the operation is a commercial off-the-shell (COTS) tool.

  Function Library. The action for the operation is either a library routine in the programming library or a shell script.

State Control. The operation is encapsulated by evoking a new P-state or by changing an A-state of a particular artifact, and the result of it opens the entrance condition of some P-state.

- ***Artifact List***. This is a list of artifacts upon which the operation is acting.
- ***Action***. This is the name of the COTS tools, shell scripts, or library routines.
- ***Role List***. This is a list of roles that may perform the operation.
- ***Post-Condition***. This is the same as the pre-condition.

3.1.5. *Analysis definition form template*

Similar to an operation, an analysis is defined on top of a method/service of object classes. Table 9 shows the template for the Analyses Definition Form. The definition of an analysis (class) should cover:

Table 9. Analysis definition form template.

Analysis Definition Form	
Name	
Synopsis	(English description here)
Information Artifacts	
Analysis Function Name	
Analysis Type	(management, quality, consistency, process_status, or user-defined)
Artifact	
Analysis Function	
Role List	
Trigger Type	(state_entrance, state_exit, user, periodical, or operation)
Result Type	(file, data_structure, diagram, table, text_report, or form)
Action Type	(prompt_message, save_to_file, or mail_to_role)

- ***Information Artifacts***. This is the list of artifacts that this analysis may reference. This field is more an aid for implementation than it is used for process modeling. If the implementation is very strong, this column may be omitted.
- ***Analysis Function Name***. This is the name of the method/service for the implementation. It serves as a reference name if it is implemented out of the process model or can be used in other parts of the process model.

- ***Analysis Type.*** The kinds of analyses that can be performed include:
  Management. The analysis function generates information for management decisions.
  Quality. The analysis function generates information for the quality of the work product.
  Consistency. The analysis function generates information for the consistency of various work products.
  Process Status. The analysis function generates information for the currency of the process.
  Measurement. The function analysis shows the pre-defined data of process and products.
  User-Defined. The process modeler can define analysis function. If it is a tool, the analysis should be well-packaged as a stand analysis tool. If it is a library routine, the analysis function needs to have a further integration step (e.g., compilation) to be incorporated into the process centered environment.
- ***Artifacts.*** This is the list of artifacts that the implementation programs take as input.
- ***Analysis Function.*** This is the implementation of the analysis function.

In addition to the standard, predefined analyses given above, the process modeler may define other analyses. These analyses may be autonomous and stand-alone, or they may be partial analyses that he can combine to perform a more sophisticated kind of analysis.

- ***Role List.*** This is a list of roles who may start the analysis.
- ***Trigger Type.*** Each analysis has a trigger type that determines when the process modeler or engineer is allowed to invoke the analysis. The different types are:
  State_entrance: The analysis can be invoked by agent or automatically each time the P-state is entered and before any activity is evoked.
  State_exit: The analysis can be invoked by agent or automatically before exiting a P-state and after the post-action.
  User. The process modeler or engineer can evoke analysis function anytime he wants it.
  Periodical. The analysis can be invoked automatically at a specified period of time, e.g., a day or a week.
  Operation. The analysis can be invoked before or after a certain operation is evoked.

- ***Result Type.*** This field describes the format of the output of the analyses. It includes:
  File. This is the name of a class of artifacts with an object type that represents a file format.
  Data structure. This is the name of a class of objects.
  Diagram. A class name of objects that represents a class of diagrams.
  Table. A class name of objects that represents a class of tables.
  Text_report. A class name of objects that represents a class of formatted texts.
  Form. A class name of objects that represents a class of forms.
- ***Action Type.*** A single analysis may have more than one of the following:
  Prompt Message. There is a text string that represents a message.
  Save To File. This is a file name represented as an instance of a class of artifacts.
  Mail To Role. This is a list of roles and a text string or a file to be included in mail.

The information needed in the form should be consistent, e.g., if the process modeler specifies file as a result type, then he should also specify save to file or mail to roles as the action in the Action Type field.

3.1.6. *Action definition form template*

Table 10 shows the template for the Action Definition Form, which represents the user-defined action. The template includes the following fields:

- ***Type.*** This field may include one of the following:
  Function_library. The action is implemented as a routine in the programming library.
  Shell script. The action is implemented as an operating system command script, e.g., shell scripts in UNIX.
  Tool. The action is a stand-alone tool.
- ***Source Path Name.*** The full path name represents where the action executable is stored.
- ***Input Object Class.*** This information is necessary for tools and shell scripts and essential for programming library routines.
- ***Input Path Name.*** This information is required for tools and optional for shell script and library routines.
- ***Output Object Class.*** This information is necessary for tools and shell scripts and essential for programming library routines.

Table 10. Action definition form template.

Action Definition Form	
Name	
Synopsis	(English description here)
Type	(function_library, shell_script, tool)
Source Path Name	
Input Object Class	
Input Path Name	
Output Object Class	
Output Path Name	

- ***Output Path Name.*** This information is required for tools and optional for shell script and library routines.

3.1.7. *Role definition form template*

Table 11 shows the template for the role definition form, which is used to define the role for a process model. The template includes the following fields:

Table 11. Role definition form template.

Role Definition Form	
Name	
Synopsis	(English description here)
Member List	
Activity List	

- ***Name.*** This is the name of the role, e.g., designer, reviewer, module designer, modeler/reviewer.
- ***Member List.*** This is a list of log-in names or a list of names for the position in an enterprise, e.g., manager_validation_lab or technical lead reuse lib. If some of these names are names for other role definitions, they construct the organization structure for a software organization.
- ***Activity List.*** This is a list of activities which the specified role can activate.

3.2. *Textual language*

The process modeler will interface with the process notation through the graphics and the forms; the textural language is used for the environment implementation only. The process modeler generates the textual language representation of the process model on the back end of the form/diagram browser/editor for the process notation. He passes this textual representation to the compiler/translator/automatic-instantiator to generate the process-centered software environment. It is up to the implementation of PASTA to have the textual language or not. The compiler/translator/automatic instantiator can share the data structures/objects maintained in the form/diagram browser/editor, and the process modeler can generate the process centered software environment directly.

3.3 *Graphical diagrams*

3.3.1. *P-state and A-state transition diagram*

A P-state is represented as a rectangular box with two kinds, and only two kinds, of boxes that can intersect with it. Figure 2 shows an example. They are the entrance, and exit conditions. The difference is that the entrance condition has a P-state name subbox on the bottom of the box, but the exit condition box does not. If it is a class of P-state, the name ends with a dot (.). The P-state name can be on any edge of the P-state boxes. This gives the process modeler a lot of geometric and topological freedom to draw.

A set of cells divides the condition box. Each cell represents one artifact in one A-state which composes the entrance/exit conditions. The intersection lines between the condition box and the P-state box divides the cells into two parts. The parts outside of the P-state contain the name of the artifact, and the part of the cell within the P-state represents the A-state of the artifact. Each artifact cell may have more than one line connected to it. This means the A-state change of an artifact may affect more than one P-state. More than one P-state may affect a single P-state by promoting one artifact. An A-state transition diagram is similar to a conventional state transition diagram, where each arc represents the operation which makes the A-state change, and the node represents the A-state.

3.3.2. *Artifact and relation*

There is only one kind of box that is divided into two parts. A smaller part

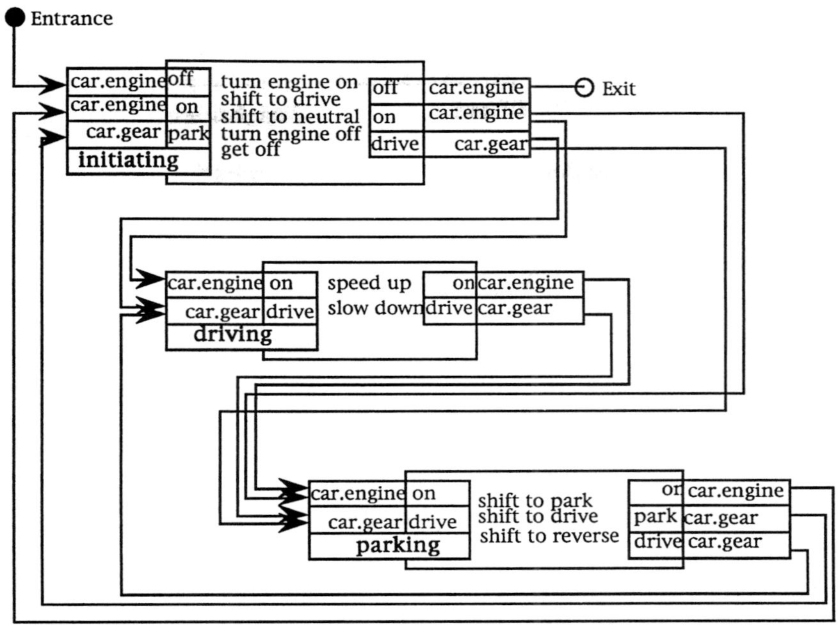

Fig. 2. P-state diagram example.

inside the box represents the name of the artifact. If it is a class of artifact, the name ends with a dot (.). The other part of the box has a list of A-states. The process modeler can draw an arrow from an artifact class to an instance of an artifact. The name of the artifact has a dot in it to connect the class name and the name of the instance. He can use an arrow which has the arrowhead at the beginning of the arrow to connect an artifact and its sub-artifacts. One artifact can have more than one sub-artifact, as well as more than one instance, but only one super-artifact. He can draw the artifact diagram with a P-state diagram. He can draw the dashed line between a class of artifacts or an instance of an artifact and a condition cell of a P-state. This is only by the request of a process modeler, and he can turn it on or off at any time. The graphical diagram (Fig. 3) is developed from very simple primary elements. The dynamic on/off options offer the process modeler the ability to perform a zoom/grow/cut query cycle when they are modeling processes.

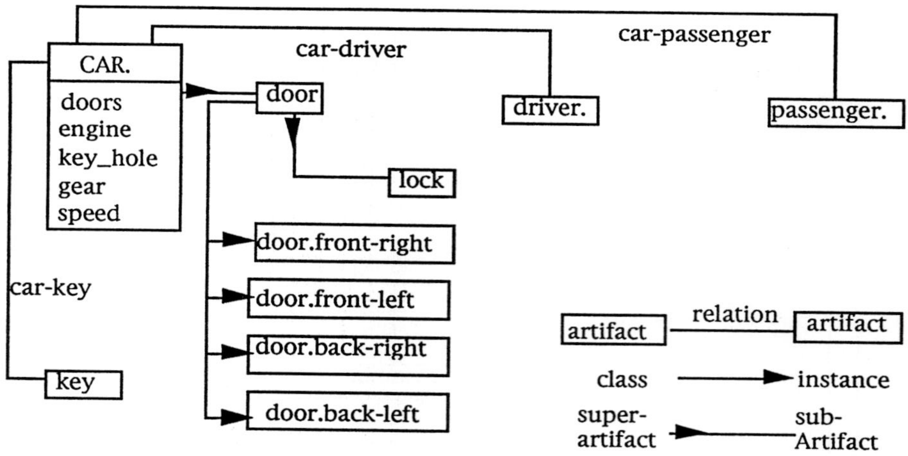

Fig. 3. Artifact relation diagram example.

4. Implementation of a Process Notation

To implement a process-centered environment for process notation, the following must be done:

- Maintain artifact states.
- Guide the sequences of decisions permitted by the P-state transitions.
  - Prevent forbidden transitions, e.g., a module cannot be done before its interface specification is done.
  - Suggest possible transitions, e.g., identify modules ready to be coded.
- Provide specified operations and analyses and provide help in performing operations that are left as manual.
- Integrate a tool set around a process.

4.1. *Using the model to build software process management tools*

The type of specification that the technologist uses in describing operations and analyses is left to the discretion of the modelers and environment implementors. There are four types of specification which the technologist can choose through the implementation of a process notation. They are:

- Tools in terms of a programming library in a high-level programming language.

- Stand-alone COTS tool.
- Operating system command-level scripts, e.g., shell script.
- Tool integration, e.g., Software BackPlane, or PCTE implementation.

The implementation reads the process notation and generates the software environment in terms of tool integration and activities coordination. For different projects, methods used, purposes and users, the process modeler uses different types at the same time. To describe the process to software developers, he may use an informal prose specification or a formal specification that describes effects in terms of state change on composite artifacts. As an example of the latter, the effect of using an editor to create an abstract interface might be specified as:

state_of(abstract_interface):=CREATED

4.2. *Interface between process model and software environment*

PASTA will precisely represent the interface between the process model and the process-centered software environment implementation. Figure 4 shows the structure of the interfaces between the process model and the implementation of the process-centered software environment. This is a world. Part of this world deals with software development and is called the modeled world. Based on the interface model, the process notation is designed so that it lets the process modeler pay most or all of his attention to the process modeling by:

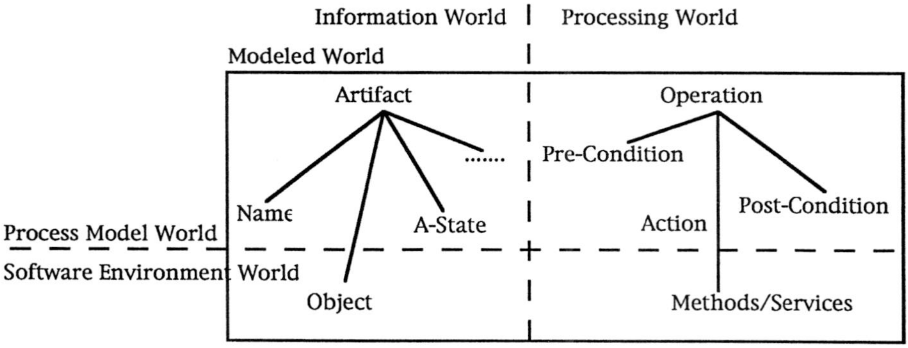

Fig. 4. Structure of the interface between a process model and the process-centered software environments.

- Defining the basic elementary artifact classes on top of the set of object classes listed in the interface/contract with the software environment world, or on top of the set of predefined object classes offered by the process notation.
- Defining the composite artifact classes on top of the elementary artifact classes.
- Defining operations/actions and analysis on top of the methods/service offered by the notation and the process-centered software environment implementation.
- Defining the interface for some environment implementation if necessary.

The software industry will be able to:

- Parallel the process-centered software environment implementation with process modeling by taking the notation as formal interface specification.
- Integrate a multiple environment implementation for a single software projects' process.

5. Using the Notation in an Organization

PASTA is being used in the Consortium's member companies as well as non-member companies. Training courses, guidebooks and tools on how to define and model a software development process based on PASTA are developed. To adopt the formal process notation in an organization, we suggest:

1. Start with a step-by-step approach, using whatever is useful, possible, and beneficial. Increase the speed of adoption when the company begins to gain something from the notation and has room to adopt more.
2. Increase the granularity with the understanding of software process. It is not necessary to describe all the details of the process in the initial model.
3. Combine the formal process notation with the use of an existing process notation. Between English and mathematics, there are different degrees of formality and notations. Start with one notation first and then combine other notations for process representation if the project benefits from the notations.
4. Start with the basic routine process because they are repeated more times than others.

Acknowledgments

This paper is a simplified and cut-down version of the Consortium's technical report "Process Definition and Process Modeling Methods." Special thanks go to David Weiss, Jim Kirby for discussion and to Jerry Doland, Mary Eward, Shawna Gregory, Jim Kirby, and Dick Werling for reviewing the document.

References

1. K. H. Britton, R. A. Parker and D. L. Parnas, "A procedure for designing abstract interfaces for device interface modules," *Proc. 5ICSE* (1981) pp. 195–204.
2. P. C. Clements, R. A. Parker, D. L. Parnas, J. E. Shore, and K. H. Britton, "A standard organization for specifying abstract interfaces", NRL Report 8815 (June 1984).
3. E. W. Dijkstra, "Co-operating sequential processes," *Programming Languages*, ed. F. Genuys (Academic Press) pp. 43–112.
4. *Evolutionary Spiral Process Guidebook, SPC–91076–MC*, Software Productivity Consortium (1991).
5. R. Guindon, "A framework for building software development environments: system design as ill-structured problems and as an opportunistic process," MCC Technical Report STP–298–88, 1988.
6. M. Kellner, "Representation formalisms for software process modeling", *Proc. 4th Int. Software Process Workshop.*
7. J. Kirby, Jr., R. C. T. Lai, and D. M. Weiss, "A formalism of a design process," *Proc. 1990 Pacific Northwest Software Quality Conf.* (October 1990) pp. 93–114.
8. R. C. T. Lai, "Process definition and process modeling methods," Technical Report, Software Productivity Consortium, SPC–91084 (September 1991).
9. R. C. T. Lai, "On a formalizing software process description: the consortium's example," *Proc. COMPSAC 91: The 15th Annual Int. Computer Software and Application Conf.* (September 1991).
10. L. Osterweil, "Software processes are software too," *Proc. 91CSE* (March 1987).
11. D. L. Parnas, "On the criteria to be used in decomposing a system into modules," *Commun. ACM.* **15**, 12 (1972) 1053–1058.
12. D. L. Parnas and P. C. Clements, "A rational design process: how and why to fake it," *IEEE Trans. Softw. Eng.* (February 1986).
13. C. Potts, and G. Bruns, "Recording the reasons for design decisions," *Proc. 10ICSE* (April 1988).
14. C. Potts, "A generic model for representing design methods," *Proc. 11ICSE* (1989).
15. B. Rendes and R. M. Stair, Jr., *Quantitative Analysis for Management*, 3rd ed. (Allyn and Bacon Inc., 1988).
16. *Software Measurement Guidebook, SPC–91060–MC*, Software Productivity Consortiumm (1991).

SOFTWARE PROCESS EVOLUTION IN MELMAC

WOLFGANG DEITERS, VOLKER GRUHN and HERBERT WEBER

Fraunhofer Institute for Software and Systems Engineering,
c/o University of Dortmund, P. O. Box 500 500,
4600 Dortmund 30, Germany

ABSTRACT

This paper describes the MELMAC approach to software process management. The MELMAC approach covers software process modeling, analysis, and enaction. The software process modeling language used in MELMAC is called FUNSOFT nets. For the scope of this paper we emphasize how MELMAC supports software process evolution. This support is based on a mechanism that allows on-the-fly modifications of software processes.

1. Introduction

Computer Aided Software Engineering (CASE) has been introduced to overcome the problem that software production often results in bad quality software, lateness, and over budgeting. CASE technology provided individual tools for supporting dedicated activities during the software production (such as system design, debugging, etc.) Furthermore, software engineering environments building integrated collections of such tools have been developed. Moreover, the definition of lifecycle models has been in focus. Several lifecycle models such as the waterfall model [30] or the spiral model [5] have been proposed to structure software development.

However, in recent years it has been recognized that the definition of software processes given by lifecycle models is too global and coarse-grained. Instead, lifecycle models have to be replaced by more detailed definitions of a software process [2, 3]. A software process is understood as the execution of the schedule of activities performed for producing a software system. The definition of a software process is called a **software process model** [11]. A software process model has to consider the individual policies and guidelines of a company and a project.

Various software process model purposes can be distinguished. These are:

(1) *software process modeling*, i.e., the development of software process models,

(2) *software process model analysis*, i.e., the investigation of errors and bottlenecks in process models before turning the process models into practice, and

(3) *software process model enaction*, i.e., the guidance of software developers during the software process.

Software process modeling, analysis, and enaction are commonly addressed as **software process management** [20] in the following.

One characteristic feature of software processes is that they are highly dynamic. This results from the fact that the software process is determined to a large extent by the work of humans. This observation resulted in Lehman's criticism [25] of a too mechanistic approach to model software processes. One conclusion from Lehman's argument is that process model evolution can only be supported by an incremental software process management approach (supporting an interleaved modeling, analysis, and enaction of software process models). This means that, it should be possible to analyze incomplete models and to enlarge or change the process model due to increased knowledge that has been gained during process model enaction.

However, the problem of process model evolution has to be investigated carefully. Although it is necessary to change process models in order to cope with the dynamic nature of software processes, it must not be possible to perform arbitrary process model changes. Since it is one basic goal of process models to introduce certain regulations (e.g., quality assurance procedures) into a software process, it has to be clearly identified in the process model what can or what must not be subject to change. Through this, the variant and invariant parts of a software process model are distinguished.

Considering the different people that are involved in software process management (e.g., software developers, project managers, quality assurance engineers) it becomes obvious that each class of user is interested in different information described in a process model. For example, a quality engineer wants to be assured that the schedule of activities performed during the software process follows certain quality regulations (e.g., ISO 9000 [27]) whereas project managers are interested in information for people, timing and budget planning. This means that, most users are usually only interested in parts of the process model. Furthermore, visibility restrictions must be implemented in a process model. For example, a software engineer should not be allowed to access sensitive data concerning the qualifications of other users. However, this information has to be put into the model for enabling an appropriate people assignment. Therefore, it becomes reasonable to split a process model into a set of views. A view is a partial process model tailored towards the needs of a certain class of users (e.g., project managers). The complete process model is then obtained by superimposing the different views.

In this paper, we introduce the FUNSOFT net approach to software process management. The FUNSOFT net approach supports different views for building software process models. These views are superimposed. The superimposition enables process model analysis and enaction.

In this paper we cannot discuss all aspects of the FUNSOFT net approach. The focus of this paper is to show support for software process evolution. Therefore, we only briefly tackle other aspects of the FUNSOFT net approach. The idea of a view based approach is more thoroughly explained in [6]. Details about process model analysis can be found in [14, 15]. A more specific discussion of the MELMAC system including a presentation of the system architecture can be found in [8].

The organization of this paper is as follows. Within Sec. 2 we introduce some views onto software process models and we show how to integrate the views into one homogeneous process model representation. Section 3 describes the software process management environment MELMAC, which is based on FUNSOFT nets. Finally, Sec. 4 concludes this paper by pointing out future plans for further improvements of software process evolution support in MELMAC.

2. Representation of Software Process Models

In order to support different kinds of users obtaining the software process model information they are interested in and in order to facilitate software process analysis and enaction, we use different representations of software process models. For modeling software processes we introduce a **user level process model representation**. This representation encompasses a set of views. The views are then integrated in an **internal process model representation** which is the basis for analysis and enaction. The user level representation is described in Subsec. 2.1. The internal representation and the transformation of the user level into the internal representation is described in Subsec. 2.2.

The examples used throughout the following sections are taken from a larger process model. This process model describes the development of the MELMAC environment itself.

2.1. *Representation of software process models on the user level*

Software process models fix allowed schedules of software development activities and they specify how these activities are to be carried out. Furthermore, process models encompass project management information. This is, for example, the allocation of sets of activities to roles. By introducing roles, responsibilities for performing activities are defined. Other project management information addresses the definition of timing conditions defining when certain activities have to be performed.

The different entities (activity definitions, timing conditions, roles, etc.) which are defined in a process model are interrelated. Within our approach we will define these different entities of process models by a view based approach [6]. Other process modeling approaches also using views are described in [22, 24]. Each view describes a part of a software process model that is of special interest to a certain class of user (for example, project management information which is of interest to project managers). The different views are mapped onto an internal process model representation (c.f. Fig. 1) that is exploited for process model analysis and enaction.

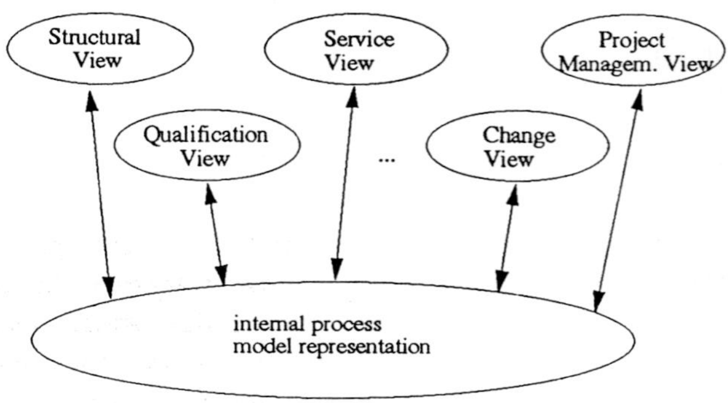

Fig. 1. Relationship between user level and internal process model representation.

In the following we describe some of the views which we have identified. The activity schedules that are carried out in the course of the software process and the types of the objects that are processed by the activities are defined in the **Structural View**. A specification of tools to be used in performing activities and a specification of activities to be carried out requiring human interaction between different software developers is given in the **Service View**. The information specified in these two views is addressed as the technical part of a process model in the following. These two views describe those process modeling aspects that usually are dealt with by other approaches (e.g., MARVEL [23], ALF [10], IPSE 2.5 [31]) too. Furthermore, we define a view that we call **Project Management View** specifying which activities belong to which roles and which timing constraints exist for activities. Due to the focus of this paper, we emphasize the existence of a **Change View**, which describes how software process models are adapted due to knowledge gained within software processes. Other views are the **Distribution View** which specifies which activities are executed at which site and the **Analysis View** which contains information about how software processes are simulated. They are not explained in more detail here. We refer to [6] for details concerning these views.

The Structural View

The heart of software processes are the objects produced in software development and the activities contributing to their production. The definition of object types and activities builds the skeleton of a software process model. Object types and activities are described in the *Structural View*.

Object types are described in a C-oriented manner. Thus, it is possible to construct complex object types from basic types and other constructed object types.

Besides an identification of the various object types, allowed execution schedules of software development activities are defined. Roughly speaking, in the Structural View the various activities and the data flow and control flow constraints between activities are defined. For defining such constraints a net-based, graphic language is used (compare Subsec. 2.2). Within a net the various activities together with their inputs and outputs are addressed by nodes. Directed edges define the data flow between different activities. In Fig. 2 an activity *change_module* is identified. This activity operates on a module that should be changed (*module_to_change*) and results in a changed module (*modules_to_integrate*).

The net-based language allows the structuring of activities hierarchically. An activity is called complex, if its details are described in its refinement.

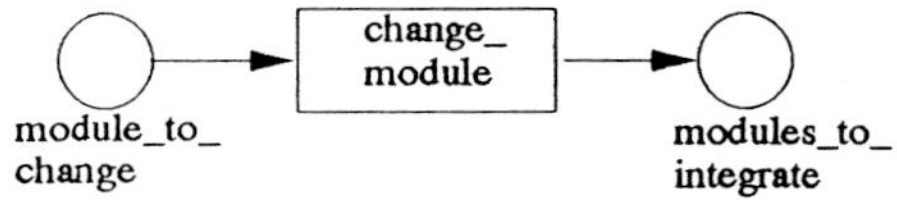

Fig. 2. Activity *change_module* with inputs and outputs.

An activity is called simple if it is not refined. As we will see later on in detail the activity *change_module* is a complex activity whereas an activity *check_system_against_requirement* is a simple one. The representation of data flow constraints given in the *Structural View* builds the skeleton of the internal process model representation that results from superimposing all the information expressed within the various views.

The Service View

Information on how to carry out simple activities is given in the Service View. In this view simple activities are attached to services. Services are either small programs or they envelop tools which have to be called when the activity is executed. Examples of such tools are text editors, debugging tools, etc. Moreover, services can be used for describing how human skill and expertise is integrated in software processes. An example of an activity which depends on human thinking and problem-solving is an activity like *review_design_document*. Such an activity cannot obviously be described in an imperative way. It is only possible to describe the types of input and output objects. This corresponds to a descriptive style of specifying activities related to human skills as suggested in [32]. We call these activities **individual interaction agencies**. Furthermore, some activities require communication between different users. Such activities are called **social interaction activities**. Services attached to social interaction activities implement mechanisms to inform the different users with whom, when, and why they have to communicate (e.g., a service notifies various users to participate in a meeting that has been settled for discussing a report).

The Project Management View

The *Project Management View* specifies information needed for people, time, and budget planning and control of software processes. In the following we describe how people are allocated to activities and how timing conditions are defined in the Project Management View.

Activity	Role
system_test	Implementer QA_Engineer
module_integration	Implementer
backup	Implementer

Role	User
Implementer	Smith, Jackson
QA_Engineer	Johnson

Activity	Objects	User
change_module	UIS	Jackson

Fig. 3. An example of people allocation to activities.

During real world software processes not all activities should be performed by the same person. In order to model this, the notion of **role** has been introduced. A role is a collection of activities that can be performed by persons who play this role. By associating an activity with a role, responsibilities for performing activities are fixed. Roles are defined in the *Project Management View*. Figure 3 shows an example of a role definition. In the first table it is defined that the activities *system_test*, *module_integration*, and *backup* are all associated with a role *Implementer*. The activity *system_test* is additionally associated with a role Quality Assurance Engineer (*QA_Engineer*). That means, this activity can be executed by a user playing one of both roles. The second table defines that the role *Implementer* is played by the users *Smith* and *Jackson*, the role *QA_Engineer* is played by the user *Johnson*. Sometimes it is not sufficient to assign roles to users, but it is required to allocate users directly to the manipulation of certain objects. This is done in the Project Management View by so-called **direct allocations**. The direct allocation given in the third table of Fig. 3 defines that the user *Jackson* is personally obliged to do the change in the module implementation for the module called *UIS*. Of course, if a direct allocation is given, the user who is allocated to an activity has to own the respective role.

Additionally, in the Project Management View timing conditions are defined for the execution of certain activities. Activities like, e.g., *backup* do not always take place when their inputs are available (in this case when the system for backup has been produced) but at a certain point in time (e.g., regularly each day, 8:00 p.m.). Such timing constraints are also specified within the Project Management View.

The Change View

The fact that software processes are highly dynamic is well-recognized [17, 19, 28]. This fact has been stressed by Lehman when formulating his *uncertainty principle for computer applications* [25]. One of the kernel ideas of the uncertainty principle is that it is impossible to specify a process model completely in advance. A process management approach has to cope with changes that occur during the enaction of processes (i.e., on-the-fly). We introduce the notion of changing a software process on-the-fly by associating refined agencies of the corresponding process model with **modification points**. Modification points identify which parts of a process model can be changed during software processes.

An example of the specification of modification points in given in Table 1.

Table 1. Attachment of modification points to complex activities in the Change View.

Complex Activity	Modpoint
check_system_against_req	MODPOINT
system_test	NO MODPOINT

2.2. *Representation of software process models on the internal level*

All information specified in the views on the user level process model representation is presented on the internal process model representation in a uniform way. This is a prerequisite for software process analysis and enaction. We utilize FUNSOFT nets [14] for representing software process models in a uniform way. That means the process model skeleton given in the Structural View is extended by the information defined in the other views.

FUNSOFT nets are high-level Petri nets whose semantics is defined in terms of Predicate/Transition nets extended by multi-sets [12]. FUNSOFT nets were designed to provide an enactable representation of software process models and to provide analysis facilities for software process models. The prevalent criteria for assessing the suitability of FUNSOFT nets is whether they enable the representation of all information given in the various views on the user level. Corresponding to the views explained in Subsec. 2.1, we point out how the information expressed in the *Structural View*, *Service View*, the *Project Management View*, and the *Change View* is translated into FUNSOFT nets. For precise definition of FUNSOFT nets we refer to [14]. Here, we aim at an overview about FUNSOFT nets.

FUNSOFT nets consist of:

- a Petri net structure (S,T,F) [29] (the S-elements are called channels, the T-elements are called agencies; the F-elements are called edges). We distinguish between data and control flow edges.
- a set of services (a service is an executable piece of software, it can be a program, a shell script or an envelope around a tool),
- a set of object type definitions (written in a C-oriented manner),
- a set of predicates (defining additional conditions needed for firing agencies),
- a set of modifications points, and
- an initial marking.

Agencies in FUNSOFT nets can be refined. The notion of refinement corresponds to the notion of transition substitution as introduced in [18]. By agency refinements FUNSOFT nets can be structured hierarchically. Services (such as *compile*, *validate_design_document*, *presented_of_results*) are attached to agencies. Object types (such as *requirements_doc*, *module*) are attached to channels. Predicates can be attached to agencies. By means of predicates it is possible to define conditions on objects which must be fulfilled in order to fire an agency. Thus, predicates correspond to the notion of preconditions as used in MARVEL [23] and ALF [4]. An agency t is enabled (i.e., it can be fired) if all channels from which t reads are marked and if the attached predicate applied to the objects to be read is fulfilled. Modification points are used for modeling that a software process can be changed during its lifetime. Modification points can be attached to refined agencies. By attaching a modification point to a refined agency, the refinement of this agency is identified as a software process model part that becomes subject to change during the software process.

In FUNSOFT nets agencies, channels, and edges have various attributes. We avoid a formal definition of all attributes, but restrict ourselves to an informal introduction to FUNSOFT net attributes here.

Figure 4 describes the uniform representation of a software process model, parts of which have been discussed in Subsec. 2.1. The sketched cut out of the complete model describes how module implementations are changed and tested. Within that activity the modules to be changed and the requirements report are extracted from the system document. The modules are changed, the changed modules are integrated and linked. A linked system has to undergo a *system test*, a copy is backed up. The test either can lead to a test failure report (in the case of an unsuccessful test) or to a tested system (in case of a successful test). In the latter case the tested system is checked against the requirements. This activity is represented by agency *t2:check_sys_against_requirements*, which is a refined one. Thus, details about that activity are described in the refinement of *t2*. The check can lead to an accepted system (in which case the test terminates) or to design failure reports, implementation reports, or bug reports. Bugs can be fixed by a new system test, other errors enforce a redesign or a reimplementation. If errors are detected all reports (the test failure report, the implementation failure report, and/or the design failure report) are merged into one failure report.

Figure 4 contains some agencies which do not have the standard Petri net firing behavior. The agency *t4* for example produces either a tested system or a test failure report. This particular output firing behavior is called *det_out*, since the value of the input object determines which kind of output object is produced. This output firing behavior as well as some input firing behaviors are described in [14]. A predicate is attached to agency *t7*. This predicate specifies that *t7* can only fire if there are objects with the same value in channel *s14* and *s15*. Thus, the activity represented by agency *t6* is triggered if, and only if, the current time, which is read from channel *s14*, equals the scheduled backup time, which is read from channel *s15*. The semantics of these firing behaviors is described in terms of Predicate/Transition nets.

In the following we explain how the information expressed in the Service View, the Project Management View, and the Change View is integrated into the process model skeleton given in the Structural View (the result of this integration is shown in Fig. 4). The information expressed in the *Project*

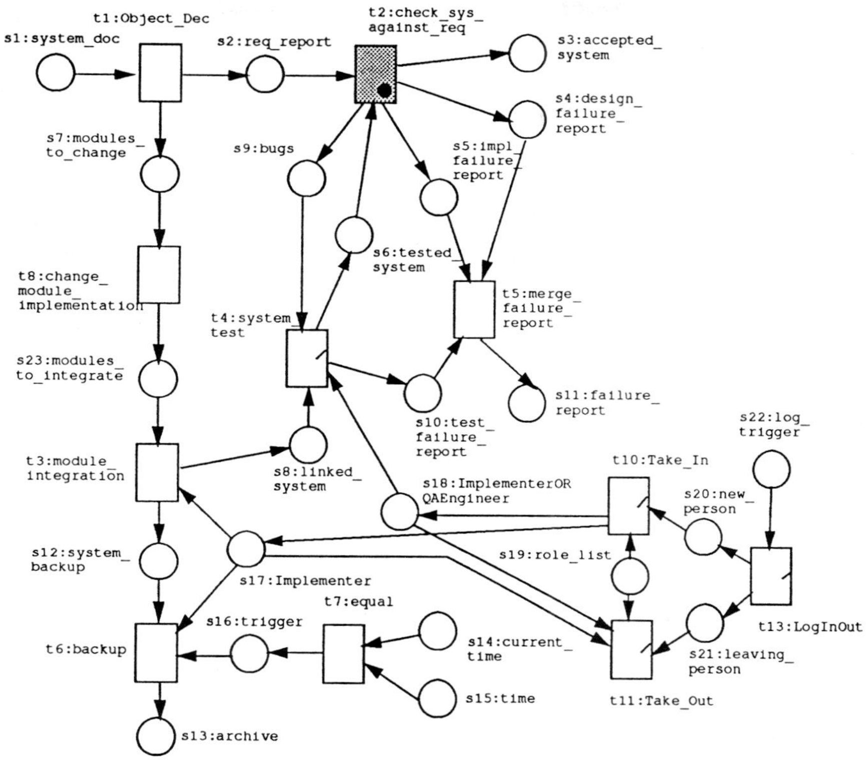

Fig. 4. Software process model representation on the internal level.

Management View is handled as follows:

Information about which activities belong to which roles is captured in net parts added to the skeleton specified in the Structural View. These net parts ensure that agencies representing activities which are assigned to roles can only be executed if people playing the required role are available. Furthermore, a net part is generated which administrates logging in and off a software process.

In Fig. 4, the role definitions are reflected by the channels labeled *Implementer* and *Implementer_OR_QA_Engineer* that have been connected to some agencies. Furthermore, for administrating different users agencies and channels have been introduced which check if people start/stop working in the software process (c.f. agency *LogInOut*) and that determine the roles of these people (c.f. agencies *Take_In*, *Take_Out*).

Information about timing constraints (as given for the *backup* activity in the *Project Management View* in Subsec. 2.1) is translated into net parts. These net parts check whether the timing condition is fulfilled. In that case a control channel is filled. This control channel is connected to the agency for which the timing constraint has been defined. Thus, the agency becomes enabled provided that all other input channels are marked, too.

In the example given in Subsec. 2.1, it was laid down that the activity *backup* takes place only at 8:00 p.m. This is implemented by a net part (c.f. channels *current_time*, *time*, *agency equal*) where a control channel (c.f. channel *trigger*) is introduced as additional input channel for the activity *backup*.

Modification points specified in the *Change View* are expressed in a FUNSOFT net by attributes of refined agencies. They are represented graphically as black dots in the right bottom corner of agency symbols (cf. agency *t2* of Fig. 4).

3. Software Process Management in MELMAC

In the following we discuss the tool support provided by MELMAC. MELMAC is a software management environment that covers software process modeling, software process analysis, and software process enaction. MELMAC has been used for several academic and industrial software process examples [6, 14, 21]. Our strongest background is in software process modeling and analysis.

MELMAC contains:

- components for modeling software processes by means of different views onto software processes (modeling on the user level),
- components for integrating information specified in different views (translation into internal level representation in terms of FUNSOFT nets),
- components for analyzing software processes represented by FUNSOFT nets,
- a component for guiding and assisting software developers, and
- a component for supporting software process evolution.

Figure 5 sketches a simplified vision of the MELMAC architecture. It shows that the four mentioned groups of MELMAC components are directed by a component called *MELMAC Ctrl*, that they commonly use a window management system (for which we have an OpenLook and a SunView version) and that all MELMAC components store and retrieve information only from

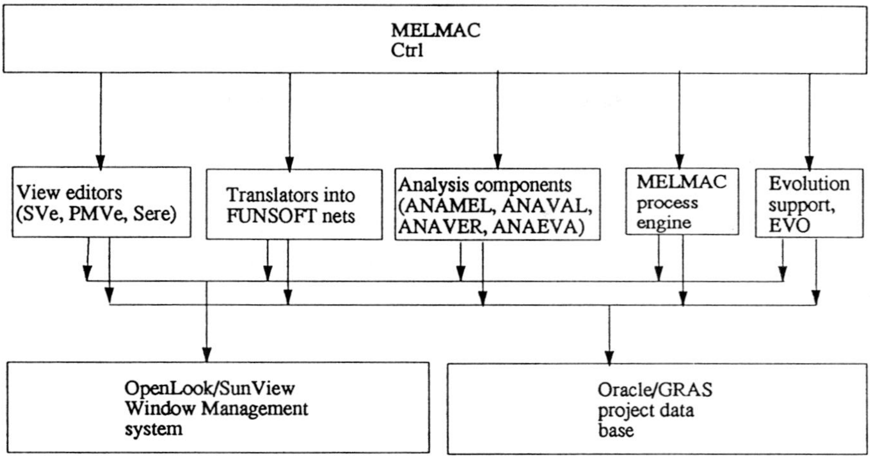

Fig. 5. Simplified architecture of MELMAC.

the MELMAC project data base (for which we have a version based on GRAS [26] and another one based on Oracle).

In the following sections we discuss software process management as supported by MELMAC components. Subsec. 3.1 describes what software process modeling in MELMAC looks like, Subsec. 3.2 focuses on analysis facilities available in MELMAC, and Subsec. 3.3 describes how software developers are assisted and guided during software process enaction. Finally, Subsec. 3.4 points out how MELMAC allows the evolution of software processes while they are enacted.

3.1. *Software process modeling in MELMAC*

The basic idea of software process modeling in MELMAC is the specification of software processes by means of different views (compare Subsec. 2.1). Therefore, several view editors are implemented in MELMAC. Examples of view editors are:

Structural View editor(SVe): The structural view editor allows the editing of software process skeletons. Firstly, it contains a syntax-driven editor for hierarchical FUNSOFT nets. The FUNSOFT net editor allows different arrangements of activities (sequential activities, concurrent activities, optional activities, etc.) and, thereby, the definition of software process skeletons. Second, the structure view editor contains an object type editor which allows the definition of object types in a C-like syntax.

Project Management View editor (PMVe): The project management view editor is used for inserting project management information. It allows the definition of roles and skills required for certain activities. Moreover, it is used to describe skills of individual software developers and to assign roles to personnel. Milestones and cost per activities can also be defined. The project management view editor is a hybrid editor. It is partially syntax-driven and allows free editing of text for the other parts. Details about this editor can be found in [6].

Service editor (Sere): The service editor is used for the definition of services which are associated with FUNSOFT net agencies. It allows the definition of C programs, shell scripts, and envelopes around tools. Details about services are described in [7].

Figure 6 shows a screendump of the software process skeleton editor and of the project management view editor. Both editors are used at the same time: While process activities are put together in the software process skeleton editor, project management information is added in the project management view editor.

3.2. *Software process analysis in MELMAC*

Software process analysis is an integral part of software process management in MELMAC. It is done in an interleaved way with software process modeling. Thus, modeling errors can be detected as early as possible. The analysis component of MELMAC is called ANAMEL [15]. It consists of three main components (ANAVAL, ANAVER, ANAEVA). The components enable a software process model **validation**, software process model **verification**, and **post-evaluation** of already finished software processes.

1. Validation of software process models is based on software process simulation. The component ANAVAL is used to simulate software processes. A simulation of a software process corresponds to looking at one specific software process example in detail, it does not show that all software processes described by the analyzed model have or do not have certain properties.

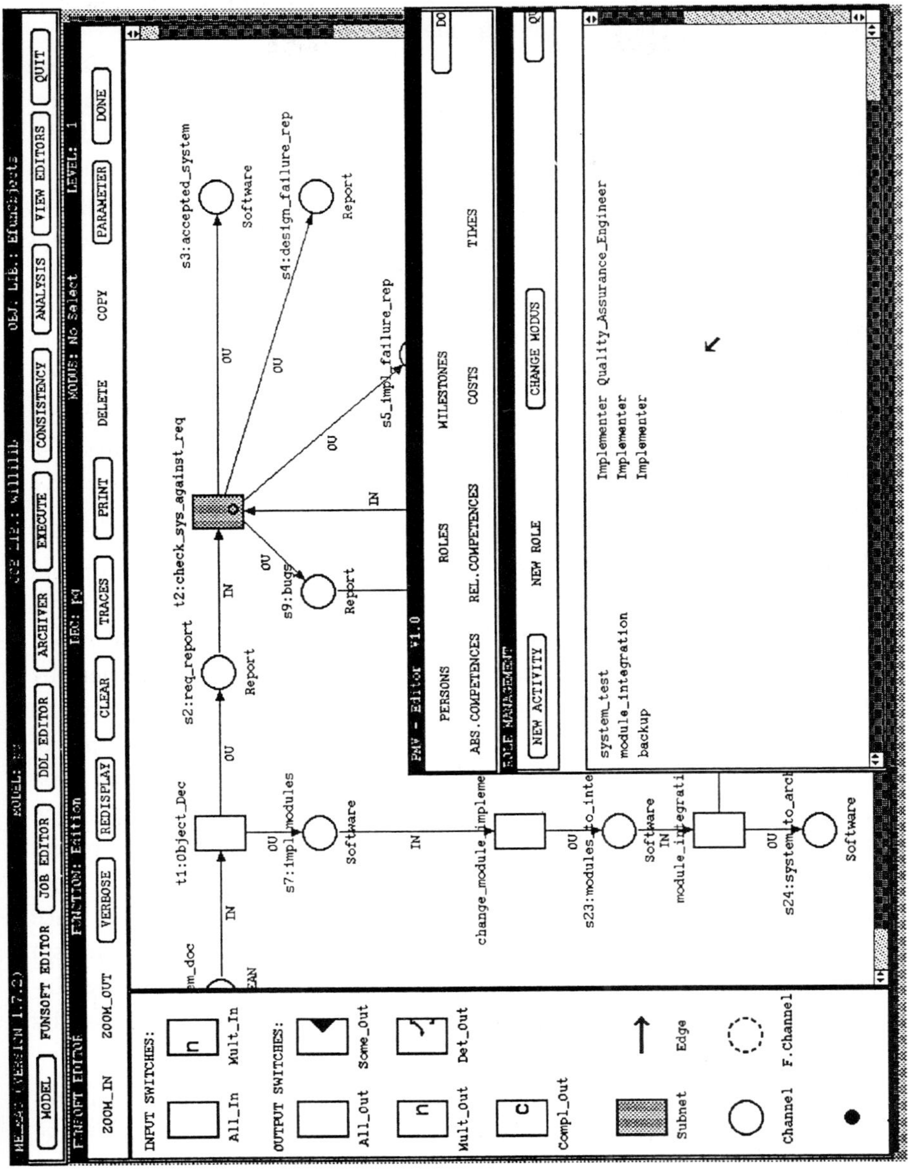

Fig. 6. Interleaved use of MELMAC modeling components.

Validation of software process models provides a worthwhile contribution to software process model analysis, because software process simulation conveys an idea about the behavior of models software processes.

In simulating software processes we try to imitate the behavior of software processes as precisely as possible. Since we do not want to waste the resources needed in software processes, we do not manipulate actual objects, but only object names in simulating a software process. For example, in the simulation of a module compilation we do not actually call a compiler, but we derive the name of the output objects from the name of the input object. Accordingly, we have to guess whether a compilation is successful or not. This is done randomly on the basis of stochastic attributes attached to output edges of the *compile* agency. Another attribute which is specific to software process simulation is the time-consumption. The time-consumption of an agency fixes how much time passes between reading objects from the input channels and writing objects to the output channels.

Simulation of software processes can be exploited in two ways.

- It is possible to observe the simulation of software processes immediately, since the flow of objects in a simulated software process is animated.
- It is possible to evaluate simulation traces. Simulation traces contain information gathered during software process simulation.

A simulation trace is produced during software process simulation by recording **basic simulation events**. These basic simulation events are the start and the end of agency firing, object flow via edges (including names of objects), and occurrence of conflicts. The information gathered during software process simulation is statistically evaluated in order to find out which activities were executed how often, how much time they took, which process part consumed which share of the overall process time, which activities were not executed because they waited for input objects. Further simulation trace evaluations focus on bottlenecks (i.e., activities that slow down the process) and on critical paths (sequences of activities that determined the process duration). Details about the structure of simulation traces and about the results which can be obtained by evaluating them can be found in [9, 16].

2. The component of ANAVER is used to verify software process model properties. It implements various algorithms used to prove numerous model properties.

By defining the semantics of FUNSOFT nets in terms of Pr/T nets, we are able to use analysis techniques that have proven to be useful for Pr/T nets. Additionally we use adaptations of well-known Petri net types verification techniques for directly proving FUNSOFT net properties.

Some examples of properties that can be proven for FUNSOFT nets are the existence of useless object types, permanently enabled activities, deadlocks of activities, and process parts in which the number of objects in channels remains unchanged throughout the process. While the mentioned properties are static properties (i.e., properties that can be proven by checking the topology of FUNSOFT nets), we also look at dynamic properties, such as the boundedness of objects in certain channels, maximum number of activities which can be fired concurrently, and occurrence of certain process states. These dynamic properties can be proven on the basis of reachability trees for FUNSOFT nets [13]. Details about the formal definition of these properties, their meaning in software process modeling and the way to prove them can be found in [14].

3. In contrast with ANAVAL and ANAVER, which are based on assumptions about software processes, ANAEVA is applied after carrying out software processes. That is why the post-evaluation implemented by ANAEVA also focuses on on-the-fly modifications which occurred in actual processes. Thus, post-evaluation helps to detect which parts of a software process model have been modified at which time and what the modified software process model looked like after the modification.

   By post-evaluating software processes in a process-centered way, we are able to reason about software processes. We are able to find out which software process model parts are frequently modified and, thus, have to be reconsidered consequently. Such results are much more valuable for the software development *culture* of a company than simply saying that the results of a particular software process have the one or the other deficiency (which is possible by post-evaluating a software process in a product-centered way).

   Results which can be obtained by post-evaluating an actual software process are similar to results that can be obtained by simulation trace evaluation. One basic difference is that post-evaluation results are more reliable. This is due to the fact that post-evaluation considers actual time-consumptions which occurred in real processes, while time-consumptions in process simulation are merely based on assumptions about how long activities last. Another difference is that post-evaluation of a software process also reveals which process model parts have been modified during the process. This information is valuable for deciding about process model parts that have to be improved for future processes.

3.3. *Software process enaction in MELMAC*

While software process modeling and software process model analysis have proven to be useful for a better software process understanding, software process enaction is less accepted by software developers. To enact a software process means to govern it on the basis of regulations written down in a process model. Thus, the work of software developers is assisted by a process model interpreter (also called a process engine [1]). Software developers fear to lose their freedom if such assistance becomes too rigid. We were aware of this danger when designing the process engine of MELMAC. In fact, it implements a careful approach to software developers' guidance and assistance.

The MELMAC process engine implements two main functions:

1. *Assistance.* The MELMAC process engine governs software processes on the basis of regulations described in FUNSOFT nets. It attempts to free software developers from menial activities in order to allow them to concentrate on creative tasks. The process engine merely offers activities to be carried out, it does not implement a rigid control of processes. In detail, it checks which activities can be executed and provides different enaction support to manual, individual interaction, and social interaction activities. This support is described below:
   - Enaction support for automatic activities is easy. They are started as soon as they are enabled.
   - For individual interaction activities, enaction support is more difficult. The MELMAC process engine offers an individual interaction activity to **all** software developers who are entitled to participate as soon as it is enabled. Offering an activity means to write the activity and its actual input parameters into the personal agendas of concerned software developers. As soon as one of the software developers chooses an individual interaction activity, it is removed from the agendas of all other software developers. Once a software developer decides to participate in an individual interaction activity, the MELMAC process engine finds out at which workstation the software developer is working and then starts the corresponding service at that station.

- For social interaction activities, enaction support is even more difficult than for individual interaction activities. The software developer who is responsible for a social interaction activity (from now on called the interaction manager) can propose a date for the social interaction. Every potential attendee can agree or disagree to the proposed date within a certain period of time (also fixed by the interaction manager). When this period of time is over, the interaction manager checks whether or not the interaction activity can take place at the proposed date. It can only be scheduled if a sufficient number of attendees accept. What is sufficient in this context is determined by the description of the social interaction activity which should encompass a description of the number and roles of software developers expected to participate. For details about such description we refer to [14] where so-called dialogue descriptions of social interaction activities are introduced. If the number of software developers who agree is sufficient, then the interaction manager can decide if he wants to schedule the meeting for the proposed date or if he prefers to propose another date. For example, this may be reasonable if he wants particular software developers to participate and if these are unable to participate on the proposed date. Once a date has been fixed, all software developers who agreed to that date get an entry in their agenda, which denotes the social interaction activity and the proposed date. When the proposed date is reached, the process engine checks if all input parameters are available and if all other preconditions are fulfilled. If so, all potential participants get a reminder, unless they are informed that the interaction has to be cancelled and the interaction manager is requested to propose a later date.

2. *Monitoring.* First, basic execution events of a software process are recorded in an execution trace. These basic execution events are the same as the basic simulation events (start of an activity, termination of an activity, conflict between two activities). In addition, the modification of the process model during enaction is recorded. Execution traces are similar to simulation traces. They are analyzed by the post-evaluation component ANAEVA (compare Subsec. 3.3).

3.4. *Software process evolution in MELMAC*

Generally speaking, software process models cannot be modeled completely before enaction. In contrast to this, software processes evolve throughout their lifetime. Therefore, the *Change View* onto software processes defines which process model parts are likely to be modified while a process governed by that model is running. Accordingly, software process models are built incrementally in an interleaved way with process enaction. On a more technical level this means that on-the-fly modifications must be enabled.

That requires a modification and extension of a software process model while being interpreted. Due to the nature of software processes, changes cannot be specified by interrupting the whole software process, otherwise the work of too many people guided by the software process model would be blocked because of changes which may be local only.

If we relate these findings to the MELMAC approach to software process enaction, FUNSOFT nets have to be modified while they are interpreted by the MELMAC process engine.

In the following we describe the on-the-fly modification mechanism implemented by the evolution component of MELMAC, called EVO, in detail:

Identification of the need to modify an agency's refinement. Certain software developers have the right to modify an agency's refinement (from now on a software developer allowed to change a certain refinement is called *process manager* for that refinement). A process manager can ask for a modification of a refinement if an agency of that refinement could be executed. This refinement is marked as being *locked.*

Shutting down the locked refinement. It has to be guaranteed that changes cannot be performed while agencies of a locked refinement are active (currently executed). This would entail the danger to lose objects that are processed. Therefore, some precautions have to be made: All information about the locked refinement should be visible for the process manager. In order not to destroy currently processed objects and in order not to lose any information about how and by whom activities are currently executed, the modification can only take place if no agency of the locked refinement is active.

The following steps are carried out in order to realize these precautions:

- no objects are passed from outside into the locked refinement,
- all agencies of the locked refinement which are currently executed are finished (otherwise some objects being currently processed in agencies could be lost), and
- no enabled agency in the locked refinement is started (otherwise the actual modification would be delayed).

Modification. The process manager has the chance to execute the modification as soon as no agency of the refinement to be modified is active. The modification is done using the different view editors (compare Subsec. 3.1).

Restart. Once the process manager terminates the modification, the locked refinement is unlocked again.

The steps described above ensure that changes can only be applied to process model parts that are passive (i.e., not under execution). Moreover, this mechanism allows to hold the passive parts as small as possible instead of interrupting software processes as a whole.

4. Conclusion

In this paper we have presented salient features of the software process management environment MELMAC. The most important feature for the scope of this paper is that software process models represented by FUNSOFT nets can be modified on-the-fly, i.e., while they are enacted. Such modifications require only minimum interruption of software processes. Software processes are disturbed as little as possible.

MELMAC support for software process evolution allows the modeling of software processes incrementally. Whenever information about software processes becomes available, it can be integrated into software process models. This helps us to use software process models as a kind of repository, always storing the current knowledge about how to develop software.

Our goal for the near future is to extend MELMAC by a mechanism that allows distribution of processes to partners located at different sites. This also would require the support of local evolution of software process parts. The idea is to identify process parts that are local to only one partner. If this partner wants to change *his* part of the process, he should be allowed to do that if the interfaces to other process parts remain unchanged. Besides the evolution support described above, this would allow local process evolution carried out by autonomous partners.

References

1. R. Adomeit, W. Deiters, B. Holtkamp, F. Schülke, and H. Weber, "K/2_R: a kernel for the ESF software factory support environment," in *Proc. 2nd Int. Conf. System Integration*, Morriston, New Jersey (June 1992).

2. V. Ambriola and C. Montangero, "Hierarchical specification of software processes," in *Proc. European Software Process Modeling Workshop*, eds. A. Fugetta, R. Conradi, and V. Ambriola, Milan, Italy (May 1991).
3. S. Bandinelli, A. Fugetta, and C. Ghezzi, "Software processes as real-time systems: A case study using high-level petri nets," in *Proc. European Software Process Modeling Workshop*, eds. A. Fugetta, R. Conradi, and V. Ambriola, Milan, Italy (AICA Press, 1991).
4. K. Benali, N. Boudjlida, F. Charoy and J. C. Derniame, "A model for assisted software processes," in *Proc. ICCI*, Toronto, Canada (June 1989).
5. B. W. Boehm, *A Spiral Model of Software Development and Enhancement. Computer* (May 1988).
6. W. Deiters, *A View Based Approach to Software Process Management*, Ph.D. thesis, University of Berlin, (December 1992). Appeared as Technical Report No. 467/1993, University of Dortmund, F2G.
7. W. Deiters and V. Gruhn, "Managing software processes in MELMAC," in *Proc. 4th ACM SIGSOFT Symp. Software Development Environments*, Irvine, California, USA (December 1990). Appeared in *Softw. Eng. Notes* **15**, 6 (1990).
8. W. Deiters and V. Gruhn, "Software process management in MELMAC," Technical Report 51, University of Dortmund (1990).
9. W. Deiters and V. Gruhn, "Software process model analysis based on FUNSOFT nets," *Mathematical Modeling and Simulation* **8** (1991).
10. J. C. Derniame, C. Godart, V. Gruhn, and J. Lonchamp, "Process-centered IPSEs in ALF," in *Proc. 5th Int. Workshop on Computer-Aided Software Engineering*, Montreal, Canada (July 1992).
11. M. Dowson, "The structure of the software process," in *Proc. 2nd Int. Software Process Workshop*, Coto de Caza, Trabuco Canyon, California, USA (March 1985).
12. H. J. Genrich, "Predicate/transition nets," in *Petri Nets: Applications and Relationships to other Models of Concurrency*, eds. W. Brauer, W. Reisig, and G. Rozenberg, Berlin (Springer, 1987). Appeared in *Lecture Notes on Computer Science* **254**.
13. V. Gruhn, "Analysis of software process models in the software process management environment MELMAC," in *Software Engineering Environment* Vol. 3, ed. F. Long (Ellis Horwood, September 1991).
14. V. Gruhn, *Validation and Verification of Software Process Models*, Ph.D. thesis, University Dortmund (June 1991). Appeared as Technical Report No. 394/91.
15. V. Gruhn, "Validation and verification of software process models," in *Proc. European Symp. on Software Development Environments and CASE Technology, Königswinter*, FRG, Berlin, eds. A. Endres and H. Weber (Springer, 1991). Appeared in *Lectures Notes in Computer Science* **509**.
16. V. Gruhn, "Software process simulation on arbitrary levels of abstraction," in *Proc. 4th Int. Symp. Systems Analysis and Simulation*, Berlin, Germany (August 1992).

17. G. F. Hoffnagle, "Process interaction modelling and mechanization," in *Proc. 3rd Int. Software Process Workshop*, Beckenridge, Colorado, USA (November 1986).
18. P. Huber, K. Jensen and R. M. Shapiro, "Hierarchies in coloured petri nets," in *Proc. 10th Conf. on Application and Theory of Petri Nets*, Bonn, FRG (1989).
19. W. S. Humphrey, "Classes of process iteration," in *Proc. 3rd Int. Software Process Workshop*, Beckenridge, Colorado, USA (November 1986).
20. W. S. Humphrey, *Managing the Software Process*, SEI Series in Software Engineering (Addison-Wesley, 1989).
21. R. Jegelka, *Evaluierung der Software-Prozeßmodellierungs-Sprache FUNSOFT-Netze und der Software-ProzeßManagement-Umgebung MELMAC (in German)* Diplomarbeit, University of Dortmund (1991).
22. W. L. Johnson, "Specification via scenarios and views," in *Proc. 3rd Int. Software Process Workshop*, Beckenridge, Colorado, USA (November 1986).
23. G. E. Kaiser, P. H. Feiler, and S. S. Popovich, "Intelligent assistance for software development and maintenance," *IEEE Softw.* (May 1988).
24. B. Krämer and Luqi, "Petri net-based models of software engineering processes," in *Proc. 23rd Annual Hawaii Int. Conf. System Sciences* (1990).
25. M. Lehman, "Software engineering, the software process and their support," *IEEE Softw. Eng. J.* **6**, 5 (1991).
26. C. Lewerentz and A. Schuerr, "GRAS — a management system for graph-like documents," in *Proc. 3rd Int. Conf. on Data and Knowledge Bases*, Jerusalem (Morgan Kaufmann Publishers Inc., 1988).
27. International Standardization Organization, "Quality systems — models for quality assurance in design/development, production, installation and servicing," Report 1987-03-15, 1st ed., International Standardization Organization (1987).
28. D. E. Perry, "The iteration mechanism in the INSCAPE environment," in *Proc. 3rd Int. Software Process Workshop*, Beckenridge, Colorado, USA (November 1986).
29. W. Reisig, *Petrinetze* (Springer, 1986) in German.
30. W. Royce, "Managing the development of large scale software systems: concepts and techniques," in *Proc. WESCON* (1970).
31. B. Warboys, "The IPSE 2.5 project: process modelling as the basis or a support environment," in *Proc. 1st Int. Conf. System Development Environments and Factories*, eds. N. Madhavji, W. Schäfer and H. Weber (Pitman Publishing, 1989).
32. L. G. Williams, "Software process modeling: a behavioral approach," in *Proc. 10th Int. Conf. Software Engineering*, Singapore (April 1988).

Educating Software Engineers for CASE

SOFTWARE PRODUCTIVITY: THROUGH UNDERGRADUATE SOFTWARE ENGINEERING EDUCATION AND CASE TOOLS

JOSEPH E. URBAN

Department of Computer Science and Engineering Arizona State University Tempe, Arizona 85287, USA

PATRICK O. BOBBIE

Department of Computer Science University of West Florida Pensacola, Florida 32514, USA

ABSTRACT

The fundamental rationale for the increase in the use of CASE tools by both large and medium enterprises is the belief that CASE tools facilitate and enhance improved productivity and system quality. The development of CASE environments has evolved over several years. Users are demanding high-level, domain-specific interfaces to applications, easy-to-use systems, systems that offer increases in productivity/cost ratios, flexibility in multi-paradigm tools usage, and systems which are modular, portable, and robust. To meet such far ranging needs, software engineering research has become a large-scale endeavor. Thus, CASE development has become the concerted effort of academia, government, and industry. In this chapter, the academic research effort on CASE development is discussed. Specifically, the perspective of the chapter is on the effect that Undergraduate Software Engineering (USE) education has had and can have on the ability to develop timely and quality software tools. This chapter is organized along three major themes: (1) the impact of USE education on current techniques for developing CASE tools and a measurement of current CASE technology transfer; (2) the qualitative component(s) of USE education which will help in advancing tools development in the next decade; and (3) the impact of USE education in promoting technology transfer which consequently increases software productivity.

1. Introduction

Undergraduate software engineering education has had a minor role in advancing CASE technology. Cooke [7] identified several problems in CASE technology,

> "including the lack of formalisms for CASE, the lack of experimental data to indicate the benefits of CASE, the lack of understanding concerning the organizational impact of CASE tools, and the fact the true industry "shakeout" of CASE products has not taken place."

The role of USE education in CASE technology advancement has been limited due to lack of attention on the part of industry, academia, and government. Most of the focus in universities on advancing CASE technology has occurred in the graduate programs.

The curriculum structures of software engineering graduate programs emphasize the use of CASE, tool integration, and tailoring of tools to meet specific tasks, and tool interfacing, among others. At the undergraduate level, however, few universities offer software engineering course sequences, let alone grant baccalaureate degrees in software engineering. On one hand, undergraduate (and graduate) software engineering education is imperative and a necessary prerequisite to the advancement of CASE technology. On the other hand, most exciting software engineering courses do not emphasize the teaching of the "building blocks" for designing, developing, using, and enhancing CASE.

This has a specific focus on what needs to be taught to enable students to grasp the intricate parts of CASE, and the need for developing a formal USE education to achieve the former. The overall impact of USE education and CASE development on software productivity, through technology transfer, is also discussed. In the following sections, community needs and goals in CASE are discussed.

Increases in industrial software productivity is hindered by limited technology transfer from academia and government to industry. The needs of industry in the area of software engineering were addressed in the context of the US Department of Defense (DoD) and defense industry in an early version of the planning for the DoD STARS program [26]. Lucky [20] raised industry software engineering needs within the context of engineering education and industrial research and development. The software engineer position title has been adopted by many organizations. The traditional route to an entry-level engineering position of a Bachelor of Science degree in "X" Engineering is, however, not the case in software engineering. On the contrary, an entry-level software engineer can look forward to a spectrum of training types that range from no training to formal training. CASE use can range from basic programming tools to actual participation in developing software techniques/tools.

In the university setting, a typical software engineering faculty member is expected to teach, conduct research, perform university service, and provide service to the profession. Faculty course assignments are ideally in the research areas, but can include all other software related courses. In institutions with graduate programs, masters and doctoral student supervision complements faculty research activities.

Computer-related degree programs that have been providing the route for entry-level software engineers need improvement for the advancement of CASE. The field of software engineering has matured to the level of introducing many of the same mechanisms from science programs that support the other more traditional engineering disciplines. Traditional science programs provide the requisite background on which traditional engineering programs prepare students to meet industrial need. There is also a demand within industry for undergraduate software engineering programs. USE education should have a complementary relationship with traditional computer science programs, as traditional engineering does have with science programs, in order to meet the industrial need.

Industry and academia have the potential to significantly benefit each other by advancing CASE. The next section includes a discussion on the current role of industry and academia in CASE tool development. Also included in the section is a perspective on some of the current limitations on industry/university synergism; and a recommended approach for advancing CASE through greater cooperation and technology transfer.

2. Current CASE Tools Technology Transfer

Using current approaches, the period for technology transfer of software techniques and tools to industry is estimated to be seven to ten years. Technology transfer has been slow to advance given the increased emphasis on CASE tool use. CASE technology transfer in academia has been even slower than in the industry, a situation which threatens to create a weak basis for developing, advancing, and incorporating the technology in course curricula. The following subsection investigates some of the impediments to technology transfer.

2.1. *Impediments to software engineering technology transfer*

One of the major problems facing software development is the huge expense involved in [16]. For example, the US DoD spent $3 billion in 1980, while the projected estimates for 1990 were around $30 billion. Some of the reasons for such huge expenses are:

1. Requirements for new systems are complex, especially for embedded systems, where rigorous performance requirements must be met;
2. Existing computer science curricula do not incorporate the technological basis for developing and advancing CASE tools to further facilitate systems development; and
3. Software development tools and methodologies have not continued to dramatically improve productivity.

While new methods continue to raise productivity in the hardware sector, the software sector has not experienced as much improvement over the last decade. Construction from scratch has been a weak point of traditional software development. A 1983 survey of programming practices found that 85% of code produced in developing software was common, generic, and mainly concerned with developing applications on computers [17]. An attempt to standardize this 85% of code would cut down the enormous production costs.

CASE technology transfer needs to approach a level of maturity that is similar to other engineering disciplines. In other engineering disciplines, the situation is such that students use and explore with the tools of their respective discipline. USE education programs, currently, do not even approach the equivalent of other engineering disciplines. Thus, the burden has typically fallen on industry to support the knowledge gap that new graduates have regarding tool use.

The incorporation of USE laboratories within undergraduate curricula is needed as in other traditional engineering undergraduate curricula. These USE laboratories need to be much more than terminals and workstations. Functional laboratory experiments for software engineering need to be constructed for use in undergraduate curricula. These laboratory experiments will then be enhanced as experience is obtained with students. More importantly, these laboratory experiments will be extended as technology advancements come from the software tool developers efforts based on the laboratory use.

2.2. *Progress in technology transfer*

The software tool technology transfer process within universities ranges from nonexistent to extensive [26]. The extent of CASE in many undergraduate programs is limited to editors, compilers, and debuggers. Incorporation of an expanded CASE toolset throughout the undergraduate curriculum is necessary as a first step. Most of this expansion would be expected to come from the migration of graduate software engineering topics into the undergraduate courses.

The use and teaching of fundamentals of CASE in an academic setting can provide a foundation for making significant advances in software development. In other words, teaching how-to-make, how-to-use, and how-to-extend principles will provide a foundational knowledge to students. In Secs. 3 and 4, the research and teaching requisites are quintessential to developing and advancing CASE through USE education and vice versa, are discussed.

3. Software Engineering Research (SER)

Software engineering research has, in the past, been focused on system-oriented tools: compilers, operating systems, database, and file management systems. The direction of SER has changed, with more focus on user-oriented, or CASE, tools for problem-solving: graphic kernels, user-interface systems, code instrumentation, and design tools. In [25], Norman and Nunamaker discuss the increases in productivity due to adherence to development standards using CASE technology. CASE tools are not, however, silver bullets for solving problems associated with academic research and industrial code production. CASE tools, often developed with dissimilar methods, are fragmented and fail to meet SER efforts. To meet the challenges of software development, the software engineering discipline must rely on the teaching of formal methods and techniques.

SER is centered around two contexts: academia and industry. In each context, one can identify tools developed by individuals, team-efforts producing integrated environments [15, 18, 23], and student-oriented or prototypical projects. In the following subsection, the aforementioned types of SER projects and the underlying methods and integration strategies are addressed.

3.1. *Industrial tool development*

The international computer industry has created a driving force behind the advances in both hardware and software. The traditional engineering discipline has matured and produced standardized building blocks and index/calibration tables for engineering design of hardware components. It is not unimaginable for individual engineers to build breadboard or prototypical systems, and have the system tested and integrated into a production quality hardware unit. Even when hardware function changes, improved components can be redesigned, according to standards, to replace the previous ones with a perfect fit. The advances in hardware and the ability for individuals to develop tools is attributable to such design principles as reusability, modularity, and replaceability.

In contrast, the software development advances have lagged behind the advances in hardware. The reason has often been attributed to the aesthetic and complex nature of software systems. Also, unlike hardware systems which are physical entities, software systems implement complex functions which are idea-oriented and ephemeral in nature. Whenever a software user desires to change the functions, due to growth or redefinition of goals, the software embodying the functions needs to be changed. Software systems rarely come in standardized and reusable components, hence the changes often entail major ramifications, making it difficult for individuals to handle alone. There are a few documented cases of fairly large software tools that are currently designed and implemented by individuals. The 1980s was an era of software development based on structured methodologies. The trend into the 1990's points to the design and implementation of object-oriented systems. With the object-oriented approach, the potential for individuals to build transferable and enhanceable software components is beginning to appear [3].

In spite of the absence or limited use of hardware design principles in software engineering, some powerful tools have been designed by a few ardent individuals. For example, the Unix^{tm} system was conceived and developed by two individuals for system programming. Unix is currently a major and, often viewed, as a *de facto* software development environment. Pascal, Modula, and Smalltalk are examples of commonly used systems or tools that did not start by a consortium of designers or conglomerate of research and development industries but by individuals.

For SER to be characterized as an individual endeavor, it is imperative that research be focused on methodologies that support tool standardization and integration. As a consequence, the standardized tools will provide the CASE toolset necessary to foster individual tool development.

3.2. *Integrated software engineering environments (ISEEs)*

SER has achieved measurable success in the development of integrated environments through tool interfacing. The Programmers Workbench/Unix

[8], Interlisp [33], and Apollo Domain [19] are representative of unified software development environments of the 1980's. The environments have come into widespread use and improved the productivity of software development efforts. The provision of libraries of development tools, common file formats, and mechanisms for piping and filtering data between tools has precipitated the integration that is necessary to develop large-scale software. One cannot conclude, however, that the "seemingly seamless" integration of such tools solves "all" the problems of large-scale systems development. The methods for orchestrating the tools to facilitate the design and implementation of systems depend largely on the familiarity with the tools and the suitability of the tools to the systems. Insofar as the approach to the problem-solving conforms to the underlying methods of the tools, the tools provide immense support.

Most of the successful integrated environments require different tools to conform to a uniform file structure (in the same environment). But the approach does not offer opportunities for revolutionary breakthroughs or advances. When an ISEE is a network of distributed cooperative environments, the immediate problem is the ways of hiding the differences in the systems' syntactic and semantic representations. Since integrated environments are normally targeted toward some operating system or hardware platforms, the problem of global integration prevails. A feasible solution is to develop tools without incorporating the idiosyncracies of the hardware and/or the operating system. For the past few years, research focus has been directed toward the development of such a solution.

Several tools in Unix-like operating system environments are integrated using the "byte-stream" and "piping" concepts. Even so, most of the Unix-based tools cannot be characterized as "truly" multiparadigm. In the ideal situation, "true" multiparadigm tools should permit the coexistence of different language constructs in the same program units. Each participating paradigm should support constructs for offering and receiving services from the other paradigms. Currently, such integrated environments are not ubiquitous. In the area of document processing, however, such multiparadigm tools exist. For example, the Nisus^{tm} document processing tool on the Macintosh^{tm} systems allows the integration of graphics and text to coexist in a single document. The need to modify the graphics component requires a simple double-clicking on the component instead of an explicit activation of the graphics editing tool.

With the advent of multiparadigm and language system design, techniques are being developed in a manner that allows different tools to be used in a single, large project [32, 36]. Similarly, multiparadigm and language systems facilitate the specification of different language constructs in a single, large program. For example, the research reported in [32] discusses the Loops system that integrates access, function, object, and rule-oriented systems using a knowledge programming environment. The Loops system is built around function-oriented programming of Interlisp-D coupled with rule-oriented and object-oriented principles. In addition, Loops introduces the concept of programming which separates basic computations from the monitoring of the computations, referred to as access-oriented programming. The Orient 84/K is a development language that integrates modules based on objects, logic, concurrency, rules, and daemons into a framework of knowledge objects [32]. A knowledge object is capable of logic inference/deduction and performs daemon processing. In the Orient 84/K system, knowledge objects are independent and can therefore run in parallel under the control of guardian rules.

A limited form of integrating constructs of different languages is provided in a language like C (the mix of assembly and C statements). On a larger scale, the X Window system, developed as part of the Athena Project, provides a protocol-level support for application interoperability and coherence through a network transparency and device independency [6]. The integration achieved using X Windows is, however, not the multiparadigm concept expected at the language level. At the application-level, system interfaces are defined through parameterization to support applications developed in C, Lisp, and Fortran.

Using a multiparadigm approach to develop ISEEs is difficult because the choice of language paradigms and programming techniques does not follow any standards. As a result, there is always a potential for creating a semantic gap between the languages and interfaces when integrating the tools. In a traditional engineering setting, for example, in the design of a hydraulic press, the viscosity of the liquid, the exact reaction time to lifting, the requisite pressure, and the weight to lift are influencing factors. The amount of pressure to apply and the type of liquid necessary to provide a uniform force for lifting weights follows well-known principles of hydrostatics and standards. In the software world, this is not the case. An ISEE must possess a similar repertoire of tools which fit together in the same program, or project, regardless of the underlying hardware or operating system. CASE tools focused on multiparadigm

languages (i.e., the coexistence of different interoperable constructs) will precipitate the achievement of significant success in "building" software.

3.3. *Lack of student-oriented tools*

This section addresses the limited extent to which CASE tools, developed both by the software industry and through industry/academia initiatives, have been infused into current USE education. It is a general belief that the great software builders of today were yesterday's apprentices in the software industry and, to a limited extent, academia. A significant number of software engineers have therefore acquired their skills on the job using sophisticated tools. In academia, however, software engineering students need and expect tools which match their level of sophistication.

In [24], Nielsen and Richards critiqued the use of Smalltalk and elaborated on the ordeal a novice user goes through in using the environment. Nielsen and Richards concluded that, although Smalltalk is a good system, the environment is not (easily) accessible to novices (as it could have been designed).

One of the factors that inhibit the teaching of the fundamentals of CASE tools is the lack of student-oriented tools. In the industry, corporate software engineering environments can be endowed with a plethora of sophisticated and state-of-the-practice tools. However, the difficulty in understanding the intricacies of the tools hampers the learning curve, and therefore, the productivity of new users. In academia, tools are often built from scratch for experimentation and testing of ideas. More often than not, students undertake projects that do not transcend academic semesters (i.e., the lack of continuity) and as a result most projects are left uncompleted. In many cases, the knowledge gained from using the development tools dissipate quickly, and sadly, some student projects often do not become integral parts of working systems.

It is imperative that CASE development be focused also on building tools that support in-class, student projects. There are a few such tools currently used for real-time systems analysis and design in the academia [34]. Such tools must be based on paradigms that foster incremental, prototypical, and evolutionary development. Student-oriented tools must be novice versions of sophisticated, production-quality counterparts. The novice tools must support nearly all facets of the advanced tools in order to expose students to a broad range of methodologies and techniques.

Industry and academia need to work together for both areas to benefit and grow together. The prognosis for both groups not working together is not that dismal in that a slower technology transfer rate can only stagnate both groups. The advancement of CASE technology at this slower pace means there is little or no risk taking and in fact some individuals will degrade on obsolete technology.

There is more that can be done to advance both groups and support the betterment of the software engineering field. The potential for cooperation between software tool development organizations and educational programs is quite significant for software tool advancement. Likewise, the potential for cooperation between software application development organizations and educational programs is quite significant for productivity and reliability.

4. A Recommendation for an Undergraduate Software Engineering (USE) Education

Writing on great (software) designers, Brooks states that [5, p. 18]:

> "... Good design practices can be taught. Programmers are among the most intelligent part of the population, so they can learn good practices. Hence, a major thrust in the United States is to promulgate good modern practice. New curricula, new literature, new organizations such as the Software Engineering Institute, all ... is entirely proper."

In this section, the essence and state of undergraduate software engineering education is analyzed. In particular, the prevalence or absence of USE education and the requirements for accrediting programs relating software development (computer science) and traditional engineering are discussed.

It is our belief that proper and systematic exposition of students to the development and use of CASE tools be complemented by a formal education process. Having been taught the basic "building blocks", or know-how, students must be formally taught the techniques for extending and advancing the knowledge to CASE. To this end, the full potential and impact of CASE on USE education and vice versa will be realized.

4.1. *Lack of undergraduate software engineering degrees*

To grant an undergraduate degree in software engineering, a university must have a broad range of interests and offerings in computer science and engineering courses (see below). Traditionally, software engineering courses have been offered through computer science programs. In other words, software engineering is often offered as a track or, in a worst case, as an emphasis in a single course. Often, that single course covers topics in program design, coding, and unit testing.

The quality of the software engineering discipline hinges on a strong background in the fundamentals of computer science and engineering design. To provide such a synergistic background, students often take balanced courses from both disciplines. Most computer science and engineering programs, however, are established as independent entities. Often computer science and mathematics/statistics or computer science and electrical/computer engineering programs are merged within the same department/division/college. While the latter type of program structure offers the desirable faculty and laboratory resources for obtaining computer science degrees, universities often do not offer approved programs toward baccalaureate degrees in software engineering.

There are a few computer science/engineering programs that offer Masters of Software Engineering (MSE) degrees. The Software Engineering Institute (SEI) at Carnegie Mellon University, among its mission, is charged to develop and disseminate new curriculum modules and information about MSE programs [11]. Ironically, there are a few USE starting programs that specifically prepare students for the MSE education other than the traditional computer science/engineering programs. We need to start integrating the current graduate course concepts into USE programs and incorporating more theoretical foundation in MSE programs.

In the engineering discipline, it is conceivable for students to design circuits with a subconscious application of principles of electricity, Boolean logic, mathematical measurements and equations, and thermal effects of materials. The principles are ingrained early during the training of the students. Engineering graduates can conduct postgraduate design of different circuits by simple adjustments in the principles and measurements. The engineering student, therefore, has more focus on the art of design than the software engineering student because there are well-guided engineering curriculum structures.

Similarly, software engineering needs to be recognized as a discipline within a guided curriculum. The following is recommended as a minimal set of curriculum structures on which an undergraduate software engineering discipline can be based. The curriculum structures could be drawn from (among others):

Computer Science
Programming Languages, Design and Analysis of Algorithms, Data Abstractions, Systems Analysis and Synthesis, Mathematics of Soft-

ware, Discrete Mathematics, Conceptual Modeling, and Problem Reduction Methods.

Engineering Design
Breadboarding and Prototyping/Modeling, Communication Theory, Structural Design, Interface Specification and Design, and Simulation.

Mathematics
Linear Algebra, Calculus, Mathematical Logic and Boolean Algebra, Set Theory, Relation Theory, Graph Theory, Mathematical Statistics and Probability Theory, Differential Equations.

Communication Skills
Technical Writing, Editing and Reporting, Video Presentations; Organizational *Management/Skills* Behavior, Management Fundamentals, and Business Ethics.

Postgraduate/Professional Certification
Courses which prepare graduates for postgraduate or professional certification. This structure might include a requirement for an internship period prior to taking a profession examination in software engineering.

Furthermore, offering an independent baccalaureate degree in software engineering (from recognized software engineering departments) shifts the students' purview of the area from being a discipline drawn from a synthesis of interrelated courses to one grounded in design disciplines and standards (as in some engineering disciplines). In [31], Shaw recounts the evolution of some allied engineering disciplines. Shaw discusses the historical evolution and accomplishments of the software engineering discipline and concludes that:

> "... There are good grounds to expect that there will eventually be an engineering discipline of software. Its nature will be technical, and it will be based on computer science. Although we have not yet matured to that state, it is an achievable goal."

Other engineering disciplines are able to build undergraduate curricula around well established standards. Software engineering standards [9] are at a stage for a similar process to begin driving undergraduate curricula. In the near future, an undergraduate software engineering degree, when offered as an independent area of academic pursuit, will cultivate and motivate software engineering students to undertake good software design. A more comprehensive curriculum model as suggested by Parnas [27], perhaps, will provide the technical content and rigor alluded to by Shaw. The model proposed by Parnas seems to have the engineering bias which might be a basis for establishing an accreditable software engineering program. Lately, Shaw has reported on the audiences of software specialists and the responsibility of computer science departments in meeting the needs of the audiences [30].

4.2. *Accreditation*

The overall objective of accrediting academic programs is to acknowledge the worthiness and satisfiability of requirements, standards, and appreciable level of fulfillment of course content, teaching and research equipment, faculty teaching and research competence in the fields. An accreditation achievement serves as a status quo and symbolizes the quality of education programs and furthering the development of the profession in the specified fields.

There are several accreditation programs in the United States. Two such programs that impact on the quality of software engineering education are: the Computer Science Accreditation Board (CSAB) and the Accreditation Board for Engineering and Technology (ABET). In the sequel, the essence and requisites for accreditation in both disciplines are discussed.

The CSAB is an organized body of teams of "experts" drawn from the computer science field. Since its inception in 1984, the CSAB has accredited computer science programs. During the first year of the CSAB's evaluation effort, twenty-three (23) institutions were accredited. The Board operates under a set of criteria focused on: (1) curriculum content, (2) sufficiency and currency of laboratory equipment, (3) student admission, counseling, and graduation standards, and (4) an overall institutional commitment to support and advance computer science programs [4].

Among the criteria, the curriculum content has a bearing on how much software engineering is offered and the sufficiency of faculty with formal training and research focus in software engineering. Since 1984, the CSAB criteria have been revised [4]. In spite of the revisions, the expected percentage of software engineering course content in curricula is not sufficient to meet the challenges of good software design. With an established USE education, it is hoped that the CSAB, in collaboration with the ACM, IEEE Computer Society, the non-engineering computer science programs, and the SEI Education Program will consider the accreditation of USE programs in the near future.

Admittedly, the accreditation of engineering programs by ABET has matured and followed well-established standards compared with the CSAB. The disparity can be attributed to the fact that the engineering profession was established long before formal engineering programs were instituted [9]. Albeit the engineering profession shifted from empiricism to fundamental scientific basis before formal academic engineering programs flourished. The ABET draws from a wealth of practical and scientific knowledge to measure the accreditability of engineering programs.

In contrast, the software engineering discipline has often been criticized for lack of mathematical rigor and scientific basis. It is anticipated that along with the innovative curriculum models and the infusion of science and mathematics in USE education being developed [11, 12] and proposed [27, 35], will be a CSAB accreditation of USE programs. In terms of laboratory requirements, formal industry and government driven tool evaluations will provide the basis for tool selection [35]. This drive for tool evaluations whether carried out by industry or academia will impact on curriculum development towards tool selection and incorporation. Eventually, standardization efforts will result from the maturing technology, thus firmly grounding a place in the undergraduate software engineering curriculum.

In the near-term, one can argue that establishing formal, CASE-based undergraduate software engineering programs, as described above, is imperative. The need for establishing such programs is precipitated by the difficulty in developing reliable and timely large software in both industry and academia. Even so, in the near-term, CASE-based USE programs will not significantly mitigate the software crisis. On the other hand, one can therefore argue that establishing formal, CASE-based software engineering *departments* in college curricula is the long-term solution.

4.3. *Individual tool exposition*

The end-product of USE education can be measured by the exposition of software tools under such programs as Tool Fairs or Tool Showcases. In fact, it is not unreasonable for USE graduates to be instilled with software engineering design principles and encouraged to demonstrate the intricate functions of tools and skills gained from software engineering education.

In the traditional mechanical engineering discipline, students usually come out of laboratory sessions with pride over a nut or bolt they have just etched or threaded from specifications. In contrast, computer science education largely emphasizes the traditional lecture-examination mode of preparing students for the profession. The project-oriented component of computer science programs, and particularly programs without software engineering courses, is abysmal. The problem is exacerbated by the offering of USE education under computer science education, making USE education suffer the deficiency of intense, project-oriented design courses that lead to good tool development. In essence, USE education can significantly impact on CASE development if (1) software engineering courses are articulated and made project-oriented, (2) students are encouraged to participate in Tool Fairs, and (3) computer science programs currently offering tracks in software engineering shift emphasis from lecture-examination mode to tool-development orientation.

4.4. *Group projects*

Several of the successful CASE tools have been developed by groups of software engineers. For example, the Athena Project led to the development of the ubiquitous X Window system [6]. The Amoeba [22] and Andrew [21] are example systems providing local and extended network environments for instructional and research computing. The Athena project and the Amoeba and Andrew systems evolved as SER group projects in academia.

Group projects often represent the necessary team-effort to developing CASE tools. On the other hand, CASE also provides the apparatus needed for effective group projects. The complementary view of CASE tools and group projects is commonly termed "groupware" in the software engineering area. Schrage [29] describes "groupware" as the process of "shared creation". Schrage argues that while significant achievements have been realized by two or three individuals, a synergistic collaboration which entails sharing minds, skills, preceptions, and expertise is imperative to successful group projects.

Group projects in USE education, in the essence of "groupware," therefore, must require student-faculty engagement in discussions, problem-solving, understanding of design alternatives, and the use of modern design tools. In effect, a collaborative environment, from the humanistic viewpoint, is necessary to make effective use or development of CASE.

4.5. *After graduation*

The trend of undergraduate computer science education and graduation rate has been on the decline for the past few years [10]. Estimates are that about 50,000–100,000 computer specialists will be needed to meet industrial demand by the mid-21st century [28]. The current graduation rate of students, however, is at about the 50 per cent level of initial enrollment. Coupled with the World Bank estimation [28], the expected number of students to graduate with emphasis in software engineering is infinitesimal. The situation threatens to create a concern in the business community to the extent that in [10] Duke quotes a remark made by Stuart Reeves, EDS vice president in charge of recruiting and development, as:

> "I'd love to have more students with degrees in finance or anthropology or political science, ... adding that being able to think critically is more important than a computer science degree. We'll teach them what they need to know to be a computer professional."

Undergraduate students with a significant concentration in software engineering are produced mostly from liberal-arts computer science programs [31]. Such programs offer formal software engineering courses constituting about 10% (12–15 semester hours) of the total of 120 hours (on the average) required for graduation. So, while the demand is estimated to be high, the supply end is not promising. The demand-supply gap further threatens the survival and advances of the software industry. For the meantime, graduating software engineering students can look forward to opportunities due to the industrial insatiability for advanced CASE [1]. The need to establish accreditable and quality USE programs, however, cannot be overemphasized.

5. Productivity Factors

In this section, we discuss the imperatives of CASE tools and USE education for achieving significant increases in software productivity. When subjected to probity, the interplay between CASE tools and USE education, as discussed in previous sections, calls for a set of criteria or paradigms of software design by which the success of such an interplay can be measured. Hoare [14] makes the point that the programmer suffers the consequence of poor tools. Traditionally, software tools have been developed and parameterized using program characteristics. It is imperative to design and develop tools that are characterized by productivity criteria and advances in hardware technology to achieve the expected increases in productivity. It is our belief that two paradigms of software development can serve as a yardstick because of their success in traditional engineering: rapid prototyping/breadboarding and higher-order languages.

5.1. *Rapid prototyping*

Boehm and others [2] investigating the effects of CASE environments on improving productivity, indicated that increase in productivity ranged from 39 to 47 per cent. This gain was a result of inclusion of an elaborate array of tools and productivity-specific methodologies. These types of results are immediately attainable if the concern for productivity is an integral part of the development environment.

Sophisticated languages and database technology are useful for rapid prototyping of a target system, especially during the design of a system. In a typical software engineering course-project, a student can observe a working model of the system and be sure of the accuracy of the conception or request for changes as necessary. In an industrial setting, rapid prototyping is quintessential to, not only meeting project deadlines, but producing at least a demonstrable model for upper management in a timely fashion. The ability to make corrections early in software development can also save a significant amount of man-hours.

An obvious requirement of rapid prototyping is minimization of the time spent in producing the prototype itself and the time spent in learning and understanding the prototype's behavior. Such an accomplishment is feasible with higher-order languages and a complete set of CASE tools. In industry, a recovery of the initial investment occurs by using the prototype in either the current or future development effort. In academia, rapid prototyping accelerates and helps early visualization of the final system; and facilitates continuity of projects that transcend several semesters.

5.2. *Higher-order languages*

Several prototyping techniques are oriented toward very high level languages. These advanced languages offer improved ability to produce compilable instruction from unclear statements of the problem. The development of higher-order languages, and their use as a paradigm for CASE tool development, may well offer the best possibility of solving the software productivity problem. As the languages and associated tools improve the ability to rapidly produce efficient code, the task of the programmer will be greatly simplified.

The current thrust of "software productivity" research is toward nonprocedural languages. Such language paradigms include visual programming, object-oriented programming with graphic capability, e.g., Open Windows, and the like. Flexibility in specifying what a system is to do rather than how the system operates mirrors a corresponding reduction in software production effort. Often, the necessary "programming" can be done at the man-machine interface level. Consequently, experienced software engineers can concentrate on the more complex problems, making effective use of the trained personnel [13].

There are some extensions to higher-order language systems based on Artificial Intelligence (AI) paradigms. Significant advances in AI-based systems research have been realized, however, there are still subtle productivity factors which largely limit the potential widespread use of AI in large software projects. The most significant productivity impact has been in knowledge acquisition systems and applying deductive mechanisms to derive logical inferences about systems behavior. AI tools exonerate the software engineer of the cognitive effort required to develop software, thereby increasing software productivity via rapid prototyping. In a typical software engineering curriculum, the immediate concern in introducing AI techniques into software design, is the preparedness of the students in concepts well grounded in logic. Unfortunately, several USE education programs, as discussed above, hardly provide adequate formal computer science courses, let alone courses in formal logic.

This technological baseline will provide the basis for advancing CASE technology transfer and USE education. The advancement of CASE technology will be in support of industry development efforts and practitioner usage patterns. The advancement of USE education will serve as a basis for improving the situation for industry with regard to the hiring of new software engineers. There are many successful and unsuccessful efforts of industry and university synergism. Case studies of both types of efforts in the software field need to be documented to support future efforts.

In sum, centering USE education around rapid prototyping techniques is essential. Traditional engineering disciplines have always focused on engineering design grounded in prototyping, breadboarding and modeling, and have been successful. Software development can similarly be characterized to achieve the desired effectiveness of CASE education. Secondly, centering CASE tools development around the use of well-integrated, or higher-order languages and emerging technologies in AI, will not only facilitate prototyping but separate software design from implementation details. Also, higher-order languages provide a framework for abstracting advanced CASE tools usage, especially tools for novice student users as discussed earlier. The net effect is facilitating technology transfer, from USE education, to industry through such paradigms as rapid prototyping and higher-order languages.

6. Summary and Conclusion

This chapter has addressed the integration of CASE in courses to facilitate USE education and the development of formal USE degree programs as a means for advancing CASE tools. The successful introduction of CASE in academia hinges on technology transfer as a delivery and infusion mechanism. The lack of an undergraduate software engineering degree has been an impediment to the software engineering field. There is significant potential for advancing CASE tools through technology transfer into and out of USE education. The potential, however, will be precipitated through cooperation with industry, academia, and government; and can be facilitated through such paradigms as rapid prototyping and higher-order languages. While the goal may be difficult to reach, a partial implementation of the cooperation package will benefit the field.

References

1. P. O. Bobbie, "Productivity through automated tools," *ACM SIGSOFT Softw. Eng. Notes* **12**, 2 (1987) 30–31.
2. B. W. Boehm, E. D. Stuckle, R. D. Williams, and A. B. Pyster, "A software development environment for improving productivity," *Computer* **17**, 6 (1984) 30–44.
3. G. Booch, "Object-oriented development," *IEEE Trans. Softw. Eng.* **12**, 2 (1986) 211–221.
4. T. Booth and R. E. Miller, "Computer science program accreditation: the first year activities of the Computing Sciences Accreditation Board," *Computer* **20**, 5 (1987) 94–102.
5. F. P. Brooks, "No silver bullet: essence and accidents of software engineering," *Computer* **20**, 4 (1987) 10–18.
6. G. A. Champine, D. E. Geer, and W. N. Ruh, "Project Athena as a distributed computer system," *Computer* **23**, 9 (1990) 40–51.
7. D. E. Cooke, "Issues in CASE technology transfer," *Proc. 4th Int. Workshop on Computer-Aided Software Engineering—Advance Working Papers*, Irvine, CA (December 1990) pp. 78–79.
8. T. A. Dolotta, R. C. Haight, and J. R. Mashey, "Unix time-sharing system: the Programmer's Workbench," in *Interactive Programming Environments*, eds., D. Barstow, H. Shrobe and E. Sandewall (McGraw Hill, 1984) pp. 353–369.
9. M. Dorfman and R. H. Thayer, eds., *Standards, Guidelines, and Examples on Systems and Software Requirements Engineering*, IEEE Computer Society Press, Tutorial No. 1922, Los Alamitos, CA (1990).
10. P. Duke, "Jobs go unfilled as fewer students show interest in Computer Science," *The Chronicle of Higher Education* (November 1989).

11. G. Ford and N. Gibbs, "A Master of Software Engineering curriculum: recommendations from the Software Engineering Institute," *Computer* **22**, 9 (1989) 50–71.
12. P. W. Garratt and G. Edmunds, "Teaching software engineering at university," *Inf. and Softw. Tech.* **30**, 1, (1988) 5–11.
13. T. Guimaraes, "A study of application program development techniques," *Commun. ACM* **28**, 5 (1985) 494–499.
14. C. A. R. Hoare, "Programming is an engineering profession," in *Software Engineering Development*, ed., P. J. L. Wallis (Pergamon Infotech Limited, 1983) pp. 264.
15. G. F. Hoffnagle and W. E. Beregi, "Automating the software development process," *IBM Systems J.* **24**, 2 (1985).
16. E. Horowitz and B. Munson, "An expansive view of reusable software," *IEEE Trans. Softw. Eng.* **SE-10**, 5 (1984), 477–487.
17. T. C. Jones, "Reusability in programming: A survey of the state of the art," *IEEE Trans. Softw. Eng.* **SE-10**, 5 (1984) 488–494.
18. B. R. Konsynski, J. E. Kottermann, J. F. Nunamaker, and J. W. Stott, "PLESYS-84: An integrated development environment for information system," *J. Manage. Inf. Syst.* **1**, 3 (1984/85) 64–104.
19. D. B. Leblang and R. P. Chase, "Computer-aided software engineering in a distributed workstation environment," *ACM SIGPLAN Notices* **19**, 5 (1984) 104–112.
20. R. W. Lucky, "Engineering education and industrial research and development—the promise and the reality," *IEEE Commun. Mag.* **28**, 12 (1990) 16, 19–22.
21. J. Morris, "Make or take decisions in Andrew," in *Usenix Conf. Proc.* (Usenix, Winter 1988) pp. 1–8.
22. S. J. Mullender, "Amoeba as a workstation operating system," in *Proc. IEEE Workshop on Workstation Operating Systems*, Cambridge, Mass. (1982).
23. P. S. Newman, "Towards an integrated development environment," *IBM Syst. J.* **21**, 1 (1982) 81–107.
24. J. Nielsen and J. T. Richards, "The experiences of learning and using Smalltalk," *IEEE Softw.* **6**, 3 (1989) 73–77.
25. R. J. Norman and J. F. Nunamaker, "CASE productivity perceptions of software engineering professionals," *Commun. ACM* **32**, 9 (1989) 1102–1108.
26. C. Oglesby and J. Urban, "The human resources task area," *Computer* **16**, 11 (1983) 65–70.
27. D. L. Parnas, "Education for computing professionals," *Computer* **23**, 1 (1990) 17–22.
28. R. Schaware, "The world software industry and software engineering: opportunities and constraints for newly industrialized economies," *World Bank Technical Paper*, No. 104 (August 1989).
29. M. Schrage, *Shared Minds: The New Technologies of Collaboration* (Random House, N.Y., 1990).

30. M. Shaw, "Informatics for a new century: computing education for the 1990's and beyond," CMU, School of Computer Science, Technical Report CMU-CS-9-142, 1990, pp. 1–17.
31. M. Shaw, "Prospects for an engineering discipline of software," *IEEE Softw.* **7**, 6 (1990) 15–24.
32. M. J. Stefik, D. G. Bobrow, and K. M. Kahn, "Integrating access-oriented programming into a multiparadigm environment," *IEEE Softw.* **3**, 1 (1986) 10–18.
33. W. Teitelman and L. Masinter, "The Interlisp programming environment," *Computer* **14**, 4 (1981) 25–33.
34. P. T. Ward and S. J. Mellor, *Structured Development for Real-Time Systems* (Prentice-Hall, 1985).
35. J. Wordsworth, "Education in formal methods for software engineering," *Inf. Softw. Tech.* **29**, 1 (1987) 27–32.
36. P. Zave, "A compositional approach to multiparadigm programming," *IEEE Softw.* **6**, 5 (1989) 15–25.